The Cyber Patient

Endorsements

"Evolving technology and a shift to consumer-driven healthcare will continue to transform the industry. *The Cyber Patient* is a comprehensive exploration into the current and future innovations that leverage cloud-based technology to break down information system and database silos. True patient-centric care begins and ends with seamless access to these data. Similar to disruptions in other industries (e.g., Blockbuster vs. Netflix), technology and consumer demands for access and convenience will push organizations to innovate and collaborate in new ways. This book is a must-read for healthcare informaticist professionals and health systems leaders looking to position themselves for success in an ever-changing market."

Dennis R. Delisle, Sc.D, FACHE, Jefferson Health; Senior Director, Operations–South Philadelphia
President & CEO, Methodist Hospital Foundation
Assistant Program Director, Operational Excellence | TJU College of Population Health

"*The Cyber Patient* is another component of the evolution of utilizing technology within healthcare. It demonstrates how providers can now manage patients via virtual visits all within the revenue cycle. Without a doubt, it's definitely the future with IoT but, most importantly, how we in IT should start preparing for new roles within cyber healthcare environment."

Donna Hart, former CIO at Cook County Health, 2015, Recipient of the HIMSS HIT Award for enhancing patient care through health IT and achieved HIMSS 7 EMR recognition for 2017/2018

"*The Cyber Patient* describes how technology is reorganizing healthcare toward a new level of interconnectivity. But more importantly, it explains how we can ride these changes to optimize patient–provider relationships, giving us tools and time to effectively listen to patients and individualize care. This book guides us toward the conscious use of e-health to enhance, not replace, the care in healthcare."

Fran London, MS, RN
Author of *No Time to Teach: The Essence of Patient and Family Education for Health Care Providers*

"If you find yourself struggling to build a strategy that recognizes the upheavals brought about by the use of information and technology in healthcare, *The Cyber Patient* digs into the implications for case management, staff roles, payment cycles, organizational efficiency and more. This book unlocks a way of approaching a future in which data is an asset with the power to guide any strategy focused on better care and performance."

Rod Piechowski, MA, CPHIMS
Senior Director, HIS
HIMSS North America

"*The Cyber Patient* represents a vision and necessary road map for healthcare as it transforms into a digital industry. The virtual connection has the promise for connecting and delivering services with a much greater value proposition than traditional models and consistent with other industries. Rebecca hits the nail on the head with the promotion of self-service as the patient becomes the provider through advanced analytics and artificial intelligence and also becomes the destination center for health and services utilizing technology as the primary channel. A must-read for those looking to enter into the healthcare field and for those within the industry who want to lead and accelerate the advancement of health."

Craig Richardville, MBA, FACHE, FHIMSS former Senior Vice President and CIO Carolinas HealthCare System (now called Atrium Health); award recipient CIO of the Year from InspireCIO (2017); HIMSS (2015); Charlotte Business Journal (2013); Most Wired designation (14 years); HIMSS EMR adoption Model Stage 7 (2017)

The Cyber Patient

Navigating Virtual Informatics

Rebecca Mendoza Saltiel Busch

CRC Press
Taylor & Francis Group
Boca Raton London New York

CRC Press is an imprint of the
Taylor & Francis Group, an **informa** business
A PRODUCTIVITY PRESS BOOK

CRC Press
Taylor & Francis Group
6000 Broken Sound Parkway NW, Suite 300
Boca Raton, FL 33487-2742

© 2019 by Rebecca Mendoza Saltiel Busch
Productivity Press is an imprint of Taylor & Francis Group, an Informa business

No claim to original U.S. Government works

Printed on acid-free paper

International Standard Book Number-13: 978-1-138-59240-7 (Hardback)
978-0-429-49004-0 (e-Book)

Library of Congress Cataloging-in-Publication Data

Names: Busch, Rebecca S., author.
Title: The cyber patient : navigating virtual informatics / Rebecca Mendoza Saltiel Busch.
Description: Boca Raton : Taylor & Francis, 2019. | "A CRC title, part of the Taylor & Francis imprint, a member of the Taylor & Francis Group, the academic division of T&F Informa plc." | Includes bibliographical references and index.
Identifiers: LCCN 2018052739 (print) | LCCN 2019008213 (ebook) | ISBN 9780429490040 (e-Book) | ISBN 9781138592407 (hardback : alk. paper)
Subjects: LCSH: Medical informatics. | Technological innovations.
Classification: LCC R858 (ebook) | LCC R858 .B87 2019 (print) | DDC 610.285--dc23
LC record available at https://lccn.loc.gov/2018052739

Visit the Taylor & Francis Web site at
http://www.taylorandfrancis.com

and the Productivity Press site at
http://www.ProductivityPress.com

To My Poet -

A master of words and meaningful expression.

Contents

Preface

It would be possible to describe everything scientifically, but it would make no sense; it would be
without meaning, as if you described a Beethoven
symphony as a variation of wave pressure.

Albert Einstein

Several of my earlier electronic healthcare publications focus
on professional considerations in utilizing technology to document healthcare information. This publication is focused
on considerations to help patients navigate a cyber-driven
healthcare commerce economy. The journey to the writing
of *The Cyber Patient: A Digitally Aware Consumer Navigating
Electronic Healthcare Commerce* has its genesis in my first
exposure to the world of healthcare.

In the summer after 8th grade, I left my house every morn-
ing at 6 a.m. to go to my local community hospital. There,
I would sit at my grandmother's bedside for the whole day,
returning home in the evening only when my father, a physician, was done caring for his own patients. I observed the
supervision of my grandmother as she recovered from a
stroke: bedridden, unable to speak, and unable to understand
English. Bedside monitors sent data to a central station; the
nurses kept notes on a chart; doctors spent barely 2 minutes

at her side, then left to write notes at the nurses' station. The only people I saw working were the nurses and their assistants. The doctors came and went and spent little time with the patient. What is different today is that nurses and their assistants spend *less* time at the bedside. Doctors continue to come and go, but the overall volume of patients seen in a day is down. Why? Electronic health record content requirements. Providers are spending more time documenting patient care specifications (not previously required) versus face to face time. Couple this with lower reimbursement rates, providers are being hit hard in the pocketbook.

Soon after this experience, I started working in a hospital in various support roles and was exposed to almost every aspect of a hospital and clinical area as a nurse's aide. For the next 30 years, my observations remained unchanged: healthcare professionals do not spend enough time with their patients.

Unfortunately, after 40 more years as an intensive care nurse, medical claims auditor, patient advocate, and forensic expert, I can see that the dynamics of a healthcare professional not spending enough time with the patient have endured. But why? After all the investments in technology aimed to produce better outcomes for patients at lower cost, why is there still a lack of effective communications between the patient and the provider, creating gaps in services provided and lower quality care than would otherwise be possible? This book seeks to provide an answer.

But this book will do more. I have previously written on: (a) fraud in the healthcare marketplace, (b) information security as health records transition from paper to computer, (c) silo-busting to enable professionals to draw together multiple types of data stored by different market participants in diverse systems, (d) patient advocacy and the need to present alternative treatment options and their associated costs, and (e) enabling consumers to use information to be their best healthcare advocate. The emergence of the cyber patient has implications in all these areas, and I have provided appropriate updates to the insights captured in those preceding publications.

My auditing work has revealed that the environment of disconnected information and lack of intimate knowledge of the patient allow deceit and fraud to flourish. To combat this, my book, *Healthcare Fraud Auditing and Detection Guide*,[1] introduced a behavioral model enabling investigators to spot lies that they would have otherwise accepted, clues they would otherwise have missed, and evidence which previously would have escaped their notice. The power of cyber considerations in applying this healthcare continuum model will be discussed herein.

Electronic Health Records: An Audit and Internal Control Guide[2] focused heavily on managing change as healthcare stakeholders moved from a paper to an electronic environment. While healthcare stakeholders continue to navigate in an electronically interoperable world, the need to provide security has exceeded the pace of the technology's adoption and the evolving electronic health practice standards. This edition of *The Cyber Patient* provides an update on one of the greatest security issues today: controlling identity theft. Further, a discussion on case management, both clinical and financial, will be re-introduced as well. This is critical because in today's environment patients continue to receive co-mingled advice from their providers. The conversations should be like this: "Your benefit plan recommends that I start you with Drug A; however, based on my clinical experience and current research, your condition appears to benefit from starting with Drug B. If you choose Drug A, the cost will be $100, and if you choose Drug B, your cost will be out of pocket and the price tag is $800." Typically, what happens today is that the physician states the first course of treatment is Drug A. When this happens the consumer is not receiving a clinical recommendation separate from a financial recommendation. This publication has incorporated updated materials from Chapters 3 through 10 within various sections of this book.

Leveraging Data in Healthcare[3] focused on transforming partitioned data into consumable and actionable data-driven decisions. Eliminating paper and creating silos of data in electronic form make data neither useful nor accessible. The market has aggressively evolved in the provision of all sorts of data analytics tools, and many have been implemented successfully. However, as these data analytics tools are deployed, the results have not met expectations. Why not? Because we have developed data tools that are being executed in environments without data strategies. A lesson I have learned from my medical audit practice is that the housing of data requires an inventory of said data, followed by the creation of a data strategy. Once that strategy is defined, then a gap analysis should be conducted to ensure that all of the data elements to achieve strategic objectives are available. Prior to execution of the data strategy, a data readiness of stakeholders should be conducted. The existence or use of a data strategy is often missed during the assessment of its storage software's readiness by the respective stakeholders. No exceptional technology will be effective if the readiness to use that tool and its analytics are not assessed first. *The Cyber Patient* has incorporated the concept of data readiness assessments at various points throughout.

In the midst of ongoing medical audit work, my company Medical Business Associates, Inc. engaged in patient advocacy support for individuals who needed assistance in navigating the healthcare system. This resulted in the development of two more publications, *Personal Healthcare Portfolio* and *Patient's Healthcare Portfolio: A Practitioner's Guide*,[4] which detail how to become a healthcare advocate. Remember: regardless of how each healthcare stakeholder pursues technology in their infrastructure (provider, payer, plan sponsor, and so forth), the patient is still getting services on a day-to-day basis. Therefore, concepts such as managing your healthcare portfolio continue to remain the same, as it helps the consumer avoid being thwarted or harmed by a healthcare system undergoing a major transition. *The Cyber Patient* has also incorporated the concept of managing a personal healthcare portfolio in various sections.

As I reflect on the current condition of healthcare, I am taken back to my academic nursing roots, which helped my understanding of the value of bonding between the caregiver and the ailing patient. I recall working in the geriatric unit with individuals in active stages of illness. Holding a patient's hand for 5 minutes, actively listening, and building trust should never be undervalued. Bonding, which creates the right environment for effective communication between patient and provider, needs to improve and be formally recognized. This is why understanding how we interact with patients is critical toward an optimal interpersonal relationship between provider and patient.

Where can this improvement begin? First, by effectively closing the gap on what conditions and circumstances we collect information on. A review of the International Statistical Classification of Diseases and Related Health Problems, 10th Revision, Clinical Modification (ICD-10-CM) index demonstrates a focus on disease and causes of death. This publication is maintained by the World Health Organization. In the context of human bonding, an entire section is dedicated to documentation of mental and behavioral health:

■ Mental disorders due to known physiological conditions (Sections F01–F09)

A patient experiencing loneliness would be documented as:

■ Factors influencing health status and contact with health services (Sections Z00–Z99)

The ICD-10 is not structured to document healthy conditions. However, it is difficult to find the ability to code a positive healthy condition. The lack of specificity of health and wellness will impede our ability to effectively measure population health metrics prior to the onset of illness. Why is this important? So we can measure and sustain practice standards that support what we are doing correctly. The World Health Organization has published ICD-11 which is utilized by countries outside of the United States. Within ICD-11, the recognition of a healthy person is moving slightly (in the right direction) as noted within this diagnostic code:

■ ICD-11 **QC21**- Healthy person accompanying sick person (*well* person accompanying sick person)

The next step in creating an environment consisting of human bonds of the healthy self and the ailing patient is to address the operational functions in which contact with the patient occurs. The theme of this book is addressing segments of healthcare that should be upended within a cyber market. It is important to include a strategy not to lose our connectivity to the patient. The infrastructure that would promote connectivity is portrayed throughout this book, emphasizing human bonds, combined with therapeutic healthy patient relationships,[5] all while navigating as a patient within the cyberworld of health. Reflecting Einstein's thoughts on Beethoven, I have taken an approach which emphasizes the importance of human connectivity aided—not replaced—by cyber technology.

Acknowledgments

In running a company since 1991, I have been fortunate to have had the opportunity to work with a multitude of talented people. My most valuable lessons in life have resulted not from SQL data pulls, but from direct experiences with my home and work families. I want to thank all who have been associated with Medical Business Associates, Inc. (MBA) over the years. I have learned something unique from each of you along the way.

I would also like to acknowledge those individuals who provided editorial assistance for this book, including Alberto Busch, Andrew Busch, Samantha Busch, Peter Elias, Dorothy Foster, Laura Krawchuk, Janet McManus, Nicole McManus, Sriram Ravi, Dina Stone and Siddharth Varadharajan. Finally, I'd like to extend a special THANK YOU to John Stanley Hamilton for his intellectual curiosity, time, energy, and thoughtful feedback during the many rewrites of this book!

The cyberworld is no substitute for human relationships—so thank you all.

Author

I've got the key to my castle in the air, but whether
I can unlock the door remains to be seen.

Louisa May Alcott
Little Women

Visionary Perspective

No doubt virtual informatics is the next frontier. All that you
see today will not exist in 20 years. The traditional roles of
medical doctor, nurse practitioner, and all of the other allied
healthcare professionals will be re-engineered. Imagine a
patient interfacing the management of their healthcare with a
self-guided virtual assistant. The self-guided medical diagnostic module with a parallel informatics specialist. The human
touch will emerge in the follow-up discussion with an infomediary specialist on the derived artificial intelligence driven
diagnostics. Treatment options performed by robotics skilled
in the craft of the most technical procedures. Real-time informatics on research, efficacy of care, outcomes management,
and adjustments to care... then you will see the future, the
cyber patient in control navigating virtual informatics and
making data driven decisions.

Professional Background

Rebecca Mendoza Saltiel Busch is a seasoned healthcare executive, registered nurse, patient advocate, and data scientist. She has a diverse healthcare consulting practice which includes various healthcare organizations, including payers, providers, drug manufacturers, and employee benefit plans. As founder of Medical Business Associates, Inc., she has created hybrid healthcare professionals by blending clinicians with finance, audit, compliance, and informatics. As a registered nurse in an acute care setting, she saw first-hand how data inundate the healthcare environment. For her clients, the devil is always in the details—data. The emergence of big data revolution in healthcare is driving health industry organizations to develop holistic policies that provide patients access to their medical information while simultaneously protecting it. Rebecca has been granted seven U.S. data analytic design patents with pharmaceutical applications, one U.S. patent pertaining to electronic health record case management systems and other patents pending on an anomaly tracking system and an interactive, iterative behavioral model, system and method for detecting fraud, waste, and abuse. An accomplished author, educator, and business developer, Rebecca has written over 56 articles and made more than 200 presentations to consumers, government agencies, corporate, and professional entities. She has published five books and contributed chapters within other publications. They include:

Patient's Healthcare Portfolio: A Practitioner's Guide to Providing Tools for Patients by Rebecca M.S. Busch CRC Press December 2017.

Leveraging Data in Healthcare: Best Practices for Controlling, Analyzing, and Using Data by Rebecca Busch, HIMSS – CRC Press December 2015.

Insurance Fraud Casebook by Joseph T. Wells (editor) "Ignorance is bliss, while it lasts" Case study on Insurance Fraud by Rebecca Busch (contributing author) John Wiley & Sons, Inc., June 2013, Chapter 25.

Healthcare Fraud: Audit & Detection Guidebook by Rebecca Saltiel Busch (author), Wiley & Sons Publications, June 2012 (2nd Edition).

Personal Healthcare Portfolio: Your Health & Wellness Record by Rebecca Saltiel Busch, Medical Business Associates, Inc., June 2010.

Legal Nurse Consulting: Principles and Practices, Third Edition edited by Anne Peterson and Lynda Kopishke, Chapter 12 pages 251–272 "Government-sponsored healthcare plans and general case evaluations," AALNC CRC Press, February 2010.

Electronic Health Records: An Audit and Internal Control Guide by Rebecca S. Busch, John Wiley & Sons, Inc., July 2008.

Computer Fraud Casebook: The Bytes that Bite by Joseph T. Wells (editor) "I Due" Case study on identity theft by Rebecca Busch (contributing author) John Wiley & Sons, Inc., August 2008.

Healthcare Fraud: Audit & Detection Guidebook by Rebecca Busch (author), Wiley & Sons Publications, October 2007.

Fraud Casebook: Lessons from the Bad Side of Business Joseph T. Wells (editor), Chapter 59 "Bodies for Rent" by Rebecca Busch, John Wiley & Sons Publications, July 2007.

Introduction

Your brain may give birth to any technology, but
other brains will decide whether the technology
thrives. The number of possible technologies is
infinite, and only a few pass this test of affinity with
human nature.

Robert Wright
Nonzero: The Logic of Human Destiny

Objective

The objective of this book is to point the systems developer
to where medical informatics needs innovation; prepare the
healthcare practitioner and patient to use such systems; and
to describe new roles in healthcare to bridge the gap between
the enormous amount of medical information potentially
available and the much more limited amount needed by a
patient to make his or her own medical decisions. Cloud-
based technology allows the infrastructure to place information in the hands of the consumer. Patient-centric care cannot
be achieved without the patient having access to all of their
information.

This publication presents frameworks for this new world
and shows the way to transition from those being used today.

A cyber-based patient-centric platform will allow the consumer access to an informatics repository to access healthcare information from across all of his or her providers, allowing for self-driven analytics—allowing, by way of example, a comparison between prices of a set of procedures, efficacy, and potential health outcomes. Beyond that, expect that the future of the cyber environment will be marked by the transformation of independent e-health information into an overarching cloud-based community landscape of health dominated by consumer and professional learning tools and service support, similar to today's Gaming as a Service (GaaS) and Software as a Service (SaaS).

Overview

An incontrovertible truth: patients cannot make proper health decisions without being able to analyze all of their current and historical health information. Patients often consult with a provider who does not have all of their health history. Advice is often given based only on the information that is readily available. Patient-centric innovative technology can enable patients to bring their information to the next provider when the provider's system cannot do it for them. This is a fundamental shift in healthcare, reflecting similar trends toward self-service in other industries. The patient has much to gain by having innovators present tools that will achieve this aim. Access to a patient's entire health history is just as important to the provider of care. Innovation is required for efficient access to their patients' complete health file, competent health standards, and current health information. Without that, they are unable to facilitate the presentation of optimal care options and the means to deliver those options to the patient.

In the preface, I made an observation about how much time a provider spent with my grandmother in the 1970s.

The current argument against the electronic documentation requirements is that increasing the amount of writing time will force the provider to see fewer patients. One way the dilemma is being addressed is by having medical assistants start writing notes on behalf of the doctor. Another way is by creating scribes to meet those documentation requirements. These medical assistants and scribes, however, may not have the skill sets appropriate to elicit the information from the patient. In the past, the provider could write one sentence or an entire paragraph. The use of electronic records (e-health) with required fields now requires the provider to include a minimum set of details within their assessments. This results in a standardization of content for a patient's written assessment. However, whereas in the past the provider could see more patients and write less, today they are seeing fewer patients and are required to enter specific documentation into the medical record—or reimbursement will be diminished. Therefore, it is not clear which environment allows the provider to spend more face-to-face time with the patient.

Technology within healthcare will evolve in a way that provides an appropriate balance between volume of patients seen and quality of care. How? By creating the means for healthcare services consumers to educate themselves—allowing for more productive and time-efficient interactions with the professionals, thus improving patient connectivity, management of their healthy self, and self in illness within a cyber environment.

In exploring the development of e-health, a foundation of knowledge regarding the cyberworld is needed by both the consumer and the healthcare professional. This book includes a discussion on how patients manage their electronic health records, data, and services technology. It also develops a deeper understanding of computer culture and virtual reality (tools in which a patient can simulate and test solutions).

The current conversation on e-health is saturated with security issues. Since security is such a threat in the cyber environment, materials within this book discuss identity theft and how to recognize its varied forms. Security and assurance business operations will be addressed from the perspective of internal control. Any topic on navigating healthcare includes a discussion on informatics (access and analysis of data); revenue cycle (how fees for services are generated); the costs of healthcare services; and internal controls (assurance that systems are not compromised).

Parallel to this is the need to recognize and have a conversation about the activities that are moving up to the cloud, as it is occurring in many industries outside of healthcare. One of which is the gaming industry, which has had long established cyber communities over the years. These players create communities of users with mutual interests. Virtual friendships, gamesmanships, and challenges are created. Cloud gaming (or gaming-as-a-service (GaaS)[6]) has its own emerging use of technology. Imagine the use of games to educate patients on options for treating a healthcare condition? Think of a credit score simulator that demonstrates what actions will increase or decrease your credit score. This could be applied to diets to address obesity, diabetes, and osteoporosis. The idea of using online gaming communities to solve known issues in professional fields has been proven to be a viable strategy. An example includes the traditional research tools by scientists to understand the structure of a protein-cutting retrovirus similar to HIV. The researchers created a game called Foldit.[7] Teams of players would fold the molecules and rotate amino acids to create 3-D protein structures. Their reward was points based on the stability of the structure. The result of the game? Scientists were able to learn the structure of the protein which allowed them to determine an effective drug to block that enzyme and treat conditions like HIV. The difference in approach? Scientists struggled without any luck over a 13-year period using traditional research techniques. The online gamers solved the puzzle within 3 weeks.[8] GaaS leverages large servers in addition to aggregating a community of users (and their collective brain power) dedicated to a particular game, which is followed by Software as a Service (SaaS) offerings.

Many emerging SaaS programs have focused on business-to-business support services such as Salesforce.com (customer relationship management tool); Microsoft Office 365 (productivity applications); Box (online workspaces); Google apps (business productivity tools); and Amazon Web Services (core e-commerce platform).[9] Now imagine a healthcare informatics, support, and delivery service moving into SaaS-based offerings. Envision in 40 years' time a cyber-souq market in which the cyber patient and cyber practitioner merge within an open cloud market to solicit or obtain healthcare services. Other support services may include consumer rating programs for doctors; shopping price; and rating health outcomes by treatment and by health conditions.

This book predicts the future of cyber-health as an overall cloud-based environment. The upcoming culture of computers, information technology, and virtual reality of healthcare stakeholders should be distinguished from the current state of "e-health." E-health is presented as individual groupings of organizations with limited electronic infrastructures. For example, Hospital System A only connects electronically with its own providers and patients. However, if Hospital B and Hospital A have a mutual patient, their electronic systems do not speak to each other so the patient has to independently seek information from each system. As stated earlier, the future of the cyber environment will be marked by the transformation of independent e-health information into an overall cloud-based community landscape of GaaS-based learning tools and SaaS for service support.

Book Abstract

In preparation for the cyber patient and cyber provider, a series of foundational concepts are addressed within this book. Chapter 1 introduces the cyber patient and trends in the development of a self-service economy. The opportunity for patient access to health informatics in a self-service economy is already manifesting itself through patient portals. Chapter 2 shows how cyber-based support services will enable traditional case management support to evolve from individual provider settings to a virtual environment with provider and user communities simultaneously linked. It further takes a deep dive into segmenting two key disciplines within case management: clinical (What is the treatment which will have the best health outcome?) and financial (What is the treatment plan which will have the best health outcome given the limited money available from patients or insurers to pay for it?).

These changes will lead to a new role in the healthcare industry—that of a cyber-nurse specialist. Such a specialist would combine traditional nursing functions and skills with new technical and informatics skills. Chapter 3 addresses current practice standards within the discipline of case management and introduction to the cyber nurse. Chapter 3 also includes a discussion on virtual world implications and case study application.

Chapter 4 reviews the development of an infomediary specialist to help consumers manage, interpret, and process large volumes of health data. Principles of cyber data strategy, analytics, and informatics, as well as the emerging roles that have resulted from the increasing need to manage data and mitigate hazards, are considered. Risks include the theft of individual, medical, professional, electronic, digital, and synthetic identities, and any data strategy designed to protect this information will need to include an assessment of the patient's readiness to manage his or her own data and the technology offerings. To introduce these ideas, Chapter 4 presents a Data Management Capability Assessment Model. In addition, this chapter reviews a methodology to capture data (behavioral continuum analytic model). This model can be adopted at any stage of technology development, level of data analytics, or user adoption.

Chapter 5 considers managing and auditing data in a cyber environment and the impact on associated internal controls. This chapter provides an example of an audit checklist to manage reviews of operations within an organization to ensure compliance. Additionally, this chapter provides a discussion on managing new data and ongoing additions of information. Once this is achieved, a processed data audit checklist and categories on how to classify data may be developed.

Chapter 6 focuses on algorithms and discusses the attributes needed to write the correct algorithm in response to questions on behalf of the user. This chapter also reviews the definition and components of the algorithm, including data elements and their behaviors. A hospital case study demonstrates the use of algorithms in understanding denial of claims and explains a data-driven revenue cycle analysis. Applications of the case study include the use of algorithms and the use of the behavioral analytics tool discussed in Chapter 4. Finally, the case study illustrates the selection of algorithms used and the general categories of the forms of algorithms by type and purpose.

Chapter 7 further explores the data-driven process with an overview of decision-making models. The knowledge models are reviewed within the previously discussed healthcare continuum model—identifying stakeholders, establishing benchmarks, and capturing the people, process, and technology data needed for any internal audit reviews. Illustrations of this model are presented from a provider, payer, and plan sponsor perspective.

Chapter 8 examines the foundational requirements of information technology to pave the way for interoperable cyber environments. It shows that infomediaries, auditors, and internal information technology departments must establish capability in managing complex systems so that cyber technology can be built upon a strong foundation.

Chapter 9 demonstrates that the market rush toward an electronic environment has been a presidential agenda item for decades. The race is beyond an electronic infrastructure; it is to move up into cyber-based platforms. The groundwork in Chapter 9 is presented by reviewing key data elements that are in active use and potential analytic opportunities that currently exist. A market evolution—with attendant growing pains— continues with the content of data that is communicated and the market standards to which those content elements are subjected. Examples of those standards are reviewed and the movement into cyber cloud-based platforms are discussed. The remainder of this chapter is dedicated to an extensive case study post mortem demonstrating the mistakes that can occur when implementing a new technology.

The patients' role in this process also must evolve. To learn to effectively advocate for themselves, they must have access to the tools and information (Chapter 10) needed to become a data-driven patient. Helpful tips and hints on how to conduct a patient-focused cyber audit is also be included, and commentaries on effective population health strategies for the cyber patient are provided. A summary of the points discussed throughout this book are consolidated in Chapter 11, and finally Chapter 12 is composed a dedicated reference guide of the tables, charts, and checklists organized into one section for quick access.

Endnotes

1. Busch, R. *Healthcare Fraud Auditing and Detection Guide*, John Wiley & Sons, Hoboken, NJ, 2nd ed., 2012.
2. Busch, R. *Electronic Health Records an Audit and Internal Control Guide*, John Wiley & Sons, Hoboken, NJ, 2008.
3. Busch, R. *Leveraging Data in Healthcare, Best Practices for Controlling, Analyzing, and Using Data*, CRC Press, Taylor & Francis Group, Boca Raton, FL, 2016, HIMSS.

4 Busch, R. *Patient's Healthcare Portfolio: A Practitioner's Guide to Providing Tools for Patients*, CRC Press, Taylor & Francis Group, Boca Raton, FL, 2017.

5 Luckmann, J. and K. C. Sorensen. *Medical Surgical Nursing*, W.B. Saunders Co., Philadelphia, PA, 1979.

6 https://www.cloudwards.net/top-five-cloud-services-for-gamers/#one accessed August 14, 2018.

7 https://www.scientificamerican.com/podcast/episode/online-gamers-help-solve-protein-st-11-09-21/ accessed August 23, 2018.

8 https://www.theguardian.com/technology/2014/jan/25/online-gamers-solving-sciences-biggest-problems

9 https://getnerdio.com/blogs/10-popular-software-service-examples/ accessed August 14, 2018.

Chapter 1

Navigating Health Informatics within the Cyberspace

This is just the beginning, the beginning of
understanding that cyberspace has not limits,
no boundaries.

Nicholas Negroponte
American Architect—the founder and
Chairman Emeritus of Massachusetts
Institute of Technology's Media Lab

Introduction

The *cyber-patient* or *cyber-health consumer* uses Internet
technology to interact with the "seller," or *cyber-healthcare
professional* to facilitate the consumption of healthcare services,
while simultaneously protecting their health information and
identities.

This new way of interacting creates a number of critical challenges not experienced before. These include:

1. How do cyber-patients access and use their health information to make informed treatment and purchase choices?
2. How do cyber-patients and providers ensure they are dealing with authenticated identities and not stolen or misrepresented ones?
3. What complications are introduced by unequal ages or sophistication of technology tools?
4. How is the purchase and sale of healthcare services exchanged between cyber buyers and sellers, and how do insurance companies get linked in?

A brief overview of how other industries have evolved into a self-service economy can serve as a guide into answering these questions.

Self-Service Economy

Either to meet consumers' desire to seek control of their environment or to reduce suppliers' costs, numerous industries have developed self-service solutions. The key to this trend is less about dumping back office functions onto the consumer, but rather, as the consumer engages as an active participant in their services, they will become more informed about what they are consuming, and thus improve their ability to make choices the next time they engage. For example:

■ **Fast Food Industry:** At McDonalds, with the purchase of a soft drink, the seller hands the consumer a cup to fill themselves. Through this, the seller reduces time (and cost) spent filling up the drink, and the consumer gains greater control over their experience through drink choice and through setting the mix of drink versus ice.

This simple step has been expanded through use of mobile phone technology as consumers now order using a smartphone mobile application program (app) and then just drive by and pick up the order. Again, sellers reduce activities the consumers particularly value, and consumers gain greater control.

■ **Travel Industry:** Flyers now make their own reservations online instead of using a travel agent. They save time and see all of their options on line, and the seller reduces time spent reviewing those options.

■ **Automotive:** Self-service pumps have replaced gas station attendants. The consumer enters their own credit card, fills the tanks, and cleans their own windows. The experience reduces the costs to the supplier, which in turn reduces the price of gasoline for the consumer. Another added value perspective: When you get out of your car and walk around it, or wash the windows, you have an opportunity to observe the condition of your car, giving you the chance to notice a new scratch or the even the status of your tires.

■ **Online Shopping:** Amazon, for example, creates a forum in which users can rate products, compare features, and get questions answered by others who have used the product.

■ **Transportation:** Uber has created a rating system whereby the drivers can rate the customers (eventually, perhaps, using those ratings to decide whether they want to pick certain passengers up or charge higher prices), and customers rate their drivers, which could lead Uber to discontinue using that driver.

Self-service healthcare will roll out in two phases. The first is electronic interaction between a patient and a provider. For example, the provider grants electronic access to laboratory test results via an online patient portal. The patient can immediately research the test, the results, and the impact, and have a better informed, deeper conversation with their provider. This will also allow the provider to be more productive on the follow-up treatment regime. In the second phase, a community of users will emerge, sharing experiences with treatments, providers, and insurers, allowing for better decisions on cost and treatments.

The Infomediary Specialist

The emergence of the cyber-patient and the increasingly necessary role of informatics in healthcare are giving rise to a new breed of healthcare professional—the infomediary specialist (IS). As we shall see throughout the book, the domain of expertise that the IS will need to have and which providing effective healthcare requires extends from being an assistant to the patient and compensated by the patient to being an ombudsman for the patient compensated by the provider to being a deeply knowledgeable information technology expert who can assist in the design and development of a provider's healthcare systems in a world where communities of patients and providers easily access and share non-confidential information—a role that might have traditionally been performed in an Information Technology department. As such, the IS, as referred to in this book, does not refer to an individual in an individual role. Rather, it refers to a breadth and depth of knowledge which will find its place somewhere in the healthcare continuum. The specific organizational structure or marketplace entity which will emerge to best provide this expertise is beyond the scope of this book.

Clinical Informatics

Clinical informatics (or health informatics) has several published definitions that involve the use of technology in managing and accessing health information. The following is an illustration of those definitions that have been summarized in the HIMSS

(Healthcare Information and Management Systems) TIGER (Technology Informatics Guiding Education Reform) Committee report dated June 2017[1]: The report contains a listing of informatics definitions from several organizations. The respective source with each definition is noted below. Some appear to be very similar, others focused specifically on their niche area of the market. The consistent theme is that informatics is the science of processing information. The cyber-patient is simply about access to the science of information processed. The infomediary specialist is the scientist that facilitates access to the information within an applied science.

- **Biomedical informatics** is the interdisciplinary field that studies and pursues the effective use of biomedical data, information, and knowledge for scientific inquiry, problem solving, and decision-making, driven by efforts to improve human health. Source: AMIA (American Medical Informatics Association[2]) white paper.
  - *The term "biomedical"* can be broken down into several subfields of study. These include, but are not limited to, public health, the study of molecular and cellular processes (genomic sequencing), bioterrorist attacks, and applications such as the National Notifiable Disease Surveillance System.[3]
  - *The cyber-patient implication:* Access to data on emerging public health conditions.
  - *Imagine* a data driven bio surveillance system that detects mild immunosuppression conditions impacting newborn children within 30 days versus years.
- **Clinical informatics** promotes the understanding, integration, and application of information technology in healthcare settings. Source: HIMSS.
  - Healthcare stakeholders must have a strategy to effectively manage the collection, storage, and dissemination of data, as well as how to interact with the patient with their health information.

- *The cyber-patient implication:* Engaging with the provider in real-time, thereby avoiding long waits in the office. The key is to enhance face-to-face interactions without a hands on examination. The increased interaction between patient and provider will also provide better feedback on the current use of electronic tools such as patient e-health portals.
- *Imagine* an advanced health data driven patient, reviewing the criteria for the selection of a diagnosis code from the International Classification of Diseases index (the rules for when a diagnosis code is appropriate) and the provider having to explain why they chose that diagnosis code over another. If a provider selects an incorrect code for the presenting symptoms, the wrong code with the prescribed treatment will skew clinical analytics on future treatment regimens.

■ **Health informatics** is the interdisciplinary study of the design, development, adoption, and application of IT-based innovations in public health and healthcare services delivery, management, and planning. Source: AMIA and HIMSS.

- *The cyber-patient implications:* Getting access to all potential stakeholders in a medium that is productive and measurable. Testing the effectiveness of the healthcare episode, the quality of management, and short and long term planning of patient care.
- *Imagine* an environment in which all activities of daily living are reconciled with your health data and can be managed from your mobile technology, or cyber highways (online portals) for not one, but multiple second opinions on a proposed treatment regimen.

■ **Health or medical informatics** is defined as the scientific field that deals with biomedical information, data, and knowledge—their storage, retrieval, and optimal use for problem solving and decision-making. Source: Stanford Medical Informatics via Open Clinical.

- *The cyber-patient implications* (ongoing) is the engagement of the user and the ability to measure effective decision-making processes by the patient.
- *Imagine* mobile technology operating in real-time: The impact of a treatment plan, immediate feedback on the efficacy of the plan, and if it needs to be modified based on the most recent clinical data.

■ **Medical information** science is defined as the science of using system-analytic tools to develop procedures (algorithms) for management, process control, decision-making, and scientific analysis of medical knowledge. Source: Shortliffe, (1984). *Medical Informatics* journal via Open Clinical.

- *The cyber-patient implications* (ongoing) is how the individual can obtain access to those conditions that are actively being researched, the context and result of that research, and the authenticity of the data. Further, the organization should have procedures as to who can have access and when to the raw data.
- *Imagine* an interactive, dynamic electronic health record that integrates communications and discussions between the patient and the provider as one consolidated e-document, instead of segregated communication channels (healthcare patient record; emails; snail mail) or having a utility function in the capacity of a USB drive that connects to the cyberworld and tracks all of your health information.

■ **Nursing informatics** is the specialty that integrates nursing science with multiple information management and analytical sciences to identify, define, manage, and communicate data, information, knowledge, and wisdom in nursing practice. Source: *Nursing Informatics: Scope and Standards of Practice, 2nd Edition.* (2015). ANA (American Nurses Association).

- *The cyber-patient implication* is the effective use of nursing practices in the overall health management

of the patient's healthy self and self in illness. With
many providers, the nurse practitioner is often the first
point of entry into a provider organization.
- *Imagine* the virtual nurse accessible at any time via a
network that can coordinate and check in on patients at
home. Social services utilize technology to check in on
foster children while they are at school. Another example involves patients with dementia. The use of facial
recognition software can confirm the identity of the
minor or elderly patient, therefore, validate the identity
of a patient who may be experiencing dementia.
■ **Nutrition informatics** is the effective retrieval, organization, storage, and optimum use of information, data, and
knowledge for food and nutrition related problem solving
and decision-making. Source: Academy of Nutrition and
Dietetics.
- *The cyber-patient implication* is navigating the
Internet domain of established nutritional sciences versus those that are driven by non-traditional sources.
- *Imagine* real-time management of food intake, analysis of content reactions, and exercise tracking through
a single mobile application which is tied to an individual's electronic health record. Something like this
would have the ability to pair with peripheral devices,
like pedometers and treadmills, from a large number
of different companies.
■ **Pharmacy informatics** is the scientific field that
focuses on medication-related data and knowledge
within the continuum of healthcare systems—including its
acquisition, storage, analysis, use, and dissemination—in
the delivery of optimal medication-related patient care
and health outcomes. Source: HIMSS.
- *The cyber-patient implication* is having access to
detailed data as to the efficacy of their own pharmaceutical regimen, specifically over the counter use.
In addition, the use of predictive genomic services

in which individuals have access to information will allow users to understand the impact of how their body metabolizes certain medications.

– *Imagine* a subdermal implant that monitors the presence and volume of certain pharmaceuticals in a patient's bloodstream. Imagine the impact on people who have delicate relationships with medicine, like diabetics and those with immuno-deficiencies. Imagine avoiding complications by giving medications in which the individual is known to lack efficacy.

Engagement of the Cyber-Patient

HIMSS suggests a series of actions for healthcare providers to take in promoting patient engagement:

▪ **Learning about the state of patient engagement and health IT**
  – Patients want to be engaged in their healthcare decision-making process, and those who are engaged as decision-makers in their care tend to be healthier and have better outcomes. Information technology supports this. The HIMSS Patient Engagement Framework[4] provides a five-milestone roadmap for health providers looking to support patients through the use of IT tools and resources: inform me, engage me, empower me, partner with me, and support my e-community.

▪ **Understanding the impact of social media and online patient communities**
  – A 2013 study[5] assessing the influence of participation on patient empowerment concluded that information utility and social support are two benefits obtained by participants in the online health communities. They also identified that online patient communities also help shape perceptions of patient empowerment among community participants.

■ **Staying current on wearables and mobile technology and incorporate patient generated data**
  – Steps are taken in the form of wearable devices and mobile health technology ("MHealth"[6]) to improve the overall health monitoring and health management for patients. These devices also serve as a novel method for data collection to perform healthcare research. The sharing of patient generated health data supplement existing clinical data and provide a more comprehensive picture of ongoing patient health, potentially reducing readmission rates.
■ **Having a strategy for health and Health Information Technology literacy**
  – According to the Agency for Healthcare Research and Quality, "Health literacy is the degree to which individuals have the capacity to obtain, process, and understand basic health information and services needed to make appropriate health decisions." Research[7] shows that patients with low health literacy are less likely to utilize educational health tools. Therefore, health literacy is therefore an essential component to support greater patient engagement in their healthcare. In addition, innovation should develop new approaches like GaaS (Games as a Service) for retention of information.
■ **Having an approach to leveraging digital strategies and a plan to address health disparities**
  – According to the discussions held at HIMSS's 2018 European summit, digital tools can be utilized to address health disparities by following these steps[8,9]:
    • Measure What You Want to Manage
    • Navigate the Digital Divide
    • Design for Your Population's Needs
    • Speak Your Population's Language
    • Build Community Relationships

In applying these concepts, it is important to first conduct a gap analysis of the current state of patient engagement within the organization, specifically in the health IT environment and where the organization would like to be in the future. An assessment of data and technology readiness by both the provider and the patient should be included.

An effective patient engagement program should parallel an effective provider engagement program. The concepts noted in this section are prepared from the patient's perspective previously published within *Patient's Healthcare Portfolio: A Practitioner's Guide*[10]; however, it has been modified in this context for added emphasis on the patient within the cyberworld.

The Cyber Management of Health Data

Within a few years since its advent, the concept of "big data analytics" has transformed into an essential component for the efficient functioning of the healthcare industry. Data analytics finds applications in the following key areas[11]:

- **Clinical data analytics and clinical decision support:** Clinical data analytics employs the use of the patient's electronic health records to identify trends and patterns on the patient's vital signs, which aid the providers to make more efficient treatment decisions for patients.
- **Quality reporting and benchmarking:** Healthcare analytic tools measure key performance indicators and clinical quality metrics that play a significant role in evaluating quality of patient care, healthcare spending, and coordinating care across disparate systems.
- **Revenue cycle, administrative, and operational analytics:** Revenue cycle analytic tools measure vital financial metrics that help facilities gauge their operational health. Operational analytics tools help healthcare

facilities improve operational efficiency by identifying improvement opportunities within their supply chain.

■ **Population health management:** Population health management is an analytics technique that involves identifying groups of patients and aggregating those patients' health data from multiple sources into consolidated patient records. Those records are then analyzed to find insights that could have clinical or financial outcomes. A number of population health management tools are currently prevalent in the market. As new strategies and healthcare initiatives evolve to affect population health management, the market will produce more robust population health management tools that are capable of further streamlining patient healthcare quality and spending.

Cyber Implication Overview

The field of healthcare analytics is rapidly changing. There are more and more tools that have descriptive, predictive, and prescriptive functionalities. This advancement is combined with cutting-edge technologies such as artificial intelligence, machine learning, and deep learning, more effectively establishing a 360-degree view of the patient. How does the practitioner even begin to help patients manage their healthcare data within a cyber-environment? As technology continues to advance, managing this information will require innovation for both professionals and patients to overcome barriers to advancement. Cyber-based technologies in the form of GaaS and SaaS (Software as a Service) will support the transition to new technologies.

Endnotes

1. file:///C:/Users/bbusch/Downloads/TIGER%20Informatics%20Definitions%20v2.0%207.6.17.pdf accessed July 3, 2018.
2. https://www.amia.org/
3. https://www.usfhealthonline.com/resources/key-concepts/bio-medical-informatics/ accessed July 31, 2018.
4. https://www.himss.org/file/1306721/download?token=m2GLGmzp
5. https://www.researchgate.net/publication/262897022_Online_health_communities_An_assessment_of_the_influence_of_participation_on_patient_empowerment_outcomes
6. https://www.himss.org/mhealth
7. https://patientengagementhit.com/news/how-digital-health-literacy-drives-mhealth-patient-engagement
8. https://www.himss.org/news/leveraging-digital-strategies-address-health-disparities-part-1-measure-what-you-want-manage
9. Ibid.
10. Busch, R. *Patient's Healthcare Portfolio: A Practitioner's Guide to Providing Tools for Patients*, CRC Press, Taylor & Francis Group, Boca Raton, FL, 2017.
11. https://healthitanalytics.com/features/how-to-choose-the-right-healthcare-big-data-analytics-tools

Chapter 2

Transcending Case Management within a Cyber-Based Environment

The first step in securing our cyber future is education, and that means everything from educating individuals to companies to the next generation of IT.

Dan Lipinski

American—Politician (born 1966) is the U.S. Representative for Illinois's 3rd congressional district, serving since 2005

Introduction

The emergence of cyber-patients will revolutionize the discipline of healthcare case management. This chapter discusses the principles of case management and strongly suggests the need to formally subdivide the management of health into *financial case management* (FCM) and *clinical case management* (CCM).[1] It also discusses *informatics*, and its integration into case management, in addition to developing an understanding of the importance of case management and informatics for healthcare professionals in their work with patients. The chapter concludes by considering the impact of patients co-mingling the use of their provider's cyber-health technology tools with their own personal use of the cyber environment to navigate their own healthcare needs.

Case Management

Case management is one of the elements behind the multidisciplinary approach to managing a patient's health plan. CCM has been in existence in various formats within the healthcare community for some time. FCM, the management of patient health from a financial perspective, is a new and emerging component of patient healthcare management. The Association of Case Managers defines case management as:

> A collaborative process of assessment, planning, facilitation, and advocacy for options and services to meet an individual's health needs through communication and available resources to promote quality cost-effective outcomes.[2]

Case management is primarily a nursing function. The American Nurses Association (ANA) defines nursing as:

> A caring-based practice in which processes of diagnosis and treatment are applied to human experiences of health and illness.[3]

As with other healthcare professionals, the definition and roles of nursing continue to evolve. The original pioneer of nursing,

Florence Nightingale, established herself as an accomplished administrator during the Crimean War with insight well beyond her era. Consider two of her famous quotes from 1859:

> It may seem a strange principle to enunciate as the very first requirement in a hospital that it should do the sick no harm.[4]

> No man, not even a doctor, ever gives any other definition of what a nurse should be than this—"devoted and obedient." This definition would do just as well for a porter. It might even do for a horse. It would not do for a policeman.[5]

Nightingale's "do the sick no harm" objective holds true today. In fact, the role of a nurse has continued to evolve over the past century and a half. Today, we recognize nurse practitioners as primary care providers and assign them approved reimbursement codes. While the practice of case management is traditionally provided by nurses, over the past decade other allied healthcare professionals, such as licensed practical nurses and rehabilitation professionals, have also been found in case management roles. However, what is significantly missing from the current practice standards and definition of case management is the financial aspect of managing patient care from the patient's perspective. The reference to "promoting quality cost-effective outcomes" does not include the patient's choice in the decision-making process.

Case management roles are well established in brick and mortar healthcare settings, but these roles will be significantly altered and expanded in the cyber-environment. The current use of telephone or—at the technological leading edge, email—to ask questions to and get answers from providers (often with a several day lag) will be replaced by patients instantaneously chatting online with their case managers.

Nurses in their role as case managers need to prepare for this increasing use of data and computer technology.

The British Medical Informatics Society, for example, specifically points this out:

> 'Health informatics' is now tending to replace the previously commoner term 'medical informatics,' reflecting a widespread concern to define an information agenda for health services which *recognizes the role of citizens as agents in their own care, as well as the major information-handling roles of the non-medical healthcare professions*[.][6] (emphasis is the author's)

It is appropriate here to introduce *infomediary specialists*. Infomediary is defined as:

> Any company or web site that gathers information from various sources, [especially] about goods for potential customers; also, a company that gathers information about consumers and markets it to other companies while preserving consumer privacy.[7]

A healthcare infomediary specialist gathers pertinent *health* information. The adaptation of case management and the integration of informatics will put healthcare infomediary specialists in a position to not only gather and provide information, but also provide patient-centric case management services. The quote from British Medical Informatics Society above introduces the idea that non-medical healthcare professionals skilled in cyber informatics could play a role in healthcare informatics. This would be a radical change to case management—akin to the data geeks who transformed baseball, as illustrated by *Moneyball*. Although the quote above also says infomediaries are data gatherers, the more powerful possibility is that healthcare infomediaries could provide the analysis of that data that changes healthcare outcomes. In other words, infomediaries have to be more than data trolls who build databases that the healthcare providers then look at. They could be the ones doing the statistical analysis which will lead to different treatment programs. The role of the deeply experienced, but non-analytic professional will be diminished in favor of the numbers jocks. The healthcare info-mediary is primed for data-driven patient advocacy. This raises the question about provider education: How extensive are the math requirements in nursing school? Even medical school? Probably very little statistics. That will change as informatics progresses.

Infomediary services may range from organizing a patient's health information into a portfolio, to researching continuity of care options, to creation of databases with analytics support.

There will emerge another important role—the cyber-health specialist—who will assist a patient in navigating the current use of computers and information technology among their providers. The cyber-health specialist will have a combination of skills not commonly found in today's healthcare environment. They will be clinically, financially, and computer literate. Resources for cyber-health specialist will be discussed in a later chapter.

Note: This role may be filled by a case management nurse with deeper analytic skills or through adding an analytics specialist to the case management team. Time will tell.

Financial Picture

The marketplace continues to experience significant pressure to control costs, and case managers will find themselves handling both clinical and financial concerns.

A provider determines an appropriate plan of care for a patient using all the clinical information available. But, how much of that plan is influenced by financial considerations? When a payer denies the use of a non-generic cancer treatment and recommends a slightly different generic treatment, is that a financial or clinical decision? When a provider consistently chooses a chemotherapy regimen with the highest rate of reimbursement, is that a financially or clinically based decision? When the system limits healthcare professionals from offering treatment regimens due to price, is the patient's welfare compromised? How should the treatment plan be presented to a patient when potentially conflicting clinical and financial influences are confounded?

Case managers currently neither separate nor delineate clinical and financial considerations and so cannot be transparent about trade-offs when discussing treatment plans with patients. Does the provider meet the standard under the Patient's Bill of Rights[8] if it does not provide full disclosure on all treatment options without any limitations due to insurance coverage? If the patient is presented with only the treatment option approved by the payer, then standards are not being met. What if a patient walks into a provider setting and "buys now" without being informed of all the costs associated with the care ordered? The expectation that the patient receives a treatment plan solely in the best interest of their clinical condition should be a minimum standard. Communication of the financial aspect of the treatment plan should be required and addressed separately.

The complex algorithms that perform predictive analytics[9] based on consumers' online behavioral patterns for targeted advertisements are significantly more advanced than patient engagement analytics among healthcare providers and payers. For example, a simple Google search on the topic of "osteoporosis" will result in a number of related sponsored advertisements. Further, within hours the cyber user will begin to find sponsored ads within future browser searches and multiple social media platforms. Platforms like Facebook and Instagram, as well as search engines like Google, employ advanced predictive modeling algorithms that choose sponsored ads from advertisers to display that are most relevant to the consumers based on their online behavior. These online platforms have developed dedicated marketing programs such as Google AdWords that facilitate digital auctions[10] for advertisement placements among advertisers. In this case, the user will now find sponsored ads from commercial entities specializing in osteoporosis treatment, based on priority determined by their submitted bids for the digital auctions conducted by the online and social media platforms. In the context of effective population health management, providers are competing with interested third parties that are reaching their patient population within minutes of a health search. Imagine what integrity and intent a pop-up advertisement possesses?

Case managers will develop new strategies for virtual worlds. They will consider how best to provide more information more quickly, cyber-health logistics, and the effective management of cyber traffic. They will use tools, developed by the infomediary specialists, to assist patients to manage multiple information technologies simultaneously to reach this information, all the while ensuring clinical and financial case management concerns are separately identified.

Case Management Environments

Hospital-Based FCM Application

FCM based in a hospital setting should ideally contain continual proactive training and educational programs to manage change, mitigate transaction errors, and assure financial integrity in an environment of complex reimbursement requirements. The following case study presents the use of the FCM model independent from CCM in a hospital setting operating without a cyber-based platform. Please note, having a separate team focusing on the financial management of the patient is not typical. Most providers integrate financial management throughout the hospital setting among staff who are providing direct patient care. By separating any financial responsibility from direct patient care providers, the conflict of choosing financial versus clinical activities is avoided.

Background Information and Provider Perspective

The FCM model was implemented at a 240-bed community hospital based in Illinois. While all direct and indirect providers of patient care focused on their core clinical competency, the hospital separated all financial duties and delegated them to a "charge team" that managed every patient within the hospital from a financial perspective.

Lost revenue, due to problems such as payer denials, inappropriate discounts, missed charges, late charges, and write-offs, hurts the financial performance of healthcare providers. Complex payer criteria, increased regulations, and an increased workload for clinicians and other personnel responsible for revenue processing contribute to the magnitude of financial challenges that providers face.

This multidisciplinary charge team, referred to as *Financial Case Managers*, follows patients from admission to discharge. The team managed the significant revenue components of the accounts receivable. They prevented or corrected errors in revenue processing at the time of patient service and assured complete, timely reimbursement for patient services provided.

The Financial Case Managers found that when multidisciplinary expertise and sufficient resources were devoted to monitoring payers, financial performance improved. The typical model for providers calls for a focus on selected managed-care or Medicare patients, instead of daily management of all payers. Addressing each and every payer—regardless of the type of insurance the patient carried or even when the patient had no insurance—proved a key factor to the success of the Financial Case Managers.

The Financial Case Managers realized key benefits: clinicians focused more on patient care, standardized revenue processing in all areas of the hospital, increased flexibility to changing payer requirements, improved compliance with payer regulations and contracts, and improved accounting for the cost of patient care.

Case Management Current State

The following Exhibit 2.1 highlights the gap that currently exists within the discipline of case management. The typical case management model is not divided into two core competencies. This summary also highlights the need to level cyber-based tools for both the patient and the discipline of case management.

Virtual Case Management Application

In healthcare, financial data include the proper documentation of diagnosis and procedure codes. The charges reflect utilization of services to treat health conditions. This data support the evolving population health programs that are being implemented. An integrated cloud-based platform would allow access to aggregated utilization and opportunity for analytics. Clinical case management can use this information in giving patients options based on prior claims history. The next evolution are real-time analytics while the patient is still in house. As charges are processed and care is provided, a daily reconciliation of clinical data with financial data with historical data can send staff alerts of potential problems to allow time to enhance the overall experience and optimize quality of care.

Problem: Getting Paid Correctly for Services Provided

Getting appropriately paid in an environment of constantly changing reimbursement rules and complex payer requirements can be overwhelming. How does a provider manage its contracted revenue throughout day-to-day business?

	PATIENT IDENTIFICATION	PROBLEM IDENTIFICATION	PLANNING	IMPLEMENTING	MONITORING	EVALUATING OUTCOMES
CURRENT STATE • **ACTIVITIES** - Clinical Case Management - Life Care Planning - Discharge Planning	**Patient Identification – Current Trends** • Use a confirmation process to help match the patient and the documentation • Use a standard display of patient attributes across the various systems • Implement monitoring systems to readily detect identification errors • Include high-specificity active alerts and notifications to facilitate patient identification	**Problem Identification - Current Trends** Clinical decision support systems provide: • Evidence based guidance, response to clinical need • To entire care team—including the patient • Through the right channels (e.g. EHR, mobile device, patient portal) • At the right points in workflow for decision making	**Planning – Current Trends** • Patient diagnosis and treatment summary • Best schedule for follow-up tests • Information on late- and long-term effects of cancer treatment • List of symptoms to look for • List of support resources	**Implementation – Current Trends** **CPOE –Computerized provider order entry** • Facilitates healthcare tracking and healthcare progress • Decreases medical error, improve quality **EHR –Electronic Health Records** • Provides patients with necessary information required for optimal care • Help patients understand the complexity of medical care and participate in clinicaldecision-making.	**Patient Monitoring – Current Trends** • Enhance provider communication with remotely monitored patients • Utilize enhanced healthcare metrics, patient messaging, mobile device integration, and in-home-focused monitoring solutions	**Evaluating Outcomes – Current Trends** • Assessing Readiness To Change • Identifying Priorities for Quality Improvement • Implementing Evidence-Based Strategies To Improve Clinical Care • Monitoring Progress and Sustainability of Improvements • Analyzing Return on Investment
- Financial Case Management			Does not provide cost estimate			
CYBER WORLD						
*PROVIDER-CENTRIC TOOLS	• TeamSTEPPS® 2.0 for Long-Term Care -AHRQ	• First Databank • Truven • Cerner	• Siemens Healthineers • Philips Pinnacle 3 • RayStation	• Cerner Millenium • Eclipsys Knowledge-Based CPOE • GE Centricity CPOE	• ApexPro, GE • Honeywell, Genesis • Philips Healthcare, EncorePro 2	• Change Healthcare • Greenway Health
*PATIENT-CENTRIC TOOLS	Opportunity to bridge cost and clinical care	• HumanDx	Opportunity to bridge cost and clinical care	Opportunity to bridge cost and clinical care	• Healow, eClinical Works • MyChart, Epic systems • Follow My Health, Allscripts	Opportunity to bridge cost and clinical care

Exhibit 2.1 Case management perspective.

Note: *Illustrative vendors not meant to be a comprehensive listing of offerings.

The embodiment of both privately and publically contracted plans and legislated rules are voluminous. Are the traditional roles of case management and utilization review addressing the payer requirements in a way that assures that providers receive appropriate reimbursement? Where do delays or losses in payer reimbursement come from, and how do we prevent them from occurring? Further, specific rules associated with clinical outcomes is having a direct impact on how patients are managed within a hospital setting.

Population health metrics are moving healthcare providers into a new era in which what you do to the patient, why you do it, and measuring the results of that care will have a direct impact on what the provider is paid. Quality metrics, and measuring patient outcomes is the new metric. Separating parallel teams of professionals solely focused on clinical considerations from those that are solely focused on financial consideration would avoid conflicts of interest and time constraints to an already tasked environment. The third layer is the patient being presented with options. By separating the functions, the patient will become aware of when clinical options are being presented from financial.

A dedicated infomediary specialist can bridge the information from the financial and clinical considerations. A common area of conflict arises when the patient is about to be discharged from the hospital. The work associated with discharging a patient home is much more involved then discharging a patient to a skilled nursing facility. The provider perspective on constraints of time and resources may fill out the paperwork and transfer the patient. The patient who may be in a position to adequately receive follow-up care in the home loses the opportunity to minimize their exposure to nosocomial infections at the skilled nursing facility, reduce out-of-pocket costs, and be in a more conducive environment as they are recovering. The infomediary specialist can provide support to the patient by ensuring that the patient does not experience gaps in aggregating their health clinical or financial information.

Exhibit 2.2 illustrates the typical flow of a provider's accounts receivable pipeline from preadmission to final account payment. To the right or left of each process step are the potential sources of error that can contribute to denials, delays, or discounts in payer reimbursement. The potential to separate the roles of clinical and financial case management can be integrated throughout this pipeline.

The first potential breakdown occurs at the point of patient entry into the hospital with application of the *72-hour rule*. Medicare requires that any preadmission testing within 72 hours of admission be accounted for and included on the inpatient bill. Failure to do so may subject the hospital to payment reduction. Therefore, processing the patient into the hospital with the appropriate admission criteria, payer information, and notification is critical. In fact, providers must follow correct verification, authorization, and notification processes throughout the patient stay. The nature of healthcare tends to place a priority on the patient's medical needs and the processing of information as secondary. As a result, providers may treat patients with required services, but fail to document and process the information required to ensure appropriate reimbursement.

While clinical personnel typically perform in-house processing of charges, their intuitive interest typically aligns with the care of the patient. The increase in patient acuity, patient-to-nurse ratios, and the stress of daily activity furthers the prioritization of patient care over charge and revenue processing. Meanwhile, complexity in the management of multiple-payer criteria, verification-authorization-notification procedures, and carve out exceptions continue to increase. When a provider reconciles patient accounts with the wrong or insufficient information, they will not receive the contracted payments from managed-care contracts and may subject themselves to an insurance audit or payment reductions from Medicare. Appropriate documentation of patient services remains imperative to receiving the correct reimbursement and avoiding

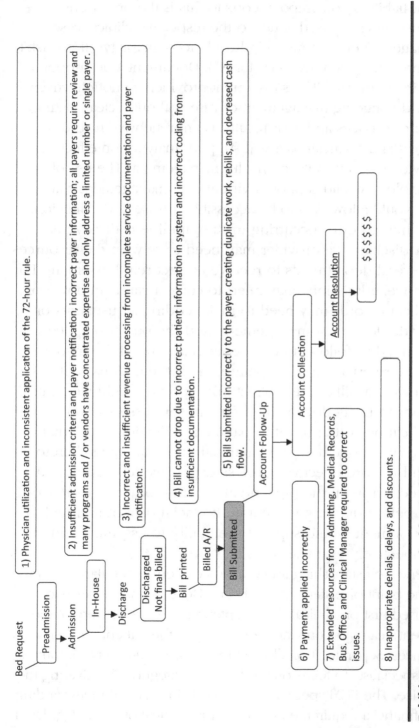

Exhibit 2.2 Accounts receivable pipeline.

audit liability. Contemporaneous to this is the opportunity to pass on care-based issues to the respective clinical case manager (There is a motto in health accountability: "If it wasn't documented, then it wasn't done!"). Documentation supports continuity of care. The subsequent provider cannot effectively provide ongoing management of care without a clear picture of prior services and their results. Comprehensive records of clinical and financial data will support analytics on effective individual and population health management. The use of technology would support a virtual case management platform that would allow data to be accessible for use and validation.

When an error occurring in the pipeline is discovered after discharge, a provider may need to rely on the resources of several departments to receive correct reimbursement. For instance, admissions may need to correct status information, medical records may need to make coding adjustments or provide document management, and the business office may need to follow up on accounts and rebill the invoice. The more errors in the pipeline, the more expensive it is to correct a bill and to collect appropriate reimbursement. Inappropriately documented patient services or payer notifications often result in payment reductions or denial of the claim altogether. The Financial Case Managers therefore found it more effective and less expensive to prevent and correct errors in the pipeline at the time of patient service and before discharge. Accurate financial data in a virtual environment would support the ability to assemble and prospectively estimate ongoing care.

Prior to establishing an FCM process, errors regularly occurred at the point of patient care delivery. Doctors and nurses had focused first on clinical documentation and the delivery of the patient's care and only after on charging the patient for their services. Separate FCM allowed for medical auditors or infomediary specialists to focus on the financial integrity of delivering the service. The FCM specialist developed skill sets in understanding the financial requirements, contractual obligations, and legislated reimbursement requirements. They reviewed the same information for reimbursement that is reviewed for quality-of-care issues. Although their tasks were rooted in financial transactions, their clinical training allowed them to recognize care-based issues and pass them on to the clinical case managers immediately.

Findings

Experienced clinical nurses and allied health support staff worked together to understand clinical diagnosis and procedures for patient care when implementing FCM processes. This team also had medical audit experience and understood hospital charge entry procedures, medical record documentation, payer contracts and requirements, and hospital operational systems. While the FCM model primarily operated to assure accurate and complete reimbursement for hospital patient services delivered, other important functions included:

- Proactively monitoring each process point of the accounts receivable pipeline *at the time of patient service* to prevent or correct errors *before discharge*
- Ensuring the correct application of all payer criteria
- Ensuring the application of verification, authorization, and notification as outlined in the FCM model
- Facilitating patient understanding of the clinical diagnosis and procedures
- Ensuring complete entry of charges
- Ensuring appropriate medical record documentation to support charges and DRG assignment
- Integrating hospital functions that traditionally did not interact: hospital services (clinical staff) and the business infrastructure (business office and finance)
- Independent, unbiased clinical staff focusing on financial integrity of the hospital
- Reporting transaction errors to appropriate departments (e.g., clinical transaction errors to clinical case managers)

Exhibit 2.3 highlights the revenue assurance objectives for payers. Providers can benefit by monitoring and preventing errors in each category of the accounts receivable pipeline. Exhibit 2.4 provides an overview of the functions associated with the financial management of patients in the provider setting.

Medicare:

✓ Appropriate documentation to support a Diagnostic Related Group (DRG) assignmentand accurate case mix

✓ Appropriate documentation for accurate observation versus admitting classification

✓ Appropriate discharge or transfer of a patient

Managed Care:

✓ Appropriate application of payer criteria to prevent Inappropriate denials, delays, and discounts

✓ Complete charges applied for percentage contracts

✓ Appropriate management of processing carve outs

✓ Appropriate documentation to support any payer audit

Commercial:

✓ Complete charges for complete reimbursement

✓ Appropriate documentation to support the bill in comparison to the record

Exhibit 2.3   Payer financial case management program revenue assurance objectives.

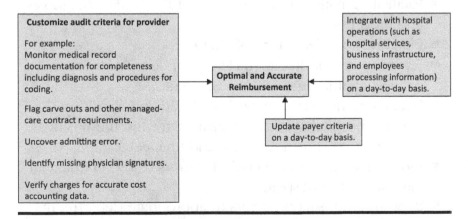

Exhibit 2.4   Highlighted functions of the FCM process.

Additional Findings

Because it assures accurate and timely reimbursement, the FCM model reduces aged accounts receivable and improves cash flow. Relieving admissions, medical records, and the business office from having to review and correct processing errors after discharge also increased hospital efficiency.

The FCM model also has an unintended beneficial consequence. Because the Financial Case Managers handle charge entry revenue processing, clinicians have significantly more time to focus on their patients. Clinical staff and patients alike have noticed the impact. With a small, specialized team of personnel monitoring the accounts receivable pipeline and responding to changes in payer criteria, regulations, and contract requirements, standardization became possible and implementation was smoother. Documentation compliance was also more manageable since the FCM team monitored patient charts during the time of service. Finally, relevant information became more available, enabling accurate determination of the true cost of patient care. Prior to the implementation of the FCM model, this hospital averaged 40 insurance audits per month. The number of audits fell to less than 4–5 per year. The most significant measurement of success, perhaps, was the hospital's return on investment: For every dollar spent on the FCM program, the hospital generated eight extra dollars.

Implementation

The FCM team's optimal hours of operation were noted on a 12-hour-day, 7-days-per-week schedule. The evening-hour activities were effectively handled during the first 4 hours of the 12-hour workday. The team gradually became integrated into the hospital through the following phases:

- *Assessment phase:* Select the appropriate qualified members for the FCM team. Provide the appropriate hospital-based finance training to the team. Place the

team in selected areas of the hospital to analyze the
accounts receivable pipeline and current problems.
Analyze previous payer denials, missed charges, late
charges, and documentation compliance. Provide a
quantitative measurement of selected criteria and current loss of revenue.

■ *Trial phase:* Implement the FCM team on a trial basis to
measure selected criteria, including efficiency of revenue
processing and effectiveness in providing complete and
timely reimbursement. Compare team results to a base-
line formulated from the assessment phase. Conduct and
report a comparison analysis.

■ *Implementation phase:* Expand the FCM model where
successful trials occurred. Continue to measure and report
effectiveness on a routine basis. A hospital may choose to
outsource FCM staff and management to an independent
medical audit firm. Utilizing such an independent audit
firm further reduces conflict of interest. CCM objectives
can be maintained by the hospital's case management
staff. As a result, both clinical and financial components
are not compromised.

■ *Retraining phase:* Provide ongoing training in market
issues and reimbursement issues and integrate new developments into the FCM model.

Although the FCM team targeted the financial management of
the patients treated at the hospital, they also received training
in clinical issues to establish a resource for the clinical case
managers, who monitor patient care. The team's clinical
expertise provided a backup resource to mitigate potential
medical errors and/or minimize the impact of a recognized
error. See Exhibit 2.5 for an illustration of the clinical services
pipeline.

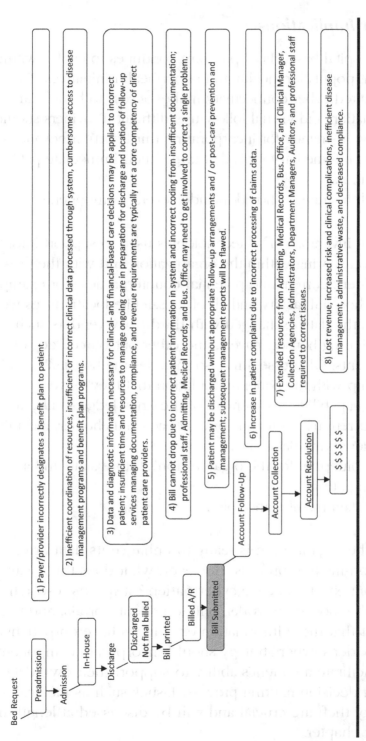

Bed Request

Preadmission

Admission

In-House

Discharge

Discharged
Not final billed

Bill printed

Billed A/R

Bill Submitted

Account Follow-Up

Account Collection

Account Resolution

$ $ $ $ $

1) Payer/provider incorrectly designates a benefit plan to patient.

2) Inefficient coordination of resources, insufficient or incorrect clinical data processed through system, cumbersome access to disease management programs and benefit plan programs.

3) Data and diagnostic information necessary for clinical- and financial-based care decisions may be applied to incorrect patient; insufficient time and resources to manage ongoing care in preparation for discharge and location of follow-up services managing documentation, compliance, and revenue requirements are typically not a core competency of direct patient care providers.

4) Bill cannot drop due to incorrect patient information in system and incorrect coding from insufficient documentation; professional staff, Admitting, Medical Records, and Bus. Office may need to get involved to correct a single problem.

5) Patient may be discharged without appropriate follow-up arrangements and / or post-care prevention and management; subsequent management reports will be flawed.

6) Increase in patient complaints due to incorrect processing of claims data.

7) Extended resources from Admitting, Medical Records, Bus. Office, and Clinical Manager, Collection Agencies, Administrators, Department Managers, Auditors, and professional staff required to correct issues.

8) Lost revenue, increased risk and clinical complications, inefficient disease management, administrative waste, and decreased compliance.

Exhibit 2.5   Clinical services pipeline chart.

Cyber Implications

The hospital-based FCM program continues to evolve within current population-health and cyber-health initiatives. Today, the limited cyber connectivity makes access to beneficiary information and virtual follow-ups difficult. Providers should develop a strategy for incorporating third-party innovations such as infomediary tools that target their immediate patient population.

Such a strategy should include several components:

- An inventory of all technologies used to support information sharing within the organization and with the provider's current and potential counterparties. For example, a hospital facility and all of its satellite locations, as well as the data exchanged with third-party vendors such as clearing houses, payers, and other outsourced departments. Of course, this also includes the hospital's relationship with the patient population that they serve.
- A capabilities assessment of the knowledge, skills, and current use of technology by each stakeholder, including identifying data gaps.
- A blueprint for the organization's future state and a migration.
- A data maintenance plan.

Now the organization is ready to enhance its data driven decision-making process. However, what does this mean in the context of an active cyber patient? It means researching cyber social networks, online patient portals, and the impact that these information exchanges have on patients. A provider's cyber strategy should incorporate components that facilitate a patient's ability to support their own data-driven decision-making process. Issues such as medical identity theft are crucial and will be discussed at length in a later chapter.

Summary

Healthcare stakeholders need to separate patient FCM from CCM. This separation removes the conflict of interest that can result when one individual makes both clinical and financial case management decisions. FCM creates a medical record-based charge capture and revenue management system. It also greatly reduces charges that post 24–48 hours after a patient leaves a facility, thereby eliminating unnecessary follow-up work for the business office. FCM ensures that providers capture charges appropriately and continually update their charge master.

Consumer-Based FCM

The consumer or patient perspective of FCM provides a foundation for a consumer to monitor market and government changes while receiving healthcare services, insurance companies, hospitals, physicians, and patients do not have a resource to predict or control the cost of an episode of care. Yet, under consumer-directed health plans, all are expected to do so. A consumer FCM application is the missing link that will help place the patient in a position to manage the costs during an episode of healthcare.

Patients are finding themselves moving from one e-health platform to another based on the connectivity of their provider. Tools aimed at helping patients manage their healthcare episodes exist in various unconnected platforms. The cyber-health market has not yet produced an offering that facilitates buying healthcare goods, managing personal health information from a clinical and financial perspective, and managing services in a world with very complex rules. Nontraditional and unclearly regulated third-party stakeholders seeking health-minded consumers are much more aggressive within social media platforms in grasping at those cyber dollars in comparison to traditional provider platforms.

Without cyber-based FCM, it is impossible for a patient to balance costs with clinical efficacy to manage their care. Our healthcare system has more than 500,000 recognized diagnoses and more than 200,000 officially established procedures. A hospital may have as many as 10,000 rules to apply to these diagnoses and procedures, and these rules may change monthly, quarterly, and annually. This case management task, then, is performed by the provider or insurance company with sufficient technology expertise and resources. The patient becomes a bystander.

When a patient enters a hospital or clinic, the doctor or nurse must be ready to assess the patient, select one or more of the diagnosis and procedure codes, and have a cost-effective plan of care ready to execute at any given notice by a government-sponsored program. How are healthcare providers able to do this? The market has provided managed care as its answer. *Managed care* is the arrangement in which an organization, such as an Health Maintenance Organization, another type of doctor-hospital network, or an insurance company, acts as intermediary between the person seeking care and the physician. It is the system that manages healthcare delivery to control costs. Hospitals expanded the roles and concepts of case management in response to managed care and other payer initiatives.

Case management, when coupled with managed care, becomes a comprehensive labor-intensive process that covers patient evaluation, treatment planning, referral, follow-up, and payment collection. Case management manages and delivers quality clinical care in a setting of constrained resources. These programs have included critical pathways, clinical maps, clinical trajectories, integrated plans of care, and quality controls—all to deliver care. The limitation of current programs is the clear separation of CCM from FCM.

Defined contribution is an alternative to *managed care.* Instead of having the payer or some other third-party drive selection and choice, defined contribution considers the patient as a consumer at the center of the selection process.

It provides patients the opportunity to specify the care they will receive and control the dollars contributed to their healthcare plan. Conceptually, defined contribution seems like a worthy endeavor. Practically, however, if providers, insurance companies, and employers had difficulty managing the selection, execution, and cost management of particular diagnoses and procedures, then how do we expect patients to understand the diagnosis and procedure selection process, the treatment choices available, and the complex payment rules necessary to make effective healthcare decisions without FCM tools?

Market Problems: The Industry as It Operates Today

Patients, providers, employers, and insurance companies face logistical nightmares in effectively managing financially related healthcare information. Effective patient management tools simply do not exist. Opportunities for follow-up care, for instance, often slip past patients and providers unrecognized. Without effective patient management tools, ongoing governmental and market changes, coupled with the intricate healthcare (diagnoses and procedures) selection and maintenance process, will continue to cause financial healthcare management to elude our patient-consumers.

Today, patients use the explanation of benefits they receive from insurance companies to manage their healthcare expenditures after an episode of care. Dave Barry, from the *Miami Herald*, captured the utility of an explanation of benefit well when he quipped:

> At some point in the past, some member of my family apparently received medical care, and now every day, rain or shine, my employer's insurance company sends me at least one letter, comically titled "EXPLANATION OF BENEFITS," which

looks like it was created by the Internal Revenue Service from hell. It's covered with numbers indicating my in-network, out-of-pocket deductible; my out-of-network, non-deductible pocketable; my semi-pocketed, non-workable, indestructible Donald Duckable, etc. For all I know, somewhere in all these numbers is a charge for Dr. Cohn's fish food. What am I supposed to DO with this information?[11]

Consumer FCM Model Application

In 1996, I began introducing patients to a specific FCM structure, which I referred to as a *Healthcare Portfolio*, to facilitate the personal management of their health. The use of a Healthcare Portfolio within an electronic personal health record supports the integration of management protected health information from hard copy to electronic environment. An introductory section of a *Healthcare Portfolio* explains the concept of self-management to patients and provides information on:

■ What is a Healthcare Portfolio
■ Why patients need a Healthcare Portfolio
■ What goes into a Healthcare Portfolio
■ How to get started on a Healthcare Portfolio
■ How to take care of a Healthcare Portfolio

Documenting a self-health history (a critical part of a healthcare portfolio) prepares patients to formulate their personal health information.

Personal health financial management helps patients manage their financial health information. It provides instructions to help patients request financial documents from providers and health insurance companies.

A Healthcare Portfolio also includes a Buyer Beware section that educates patients to manage vulnerabilities and avoid being victims of fraud. It includes where to get up-to-date fraud alerts regarding providers, payers, suppliers, pharmaceuticals, and supplements. The complexity of the healthcare environment additionally calls for patients to be prepared from a legal perspective.

Paperwork can often overwhelm patients. Even the most well intentioned personal health record infrastructures or tools often lack a resource to smooth out the bumps in the road. With this understanding, best practices for effective management of patient health information concluded with the need to utilize nurses trained in finance, case management, medical audit, and fraud to offer infomediary instruction, assistance, research, advocacy, and support services for patients. These professionals were trained as *health infomediary specialists*.

Because many healthcare issues involve pharmaceuticals (such as the coordination of care from multiple prescribing providers, the potential for medical errors, the cost associated with these medications, and medication management by the patient), the Healthcare Portfolio also devotes a separate section to pharmaceuticals.

Other sections of a Healthcare Portfolio provide information to help patients manage their healthcare episodes:

> These other sections may also be used as an infomediary audit checklist to evaluate any personal health record management system. The personal healthcare portfolio is a patient-centric health data management guide and tool principally used by the patient and supported by providers and advocates to reinforce data driven health decisions.[12]

Personal Healthcare Portfolio Application

The following case studies demonstrate how the Healthcare Portfolio assisted three patients who were stuck in the healthcare system. The first case exemplifies the ideal use of the Healthcare Portfolio, in which it prepares and empowers patients prior to the occurrence of any adverse event. The second and most common case shows how the Healthcare Portfolio helps to mitigate an issue after its occurrence and highlights the role of the health infomediary specialist as an independent advocate and resource. The third case illustrates the concurrent use of Healthcare Portfolio and a health infomediary specialist while receiving a service. Please note, all names have been change to maintain anonymity of the actual patient.

Case Study #1: Healthcare Portfolio Implementation Prior to Adverse Event

"Dina," a 56-year-old female diagnosed with breast cancer, utilized the FCM/CCM process by implementing the steps outlined above in creating her Healthcare Portfolio. Dina's healthcare encounters and history were studied and followed for several years.

Prior to receiving any cancer treatment services, Dina encountered seven different licensed professionals who each directed a portion of the assessment for her initial treatment. As she traveled between each provider, Dina realized that not one of them had a complete record of her care that incorporated information from each of her other six providers. Each provider therefore planned to make his or her assessment without complete information from Dina's other concurrent providers. Uncomfortable with this scenario, Dina began to accumulate and share her own record of information from and with each provider as she traveled between them.

Dina eventually made the decision on an initial course of action to treat her cancer. It involved a breast lumpectomy and she was given anesthesia for the first time in her life. Dina then underwent the very unfortunate experience of intraoperative awakening. Although she woke up in pain, crying in the recovery room, her physician at the time told her that "she was just dreaming."

As Dina continued her course of treatment, the anesthesia incident became part of her own traveling Healthcare Portfolio. During subsequent surgeries, Dina asked the anesthesiologist to review the operative record from her breast lumpectomy. The doctors thanked her for preventing further medical errors and she never experienced intraoperative awakening again.

In year three of her cancer treatment, Dina received her first denial from her insurance company. During this 3-year period Dina had collected a detailed history of all documents associated with her medical bills. This allowed her the ability to access all of her financial information. The sudden denial for a services that was deemed not medically necessary could be proven simply by the fact that she had been receiving the denied service for the past 3 years. Because of Dina's initial investment in FCM organization, she had all the necessary information at her disposal to advocate for herself in any correspondence with her insurance carrier and was able to mitigate the presenting issue. Specifically, she was able to provide the "medically necessary" documentation that justified continued treatment.

The combination of FCM and CCM helped Dina make a cohesive and comprehensive initial treatment option. CCM also helped discover an unknown allergic reaction to anesthesia that resulted in one episode of intraoperative awakening and prevented future medical errors by empowering Dina to share the discovery with subsequent providers. Finally, through FCM, Dina had the information to address the financial matters impacting her ongoing care.

Case Study #2: Healthcare Portfolio Implementation after Adverse Event with Health Infomediary Specialist Support

"Kevin" was about 2 1/2-years old when his parents requested patient advocate support. Kevin's history included serial ear infections and subsequent procedures since birth. Due to the nature of the ear infections, Kevin was not progressing in his motor development—particularly for crawling and being mobile—and resulted in atrophy of his muscles and stunted development. Kevin's doctor ordered physical therapy, but the insurance carrier denied the treatment on the basis that developmental delay was not a covered item and that the issue was not medically related. Due to the severity of atrophy, Kevin's parents initiated his physical therapy treatment out-of-pocket as directed by their physician. During this time, they also continued to pay Kevin's insurance premiums for his policy, which they purchased independently as small business owners.

Kevin's parents reviewed their predicament with their patient advocate. They were advised to retroactively implement Healthcare Portfolio's FCM and CCM processes from the time of Kevin's birth. The clinical data collected demonstrated that Kevin's condition indeed resulted from medical problems associated with his ear infections.

Kevin's parents also collected 2 years of correspondences with the insurance carrier to review with their patient advocate. The advocate in the role of a health infomediary specialist noted that these letters lacked specific correspondence language that ensures a patient's right to their health information. Patients (guardians) have a *right to their health information (Individuals' Right under Health Insurance and Accountability Act of 1996 to Access their Health Information 45 CFR § 164.524*[13]*)*. Specifically, information included in the right to access is referred to as the "designated record set."

> Individuals have a right to access protected health information in a "designated record set." A "designated record set" is defined at 45 CFR 164.501 as a group of records maintained by or for a covered entity that comprises the:
>
> ■ Medical records and billing records about individuals maintained by or for a covered healthcare provider;

- Enrollment, payment, claims adjudication, and case or medical management record systems maintained by or for a health plan; or
- Other records that are used, in whole or in part, by or for the covered entity to make decisions about individuals. This last category includes records that are used to make decisions about any individuals, whether or not the records have been used to make a decision about the particular individual requesting access.

  The term "record" means any item, collection, or grouping of information that includes protected health information and is maintained, collected, used, or disseminated by or for a covered entity.[14]

The infomediary specialist wrote a letter on behalf of the patient's guardian to the private carrier disputing the denial. Although the next correspondence from the payer resulted in a continued denial of service due to services not covered for developmental delay, the letter finally included information on the patient's right to appeal to the State Department of Insurance. The next step in the process involved submitting a letter on behalf of Kevin to appeal the payer's denial with the State Department of Insurance. Several weeks later, Kevin's parents received a letter from the state noting that the carrier reversed the denial and confirming payment to the hospital. Eventually, Kevin's parents were able to reclaim their original out-of-pocket expenses from the provider.

Kevin's parents received the requisite instruction to manage health information through FCM and CCM; education and training under the Individual Rights under Health Insurance and Accountability Act of 1996 to access information; advocacy support pertaining to appeal rights with the Department of Insurance; and support while obtaining a refund from the hospital for paying covered expenses out-of-pocket.

Case Study #3: Concurrent Implementation of Healthcare Portfolio and Health Infomediary Specialist Support

"Laura" was a 36-year-old mother of two. When the time came for Laura to be admitted into the hospital for a medical (not fertility-related) hysterectomy, she already had established a relationship with her infomediary specialist. Laura was visited by her infomediary specialist (IS) in the hospital on the first day following surgery and initiated both the FCM and CCM processes.

During this initial post-surgery visit, it was observed that Laura was receiving intravenous Pitocin—a medication often utilized to induce labor. When an evening-shift nurse entered the room, the IS questioned the purpose of the medication. Before leaving the room, the evening-shift nurse replied, "She is not getting Pitocin...the drug is just mislabeled."

Eight hours later, Laura was still on Pitocin and began complaining of severe migraine headaches. When the day-shift nurse came in, she apologized to Laura and promptly removed the Pitocin, replacing it with normal saline. The day-shift nurse explained that she had been working a 12-hour shift and must have inadvertently hung the Pitocin as a result of implementing routine standing orders.

Frightened and unaware of what complications might result from the nurse's error, Laura turned to a professional she knew and could trust. She turned to her health infomediary specialist—as a professional who would put her own interests first and who could advocate on her behalf. After contacting the drug manufacturer, it was determined that specific research on the impact of Pitocin on women without a uterus did not exist.

Ever since surgery, Laura had continued to experience adverse issues with her bladder. (Although she never filed a medical malpractice claim, the hospital never submitted a bill for the surgery.)

Laura's active CCM support services mitigated the damages of an active medical error and was a resource for Laura's clinical questions not sufficiently answered by her provider. Of interest, the advocate continued to support Laura during this confinement and helped her through three other errors relating to this hysterectomy surgery. The infomediary specialist shifted to FCM functions in order to obtain approval from the payer for subsequent care related to the post-operative complications.

Cyber Implications

Patients are seeking third-party support in the form of infomediary specialists—who also specialize in the role of patient advocate—to help others manage their healthcare services. Currently patients move from one provider electronic portal to another. Within the cyberworld, consider the development of global online shopping malls for healthcare support services. The Healthcare Cyber Specialist will be in the best position to provide the patient cyber support in navigating the Internet to find and utilize available services. In obtaining support, consumers need to learn to distinguish resources that provide financial support (FCM), clinical support (CCM), and those resources that have the ability to provide *both* financial and clinical support. Further, the notion of "buyer beware" is very important to include in teaching materials since most patients seeking help may be more focused on their healthcare needs and, as a result, are more vulnerable.

Virtual Case Management

We have presented above a seemingly unsolvable problem: How can patients be empowered to integrate clinical recommendations with financial practicalities so as to control their own health when the data and systems requirements to do so are so complex and onerous as to be outside the capabilities of almost all consumers? *Virtual case management* (VCM), *which* presents separate financial and clinical case management options and then assists patients to integrate them, provides the answer. VCM and infomediary specialists will provide patients the resources to select, manage, control, and predict the cost of an episode of healthcare.

VCM is case management where the communication of information and provision of services function in a true state of interoperability. VCM will automate the decision-making process, facilitate recommendations, and communicate personalized information and advice. It will create the infrastructure desperately needed to manage healthcare services in a defined-contribution or managed-care environment. Cyber-health infomediary specialists will test to ensure that VCM tools empower patients, encourage access, mitigate errors, and provide patients with ability to advocate for themselves. The ideal model for VCM in the cyber-health environment will vary depending on the market player at hand.

VCM Payer Model

The VCM *payer model* addresses the management of patient requested services, the fees associated with those services, and ensuring appropriate capture of all associated payment criteria. For example, a request for a hip replacement typically involves either a telephonic, facsimile, mail, or electronic submission from a provider. A service request could also be directly submitted by a patient. Payer service request responses therefore involve labor-intensive manual processes. They are dependent on specific users such as review staff or claims adjustors to interpret payment criteria, which can result in inconsistent application of those criteria. In addition, the staff may not effectively separate financially based decisions (e.g., denying service because it is not covered by the patient's plan) from clinically based decisions (e.g., denying service because it is not medically necessary). A VCM payer model should recognize and separate the concepts of CCM and FCM to gather data intelligence about how their beneficiary decisions are made to better serve the insured and reduce risk resulting from inappropriate claims handling.

Payers find themselves in the uncomfortable position of preventing conflicts of interest from occurring when making decisions on coverage. Conflicts arise when denying a patient's health service results in direct financial gain for the insurance company. Therefore, payers will constantly wrestle with well-defined processes that protect the insured from receiving medically unnecessary services versus those that thwart costly medically necessary services. Payers must also bear the burden of continuously screening claims to catch false claim submissions. Unfortunately, the screening can compromise legitimate patients with legitimate diagnoses that are being treated by legitimate providers.

VCM Patient Model

A VCM *patient model* will support a new healthcare environment where patients acting like customers will drive the treatment selection process using an intelligent electronic web-based application, equipped with tools for comparative analysis and interactive decision-making. These tools will engage patients and will, over time, learn to address patient needs and concerns.

The VCM patient model should allow patients to control the selection and management of services within and out-of-network. The VCM patient model should address CCM, FCM, and the other issues covered by the Healthcare Portfolio. Although numerous vendor offerings promote personal health management record systems, self-directed patient case management tools do not exist. The direction of the cyber community calls for the ability to effectively manage health information, finances associated with healthcare support, and the integration of infomediary specialists.

VCM Hospital Model

The referenced FCM *hospital model* in the community-hospital case study earlier in this chapter demonstrates how the separation of FCM and CCM causes significant improvements in efficiency while patients are in the hospital. Separating FCM from CCM also improves efficiency after patient discharge by enabling hospitals to better manage future services and reimbursement issues. When a hospital performs hip-replacement surgery on a patient, for example, it may miss the opportunity to provide rehabilitation services to the patient upon discharge. Hospitals have various case management methodologies for inpatient monitoring, but managing post-operative care and general subsequent care can be a logistical nightmare. Managing outpatient care is currently a manual, disconnected process where individuals must make phone calls and depend on laborious facsimile transmissions on a case-by-case basis to place patients. However, automated post-discharge case management tools are slowly evolving through population cyber-health initiatives.

VCM Physician Model

A VCM *physician model* should allow physicians to better manage future services and reimbursement issues once they determine a patient's diagnosis and treatment plan. The separation of CCM and FCM, with a trained physician and an informed patient, will help both parties in organizing, structuring, and advocating active and future care.

For example, when a physician diagnoses a patient with a severe arthritic condition of the hip and recommends a total hip replacement, the physician cannot proceed with his plan of care without the coordination of the other players in the marketplace. A payer might decide that it will pay for only 3 days of rehabilitation, but the physician plan of care might require 7 days of rehabilitation for optimal outcome. As a result, a physician could place surgery on hold until completion of the entire plan of care. When physicians recommend a plan of care, they should present the patient with two separate plans: a CCM plan defined by the prescribed regimen and an FCM plan that explains the current financial obligations, determinations, and implications. When patients have this information, they can then make informed decisions when considering their treatment plan. Because patients would know the finance issues that might be in dispute with their insurance carrier, they would be able to initiate an appeal with their carrier based on the two separate plans of care.

The current problem in the marketplace lies in convolution of clinical decisions arrived with financial determinations. The patient has a right to both sets of information and assurance that one set of criteria does not impact the other. The VCM physician model provides coordination of approved services and options to facilitate the financing of non-covered services. As major health systems incorporate population health tools, the ability for cyber communications between the patient and provider should evolve with the adaption of technology tools. Effective, mobile, patient-centric offerings will continue to be segmented among defined professional stakeholders.

VCM Allied Health Services

The market focuses heavily on services provided by physicians and hospitals. However, the delivery of patient care involves numerous other services. *Allied health services* providers such as physical therapists, dialysis technicians, and other non-traditional professionals will also benefit from a VCM model. For example, when a patient has a total hip replacement, insurance coverage may allow for in-home physical therapy. The VCM allied health services model will enable these types of providers to better manage services and reimbursement issues.

VCM Non-Traditional Health Services Model

The science behind many of the benefits of non-traditional provider care services has been around for well over a 100 years, if not longer. But due to limitations of payer coverage, patients typically finance these services directly. Non-traditional services providers therefore have a leg up in the marketplace because, unlike traditional providers, they are not dependent on payers for their revenues. A VCM *non-traditional health services model* will nevertheless enable better management of services and reimbursement issues in this segment of the market. When a patient has a total hip replacement, for example, policy coverage may provide for some type of limited chiropractic rehabilitation services or acupuncture for pain management. The VCM non-traditional health services model will help integrate the information generated by the non-traditional providers with that of traditional care providers, whose services are typically recognized by the payer community.

VCM Other Business Services Model

With the advent of cyber-health, it is important to recognize other types of related services in the marketplace. For instance, healthcare infomediary specialists facilitate management of patient services, ensure policy requirements, and resolve reimbursement issues. Other business providers could include disease management firms that provide supplemental information to any one of the market players or a nursing home that temporarily discharges a patient to a hospital for a total hip replacement. Upon patient discharge, the nursing home does not currently have the capacity to directly manage any rehabilitation process. The logistics of finding interim care and lodging for this patient are therefore manual, cumbersome, and limited. Another business provider may include a school system that manages the health records of the children within its school district. The VCM *other business services model* would simplify and automate these processes. Integrating these services into FCM and CCM will promote a comprehensive, effective patient-driven cyber-health environment.

Cyber Implication Overview

Virtual case management will allow patients and infomediary specialists to leverage technology to delineate and integrate the patient's treatment options. The patient will enhance their ability to make informed decisions by separating clinical and financial considerations. As stated previously, the data associated with clinical options should be presented, with separate alternative options which reflect financial considerations. Separating FCM from CCM in the VCM model will set the stage for developing conflict-of-interest controls throughout the healthcare continuum. Further, tools to assist patients in a virtual environment is the next wave of informatics in healthcare. This chapter has outlined those roles within various types of virtual case management programs. The next chapter will introduce the role of the cyber nurse case manager, review current case management practices, and the subject matter expertise relevant to perform the function. The next chapter will also include virtual world implications of case management.

Endnotes

[1] Busch, R. *Electronic Health Records an Audit and Internal Control Guide* John Wiley & Sons, Hoboken, NJ, 2008.
[2] http://www.cmsa.org/who-we-are/what-is-a-case-manager/ accessed July 18, 2018.
[3] https://www.ncbi.nlm.nih.gov/books/NBK232401/ accessed July 18, 2018.

[4] https://www.brainyquote.com/quotes/florence_nightingale_101985 accessed July 19, 2018.

[5] https://www.bmj.com/content/bmj/288/6412/216.full.pdf accessed July 19, 2018.

[6] University of Iowa Health Informatics, © 2005, University of Iowa, http://www2.uiowa.edu/hinfo/academics/what_is_hi.html, accessed December 11, 2007.

[7] Infomediary (n.d.). Webster's New Millennium™ Dictionary of English, Preview Edition (v 0.9.7), retrieved December 11, 2007, from Dictionary.com website: http://dictionary.reference.com/browse/infomediary.

[8] https://www.cms.gov/CCIIO/Programs-and-Initiatives/Health-Insurance-Market-Reforms/Patients-Bill-of-Rights.html accessed July 27, 2018.

[9] Predictive modeling of consumer financial behavior using supervised segmentation and nearest-neighbor matching https://patents.google.com/patent/US7165037B2/en

[10] How do Google's and Facebook's Online Ad Systems Work? https://www.nytimes.com/2017/10/12/technology/how-facebook-ads-work.html

[11] DATE: Sunday, October 8, 2000 Miami Herald EDITION: Final SOURCE/CREDIT LINE: By DAVE BARRY, Herald Columnist

[12] Busch, R. *Patient's Healthcare Portfolio: A Practitioner's Guide to Providing Tools for Patients*, CRC Press, Taylor & Francis Group, Boca Raton, FL, 2017.

[13] https://www.hhs.gov/hipaa/for-professionals/privacy/guidance/access/index.html accessed July 27, 2018.

[14] Ibid.

Chapter 3

The Cyber-Nurse Case Manager

I feel sort of really aware of how the ... online cyber world has begun to take over reality.

Brad Paisley
American Country Musician, songwriter. Born: 1972

Introduction

"I feel sort of really kind of aware" is the theme of healthcare providers navigating technology and most certainly that of patients trying to use their providers' e-health platforms. Both patients and case managers are struggling in the management of and access to information, and there have arisen new healthcare roles and tools to bridge the gap between current capabilities and future opportunities. The role of the cyber-nurse case manager (CNCM), the current case management practices he or she will use, and the subject matter expertise needed to perform that function, will all significantly change as cloud-based technology saturates healthcare. The progression of informatics tools available to providers has lagged those available in other industries, and the inability of general purpose tools like Internet browsers to distinguish credible information from the rest will create the need for infomediary specialists. The demand for online tools has accelerated the pace of provider production of informatics technologies. The practice standards, skills, abilities, and experiences in traditional provider- and payer-based environments will be so fundamentally transformed as to appear newly created. The transformation is not about performing tasks via a computer instead of telephone or the task of filling out online forms instead of paperwork. The transformation of case management requires the ability to download, analyze, and interpret numbers, outcomes from an unfamiliar source instead of simply using one's own prior experience.

Case Management

Case management can be carried out by individual providers or by a series of providers acting in collaboration to support the needs of the patient. The services may be prospective, contemporaneous, or retrospective (as an examination of claims denied as medically unnecessary).

The Case Management Society of America[1] (CMSA) is a professional association that supports the ongoing practice standards for case management. The CMSA healthcare continuum model is illustrated in Exhibit 3.1.

Note specifically the role of case management in coordinating social support, financial support, providers, and understanding ethical and legal considerations. Further case management functions include assessment, planning, collaboration, implementation, monitoring, and evaluation. Case management crucially reduces the fragmentation of care that is often experienced by clients who obtain healthcare

Exhibit 3.1 Case management model.

services from multiple providers. The fragmentation includes geographic considerations, as CMSA points out:

> The case manager practices in accordance with applicable local, state, and federal laws. The case manager has knowledge of applicable accreditation and regulatory statutes governing sponsoring agencies that specifically pertain to delivery of case management services.

Technology standards for practices and laws will be driven by the geographic location of the patient. As the cyber-nurse operates in a virtual world with increasing likelihood of being physically removed from the patient, he or she will need to be knowledgeable of the laws and state requirements in which the patient is based rather than the location of the case manager (National Council of State Boards of Nursing[2]).

The CNCM should anticipate ongoing updates on how the market will be managed during the global integration of cyber-health delivery and/or the coordination of services. With the use of telemedicine, the two-way real-time interactive communication between the patient and provider occurs with the effective use of camera, sound, and approved diagnostic equipment from any location.

Advances in the cyberworld have profound implications on case management since the CMSA published practice standards in 2010, including patient/client identification and selection of case management services, problem identification, planning, implementing, monitoring, evaluating, and outcome identification. A cyber-nurse will have to recognize and understand how technology advances change traditional case management tasks.

Key Issues in Cyber Case Management

Identity Proofing: The in-person process of identifying the patient and the patient's ability to validate the provider, which we currently have, will give way in a virtual world. The complexity of identity theft has implications that go well beyond the use of identity for financial purposes. This will introduce a new type of risk, specifically the accidental referral of an illicit party who misrepresents themselves, resulting in financial loss in addition to bad outcomes from the delivery of unlicensed or uncredentialled care.

Professional Code of Conduct Within the Virtual World: These considerations will be driven by respective professional code of conducts within each professional designation. For example, registered nurses are subject to the code of conduct within their respective state licensure and practice standards of their professional organizations. In the cyber environment the process of identity proofing and confirmation of the identity will need to be established. How will licenses be validated? Practice standards may be found within professional organization such as Healthcare Information and Management Systems Society (HIMSS) and other technology-based professional organizations.

Privacy and Confidentiality: Healthcare literature on the subject of privacy within the cyber environment is focused on cyber security and breaches. The CNCM will have to take into consideration the security of the "cyber-mall" environment in which communications takes place, while security professionals will have to ensure the requirements under HIPAA[3] are met.

Financial versus Clinical Case Management[4]: There is a significant amount of pressure on case managers to control the cost of managing a patient's illness. When a provider determines an appropriate plan of care for a patient, both clinical variables and financial considerations equally impact the formulation of the plan. The expectation that the patient received a treatment plan solely in the best interest of his clinical condition should be a minimum standard. Communication regarding financing of the plan should, nevertheless, be included.

Provider financial case management creates a records-based charge capture and revenue management system to capture charges appropriately and calculate revenue. Financial case management deals with issues such as payer denials, inappropriate discounts, missed charges, late charges, and write-offs, these can cause revenue loss, which hurts the healthcare provider's performance. Complex payer criteria, increased regulations, and an increased workload for clinicians and other personnel responsible for revenue processing contribute to the magnitude of the financial challenges that the providers face.

Provider clinical case management deals with issues such as mitigation of potential medical errors and minimizing the impact of a recognized error. The clinical case management aims to enhance patient care by focusing on details such as increasing patient acuity, patient-to-nurse ratio, and stress of daily activity.

To reiterate the argument made in Chapter 2, hospitals need to separate patient financial case management from clinical case management. The separation of services removes the conflicts of interest that arise when the same individual makes both financial and case management decisions. The cyber-based implication is effective use of technology to access information and analytics virtually.

Subject Matter Expertise within Case Management

Case management practice varies in intensity and complexity based on four factors (Powell[5] and Tahan, 2008[6]; Tahan, 2008[7]; CMSA Standards of Practice for Case Management 2016[8]). According to the CMSA Standards of Practice for Case Management 2016, these four factors are the context of the care setting (e.g., wellness and prevention, acute, subacute, and rehabilitative, skilled care, or end-of-life); the health conditions and needs of the client population served, including the needs of the client's family or family caregivers; the reimbursement method applied, such as managed care, workers' compensation Medicare or Medicaid; and the healthcare professional discipline of the designated case manager such as, but not limited to, a registered nurse, social worker, physician, rehabilitation counselor, or disability manager.[9]

The high utilization of mobile phones by clients makes knowing the physical location of the client problematic for the case manager to practice nursing according the appropriate state's licensure laws. As telehealth becomes more accepted, physicians are making inroads to having their licenses recognized across state lines. Now, a registered nurse has to live in a compact state in order to have the license recognized in the other compact states (Nurse Licensure Compact approved by the May 4, 2015 Special Delegate Assembly of the National Council of State Boards of Nursing).

The inclusion of case management in hospital emergency rooms to reduce unnecessary hospital admissions through referrals to community resources has been instrumental to safe cost reduction programs. Many hospital emergency rooms have implemented programs to enroll the indigent into government programs such as Medicaid in order to support outpatient resources. Private payers have also added referral services in the emergency room in order to direct clients to care within the health plan. The goal of hospital-based care management is a safe transition of care to the appropriate level of care at the right time. It is equally important to formulate back-up plans with the caregiver should he/she be unavailable to perform the caregiver role for even a short period of time. Quick access to information on the patient's payer is necessary for many of these referral programs to work effectively. This is facilitated by advances in cyber technology.

Virtual World Implications

The cyber-nurse may participate in or collaborate with a professional who creates life care plans for patients. Having a credentialed life care planner skilled in the remote virtual process (cloud-based cyber platform) of case management may continue to assist a family or caregivers in managing ongoing health issues. In particular, post discharge often results in a sense of ambiguity, although the patient continues to benefit from the expertise of a case manager while receiving the required relevant care. Issues in which a case manager can provide support may include access to ongoing medical issues, managing supplies/equipment/caregivers, and all the other items set forth in the life care plan. The family may require expertise such as understanding insurance and other resource options. Upon the successful funding from a payer, a case manager may assist in the effective management of ongoing resources and requirements.

Hard thinking and thorough planning at the outset of a case can result in accurate predictions of the monies needed for the "life care" of the patient, which helps to maximize budgets and efficiently allocate money. Many times individuals find themselves at a loss on how to effectively maximize their resource potential, minimize excess, and effectively negotiate pricing on future services.

The CM, in their role as case managers, can perform in various capacities that range from simple (like ordering supplies as in the case below) to complex (like high level of involvement at the level of financial management and allocation of the funds).

Case Illustration: Mr. Jon Doe

Jon Doe's mother (Mrs. Jane Doe) complained about getting supplies on a timely basis. She cited two examples showing that the cords on the suction equipment used for her 5-year-old son were wearing down rapidly. Before her son was admitted to the hospital for a respiratory infection, she was running short of oxygen supplies. The CM recommended an oxygenator (cost-effective solution). The CM assessed the need, relied on data and feedback from a virtual network of other providers who have patients with similar conditions, picked the best supply house to obtain the oxygenator, discerned the insurance requirements, assisted with procuring the device, and finally monitored Jon Doe's use.

Jon Doe's family also had to make major modifications to their home by including facilities suitable for their growing son. Some modifications included making the bathrooms accessible, widening the entrances and exits, installing ramps, and outfitting the family vehicle with a ramp. Data were obtained from a virtual network of options and prices for modifications to guide the decision-making process.

Medical and daily care must also be planned and implemented. Physician/therapy visits as well as daily care services should be continued and, in Jon Doe's case, increased as he grows older. Data-driven decisions are supported by shared experiences within a virtual network. The CM will continue monitoring and implementing the life care plan—i.e., setting up the caregivers/nurses, ordering the medical supplies and equipment, and making sure they arrive on a timely basis while making sure that the dollars are spent wisely.

Apart from the physical nature of managing funds and healthcare, the CM must also tend to the emotional needs of the patient and the family faced with many changes and uncertainties.

For example, a patient may have to transition to a different home or a different facility as his or her needs require. Mrs. J is 91 years old and wants to stay in her home as long as she can. She feels that if she leaves her house of 50+ years, she will just wither away and die. Patients are often overwhelmed with feelings of sadness, regret, or indecision. This is where the CM's finer case management and patient advocacy skills are put to the test.

The evolving role of a patient advocate as a navigator, story teller, infomediary specialist, and educator is in great demand. Simply stated, the patient advocate seeks to inform and empower the patient to take control of their healthcare.[10]

Qualities that define a passionate, qualified CM:

- Respectful—CM must know how to create an atmosphere of TRUST with the patient and their family.
- Enthusiastic, accessible—CM must be eager to support the patient, even when it might be on an "off-schedule" occasion.
- Subject Matter Expert—The best patient advocates never stop learning. They research the pros and cons of recommended treatments/procedures and relay their knowledge to the patient in terms they can easily understand. The advocate's passion for learning can encourage the patient to take a greater interest in his or her well-being.
- Collaborator—Many times, the advocate acts as a type of surrogate, helping a patient understand what is said to them and to understand their care directives. They can pick up cues from other caregivers and help the patient and family spot those cues as well.
- Resource—a patient advocate maintains access to a multitude of resources. He or she can help the patient through the legal and financial mazes that result from a lawsuit or a debilitating medical condition.
- Cheerleader—the CM's mantra is "nothing but the best" for their patient's health. They will encourage and support the patient and their family as the family navigates through a healthcare crisis.

Cyber Implication Overview

This chapter provided an overview of the brick and mortar case management function. The practice standards established within traditional settings established the foundation for practice standards within a virtual setting. The cyber-nurse role in a virtual environment can support the information overload and foreign territory that patients will continue to experience. The push for cloud-based technology has saturated healthcare, setting the stage for the cyber-nurse to also become proficient as an infomediary specialist. This includes the provision and access to services such as case management. As mentioned in the introduction, the CNCM is the ideal role to facilitate the coordination and continuity of care for patients in an environment where health functions, information, and support continue to move into the cloud. At every stage the opportunity for the patient to become a data driven consumer will increase. Specifically, the data driven patient will increase the use of analytics in managing their healthy self and their health in illness. The cyber nurse will continue to support the patient with the use of analytics within the function of case management.

Endnotes

[1] http://solutions.cmsa.org/acton/media/10442/standards-of-practice-for-case-management accessed August 8, 2018.
[2] https://www.ncsbn.org/index.htm accessed August 8, 2018.
[3] Health and Human Services (2003, April 14). *Protecting the privacy of patients' health information.* Washington, DC: U.S. Department of Health and Human Services.
[4] Busch, R. S. (2008). *Electronic Health Records: An Audit and Internal Control Guide,* Hoboken, NJ: John Wiley & Sons.
[5] Banja, J. (2008). Ethical issues in case management practice. In S. Powell & H. Tahan (Eds.), *CMSA Core Curriculum for Case Management,* 2nd ed (pp. 594–607). Philadelphia, PA: Lippincott Williams & Wilkins.
[6] Shoenbeck, L. (2008). Geriatric case management. In S. Powell & H. Tahan (Eds.), *CMSA Core Curriculum for Case Management,* 2nd ed (pp. 479–496). Philadelphia, PA: Lippincott Williams & Wilkins.
[7] Muller, L. (2008). Legal issues in case management practice. In. S. Powell & H. Tahan, *CMSA Core Curriculum for Case Management,* 2nd ed, Philadelphia, PA: Lippincott Williams & Wilkins.

8 http://solutions.cmsa.org/acton/media/10442/standards-of-practice-for-case-management accessed August 10, 2018.

9 http://solutions.cmsa.org/acton/media/10442/standards-of-practice-for-case-management

10 Busch, R. M. S. (2017). *Patient's Healthcare Portfolio: A Practitioner's Guide to Providing Tool for Patients.* Boca Raton, FL: Taylor & Francis Group.

Chapter 4

Cyber Data Strategy, Analytics, and Informatics

What gets measured, gets managed.

Peter Drucker
Management consultant, educator, and author
1909–2005

Introduction

The healthcare infomediary specialist (IS) is, above all, a data and information expert. He or she will research authoritative, accurate, and informative data, follow up with critical review, then measure performance, outcomes, and success.

A skilled IS starts with an aggregation of data, which is created via an effective data strategy, then analyzes the organized data. Informatics allow him or her to extract useful information, which subsequently enhances case evaluations. This chapter will delve into the world of data and its use in managing our health. This chapter also includes a data readiness assessment methodology, appropriate to consider in assessing a patient's ability to receive and manage their ongoing health information.

Key Information Definitions

- **Data** are qualitative or quantitative factual values that can be used as a basis for reasoning, discussion, or calculation.[1]
- **Information** is knowledge generated from processed and synthesized data. Information should be defined in its context, condition, and can be a snapshot in time or evolving. While data are always correct, information can be wrong if the data elements were not processed in their proper context[2] (Johnson, 2014).
- **Analytics** "…is the discovery and communication of meaningful patterns in data. Especially valuable in areas rich with recorded information, analytics relies on the simultaneous application of statistics, computer programming, and operations research to quantify performance. Analytics often favors data visualization to communicate insight" (Get it Done, 2017, p. 1).[3] The IS will both collect the relevant data as well as analyze it. Collecting data requires ensuring controls over the methodology prescribed, process followed, and documentation. Data analytics includes detailed documentation of elements and algorithms utilized.
- **Informatics** is the science of computer information systems, an academic field which involves the practice of information processing and the engineering of information systems. This field encompasses the interaction between humans and information as well as the enabling construction of interfaces, organizations, technologies, and systems[4] (Johnson, 2014).

Current State of Managing Data

Data management plays a significant role in an organization's ability to generate revenue, control costs, and mitigate risks.[5] It is also critical for effective management of an individual's current and ongoing healthcare. Data management is critical in assuring sufficiency and relevancy when conducting a risk management assessment.

Most organizations today barely tap the information already available in their stored data, and the emergence of an ever-increasing amount of compute power and data storage capability suggest the unrealized potential of those data will only grow. Hence, it is vital to decide the most relevant data for the enterprise and develop practices to manage that data. To this end, the challenges organizations face include:

■ Fragmented, uncategorized, and incomplete data;
■ Increasing data volume; and
■ Analytic results misconstrued to be conclusive, but which are not due to the fragmented data sources.

Managing data focuses on defining the data element (e.g., payer remittance, electronic health records, and clinical research) and how it is structured, stored, retained, moved, and, ultimately, destroyed. At minimum, the IS should be able to document these processes. The IS will also need to develop skills in evaluating the quality, sufficiency, and integrity of the data being collected and used for analytics.

Current State of Managing Information

Information management is concerned with the security, accuracy, completeness, and timeliness of multiple pieces of data, and the effective management of information is a key focus area across all organizations.[6] In many cases, effective information management has meant deploying innovative solutions such as data warehousing and access to that data via portal applications. Organizations aim to deliver an integrated information environment and face several challenges, as follows:

- Large numbers of disparate information management systems
- Little integration or coordination between information systems
- Range of legacy systems requiring upgrading or replacement
- No clear strategic direction for the overall technology environment
- Limited and patchy adoption of existing information systems by staff

The IS should understand the context and condition of data receiving, data generation, and data storage, and that the practice and/or organization has an established policy and procedures on managing information.

Current State of Managing Analytics

Increasing levels of digital information and sophisticated analytics are radically changing the world of business.[7] With the right approach, analytics can alter how decision makers think about business problems, reveal new opportunities, create competitive advantage, and steer organizations into more innovative directions. However, organizations face several challenges in managing analytics, such as finding the right resources and skills, and choosing the right technologies. Other challenges involve the selection of the analytic itself.

What metric will be measured and what values indicate organizational health?

An effective IS will stay current on innovative technologies used to manage and take care of patients. HealthIT.gov and other industry organizations, such as Health Information and Management System Society, will provide a point of reference on emerging utilization and practice standards, and further distinguish technologies open to the public. The IS should be mindful of technologies, proprietary tools, and database platforms such as statistical, computing software like R (https://www.r-project.org/), open-source relational data base management systems tools such as MySQL platforms, or SQL Server in which algorithms may be processed.

Emerging Data and Informatics Roles

Data proliferation has resulted in the expansion of roles by title and function. Exhibit 4.1 shows the functional leadership positions affected.[8]

To the traditional leadership roles of CEO, CFO, CMO, CCO (compliance), CSO (strategy), and CIO are added new

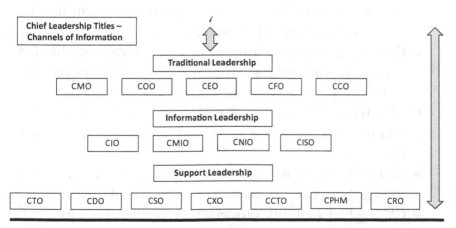

Exhibit 4.1 Leadership roles by title.

roles representing a segmentation of deep industry experience and more core competencies that has not existed heretofore:

- ■ CCO (chief cyber officer): Senior level executive focused on the deployment of defenses in the context of cybersecurity, third-party communications, and board level communications.[9]
- ■ CISO (chief information security officer): Senior level executive responsible for establishing and maintaining processes across the organization to reduce information and information technology risks.
- ■ CTO (chief technical officer): An executive level position in a company or entity whose occupant is focused on scientific and technological issues within an organization.
- ■ CNIO (chief nursing information officer): Nursing healthcare executive responsible for health informatics platform to work with clinical information technology staff to support efficient design, implementation, and use of health technology within a healthcare organization.
- ■ CDO (chief data officer) or CAO (chief analytic officer): Transforms data into information, physicians can use, to make better-informed decisions.
- ■ CPHO (chief population health officer): Responsible for overseeing development and implementation of the organization's population health management strategy.
- ■ CKO (chief knowledge officer): Assigned to turn raw data into usable knowledge for organization to use in innovative ways.
- ■ CIO (chief incentive officer): Examine ways hospitals can change behaviors to meet cost savings goals.
- ■ CMO (chief mobility officer): Investigate, plan, and implement mobile strategies for the organization.[10]

Data Integrity and Security Risks

Data Validation

In a data-rich environment, a critical risk is not collecting the relevant information for a review and/or classifying information incorrectly. An approach to ensure the integrity of the data collection and validation process is to create a workflow for the entity or function, for which the IS is intending to collect information. The work flow diagram should include the movement and generation of data within the organization. For example, the patient obtains their prescription from two different pharmacies. Do they have access to the medication list electronically? How many providers prescribe the same or diverse set of medications? Where does the patient buy medications (online versus retail)? This will help in accurately identifying all relevant information to be collated. The concept of detecting "normal" within an organization means anything outside of the workflow parameters is assumed abnormal. This will help identify all the categories of data to collect.

Upon receipt of the data, a process should include validating its content. For example, upon collecting claims data in electronic form, the IS should validate the data fields and the actual values within the fields. For example, if a data field is referenced as "last name" the values within the field should be the actual last names versus a street name of an address of the patient. Any process, at minimum, should include authenticating data elements, content configuration, and authenticating identities associated with the data. This cumbersome task could be accomplished with efficient cyber-based tools. The type of data most damaging in the event of a breach is personally identifiable information. Providers should have educational programs of the types of identity theft that exist in addition to programs to educate their patients. Considering the misuse of identities is the fastest growing area of organized crime, a dual educational program among providers and patients is critical to early detection and recognition of any type of breach.

Review of Identities

The theft and misuse of identities is the number one threat within the cyberworld. What is the value of identity? It is important to understand that individuals have multiple identities:

■ An individual's basic identity commonly referred to as personally identifiable information or sensitive personal information. These are comprised of data components which, when combined, link a person to sensitive information such as social security (government issued identification card), age, marital status, and demographic information.
■ Medical identity: data elements that identify individuals in the context of their health, healthcare services, and other biometric identifiers.
■ Professional identity: professional licenses, such as connecting an individual to a medical license, nursing license, and/or certified public accountant certification.
■ Organization or business identity: could be the name or company logo.
■ Electronic identity (e-identity): usernames and other various aliases utilized by online consumers and users of social media platfoms.
■ Synthetic identity: an artificial identity, created by co-mingling of real and false information, the sources of which might be another's stolen identity.

The following reviews the potential misuse for each identity type.[11]

■ **Individual Identity Theft:** A social worker at a hospital steals the baby's social security number, name, and date of birth, and then opens credit in this individual's name (https://definitions.uslegal.com/i/identity-theft/).

■ **Medical Identity Theft:** A brother used his brother's identity to obtain open-heart bypass surgery because he did not have insurance. The result is the co-mingling of protected health information under an assumed name in addition to depletion of benefit plan dollars (https://definitions.uslegal.com/m/medical-identity-theft/).

■ **Professional Identity Theft:** An individual assumed the registered nurse (RN) licensure of a nurse, was hired, and worked within a healthcare facility, taking care of patients under an assumed license. The result: the individual was criminally prosecuted. The healthcare facility had to refund Medicare and Medicaid on monies received for treating patients by the unlicensed individual[12] (Burkhalter and Crittenden, 2009).

■ **Corporate/Business Identity Theft:** A criminal organization slightly modified the name of a well-known insurance company and pursued victims, sold fake insurance policies, and collected premiums. The outcome was eventual criminal prosecution and numerous victims, expecting coverage, with very high healthcare bills. (https://definitions.uslegal.com/t/theft/).

■ **E-Identity Theft:** Obtain access to online bank account and transfer financial assets. Other modes of theft are viruses attached to emails that will leave behind key logger software to collect individual's interactions with electronic mediums.

■ **Digital Identity Theft:** An employee left a computer on at work and a co-worker accessed an Amazon account to obtain data identifiers that would support the retrieval of a lost password. The perpetrator made changes, but forgot to alter the delivery address, and so did not retrieve the package in time from the real owner of the Amazon account.

■ **Synthetic Identity:** An individual with a newly created hybrid identity opened a series of credits cards, shopping until the bank denied issuing a credit card to the individual. The consumer is left sifting through details of their credit report and having to evaluate what is real and what is not (https://definitions.uslegal.com/s/synthetic-identity-theft/).

Data Management Principles

Data management as a scientifically based discipline is evolving in form and pace in various industries. A data management plan, which is often lacking in organizations, includes an assessment of the capacity of that organization, or individuals within that organization, to effectuate the management of data. To improve an organization's data management capabilities, a model will be presented in this chapter which is an extension of the Data Management Capability Assessment Model (DCAM). The DCAM was created collaboratively by members of the Enterprise Data Management Council, a trade association that focuses on data management standards and best practices.[13]

DCAM focuses on a set of criteria that identify and measure the capabilities needed to develop and sustain an effective data management program. Although originally introduced into the banking industry, the concept of managing information via a set of standard capabilities is gaining value across industries. For the patient advocate, these concepts can help in developing a tool to assess a patient's capability and sustainability in managing their own healthcare data. The DCAM model was applied in the context of managing a personal healthcare portfolio (PHP), and the same attributes may be used when reviewing a patient's individual healthcare records within a case review.

The IS may be involved in assisting the individual patient (or case review of an individual's set of health records) to organize his or her personal healthcare records into their overarching PHP. A PHP is a patient-centric health data management tool, used by providers, advocates, and most importantly the patients themselves. The PHP provides a practical illustration of how to create, validate, and update patient-centric health information in a meaningful way to ensure an individual's defined health objectives are met.[11]

PHP Objectives

PHP objectives should include qualitative and quantitative goals that can be continually measured and updated and that enable effective self-advocacy, thereby helping the patient to make the best-informed healthcare decisions, manage ongoing health and costs, and avoid adverse health and financial events. They should also maximize patient and provider integration and understanding.

PHP Illustration: Patient Capability Assessment Model
Patient capability assessment model (PCAM), like the DCAM from which it was derived, provides patient advocates a mechanism to assess patient readiness to manage their own health data. Below follows the main ingredients of a PCAM:
Objectives:
■ All objectives are incorporated in the healthcare decision plan.
■ The objectives are approved and validated by all stakeholders, and stakeholder access to health data has been defined and approved by the individual.
■ All health provision objectives are prioritized.
■ The objectives are measured and evaluated.
■ The individual has the resources and mechanisms to achieve the objectives.

■ Communication and/or educational gaps, to include necessary or required training that effectively and efficiently support identified patient care objectives.

Processes for managing health:

■ Wellness management integration—patient sets up an active wellness program.
■ Finance management integration—patient has or establishes a health financial plan and understands current coverage and/or limitations.
■ Personal health assessment integration—patient actively monitors ongoing health needs.
■ Assess patient engagement gaps and facilitate plans that guide the patient to effectively manage health information[14] (Busch, 2017).

Process for managing data:

■ Patient will demonstrate an understanding of personal health information attributes that are collected.
■ Health data integration—patient collects any/all healthcare records.
■ Patient health data integration within stakeholder team defined and validated by patient and advocate.
■ Patient collects relevant policy and procedures of the stakeholders involved with managing their care and information.
■ The currency of the third-party patient support is identified.
■ Patient demonstrates a process to determine and validate access to their personal health information.
■ Patient demonstrates a process for organizing the information collected.
■ Patient demonstrates which information will be accessible and to whom.
■ Patient will validate who is utilizing their personal health information, how, and to what degree (do they understand it).

- Patient demonstrates an interactive approach to ongoing updates of personal health information.
- Data control(s) defined and validated by patient and advocate.
- Data controls and data management life cycle support established by patient and advocate.

Individual data elements:

- Readily available to relevant end users.
- Protected from unauthorized access.
- Easily captured, stored, mined, and analyzed.
- Needed for decision-making in both the clinical and business areas.
- Fluid and responsive to emerging market trends.
- Consider compliance and changing legislation.
- Patient centric.

Health data technology:

- Patient defines the technology architecture used in managing their health information and understands the technology used by information providers. Data technology tool identified, defined and validated by patient and advocate.
- Data storage management strategy, defined and validated by patient and advocate.
- Risk planning defined and validated by patient and advocate.
- Data quality program—for both data that are already collected and data which will be newly monitored—defined and validated by patient and advocate.

Making this assessment can be as complex as learning to navigate the overall healthcare system itself. The advocate may start by creating a data workflow of how the patient currently interacts with the healthcare system, in addition to a detailed inventory of all healthcare stakeholders that patient interacts with.

Data Integrity:

Garbage in, garbage out. The effective use of the PCAM model requires the data collected come from authoritative sources, be stored and maintained with integrity, and used in accordance with scientific principles. It is the role of an internal audit team to answer these questions:

■ How can we count on our analytics to be correct?
■ What are the new roles, who are the fresh players?
■ How can we better manage data?
■ How do we rise above the mass chaos of ever-exploding data to find what we need?

Illustrative Data Strategy Application

For the patient, the PHP model helps obtain, consolidate, organize, and process all personal health information so as to achieve a full accounting of medical or health status. The word data implies static numbers, text fields, or symbols that blandly stare back at us as if we were looking at an old photo. Looking at such data from an unfamiliar perspective, this same stagnant information morphs and mobilizes through processes of identification, correlation, and integration into patient and provider insight. The key is, *you don't know what you don't know...it is there, so find it, validate it, and put it to use*! That is the goal of the data strategy.

Comprehensive and accurate personal health information leads to prompt, focused, and correct care. In some cases, healthcare may define life's immediate path forward and *time can be of the essence*. That is not the time to begin a search to consolidate a lifetime's worth of medical or health records scattered across the landscape.

From a provider's perspective, raw data are useful only when they can inform or improve decisions or other business processes.

Strategy Components

The fundamental behavioral principles (continuums) that must be understood when determining data points fall into the following categories[15]:

- **Player Component:** A person, place, or thing that takes part; a participant, provider, or entity.
- **Benchmark Component:** The identified player's standard(s), point of reference, and/or measurement(s) for each identified player, as well as within and/or among each component within the behavioral continuum.
- **Functional Information Component:** All relational knowledge derived by persons, communication systems, circumstances, research, processes, technology, and/or behaviors realized by each identified player, as well as within and/or among each part within the behavioral continuum.
- **Rules-Based Component:** All related principle(s), regulation(s), governing conduct(s), action(s), procedure(s), arrangement(s), contract(s), legislature, dominions, and control(s) generated by each identified player, as well as within and/or among each part within the behavioral continuum.
- **Transparency/Opaqueness/Obstruction Component:** The identification of the quality of being transparent, opaque, and/or obstructed (barrier[s], impediment[s], obstacle[s], stoppage) by each player, as well as within and/or among each component within the behavioral continuum.
- **Consequence Component:** The identification of issue(s), upshot(s), sequel(s), damage(s), act(s), instance(s), effect(s), result(s), outcome(s), conclusion importance, significance, rank, position, monetary value, or state of being of each player and within and/or among each component within the behavioral continuum.

This behavioral checklist approach ensures all types of data are collected from all roles involved with the review of any matter. For example, by consistently identifying a player, each player should then be tied back to a market or practice standard. The players have a workflow: what tools do they use to conduct the work being reviewed. This is followed by adding on any rules (such as Health insurance Portability and Accountability Act) or contracts that dictate what the players must and/or shall do within a set of events. The continuum then follows the documentation or notation of any transparency issues. For example, the patient is deceased and cannot be interviewed. What other avenues are available to mitigate this roadblock? A review of patient documented statements? A prior video of the individual? Finally, each layer has a potential damage. This should be identified and contributed to any damage calculation by type and value.

People Process Technology

This consulting term of art "people process technology" refers to a process of creating work flow diagrams in order to identify all relevant people, processes utilized by those people, and the technology used to conduct their work. Detailed workflows and data roadmaps should be delineated to include all people, process, and technology components. The following components should be highlighted:

- Data capture that identifies and defines all workflow
- Mechanism of data and their movement
- Data workflows mapped
- Drivers of data components
- Activity of daily functions associated with workflow
- Business intelligence data flows
- Clinical intelligence data flows
- Revenue cycle data flows
- Operational data flows

- Service delivery data flows
- Product delivery data flows

The efficacy of the work conducted by an IS and, ultimately, the final deliverable, will be impacted by utilizing relevant data strategy components. For example, in the context of a life care plan, understanding a patient "health work flow" will ease obtaining a complete accounting of the patient's healthcare activities. In the review of any type of fraud, waste, and abuse matter, the entity's workflow will facilitate obtaining evidence that supports the mechanism of theft among the illicit parties.

Creating a Data Strategy

The healthcare continuum models serve as a framework to address the questions an IS may consider when implementing a successful data and information strategy for conducting a detailed deliverable. The model is structured to provide a comprehensive listing of critical components and includes all relevant sources of information, as well as all parties and processes that rely on information collected by the entity. The six components of the healthcare continuum model (HCC) are broken down by key behavioral components and illustrative operational considerations:

Primary-HCC

Primary-HCC analysis identifies the parties that provide direct or indirect healthcare services, how they work together, and the information shared. Included would be the identification of any online healthcare portals, electronic access to both clinical and financial data.

Secondary-HCC

The secondary-HCC identifies each entity that uses information generated from the primary-HCC for clinical and financial case management of the patient. The secondary continuum describes the mechanics of how to implement required clinical metrics for evaluating patient care.

Information-HCC Definition

The information-HCC analysis identifies the operational issues within the entities of the primary-HCC and the users and "uses" of the secondary-HCC. It is important to understand the current operating practices and procedures, and how they interact with other parties within the healthcare marketplace. It is also necessary to identify electronic interoperability drivers such as compatible internet, intranet, and extranet systems and electronic interoperability impediments such as incompatible and/ or detached electronic and paper systems.

Consequences-HCC Definition

Consequences-HCC analysis identifies and measures risk of all associated behaviors and activities to ensure all required processes are present in the healthcare marketplace and any adverse potential complication the patient may have. For example, a family urgently took a family member from a nursing home to an acute care facility because of patient neglect concerns. Medicare is denying payment for the hospitalization because the family member was not transported via ambulance.

Transparency-HCC Definition

Transparency-HCC integrates risk. It identifies transparency issues that may exist for any number of reasons and affect numerous market player processes. Transparency issues can pertain to both business and personal disclosures and are motivated by social assumptions, laws and legislation, limitations of access due to technology, contracts, and other intentional and unintentional constraints. The purpose of the transparency continuum is to recognize any roadblocks that would impact the operational objectives. Therefore, the inclusion of a mitigation strategy to address roadblocks and settle on opportunities to evaluate how to mitigate those roadblocks should be incorporated to be vigilant and minimizes the impact of any ongoing threats.

Rules-HCC Definition

The rules continuum incorporates an understanding of "rules" that all market players are subject to. The rules consider the monetary and business drivers that may be contractually driven or simply a business practice. The data information strategy must incorporate and update any new requirements contracted or legislated.

A comprehensive data driven IS review should consider effective identification of all critical data elements by type, involved within the matter at hand. If the review involves an episode of care, then it is important to identify the stakeholders involved in the patient's care; the benchmarks those parties are accountable toward; the relevant workflows impacting a patient's future or current care; and the impact of any risk, damages, or identification of roadblocks impacting the delivery of that care.

The Role of the IS Related to Data Strategy, Analytics, and Informatics

In a data driven environment with evolving informatics and analytics, the IS may find developing roles in managing data and information, including:

■ Synthesis of data and enhanced life care planning activities that include the development of a personal healthcare record in addition to a life care plan.
■ Developing sub-specialties in mitigating medical identity theft. Specifically, the IS may play a role in separating real from fake health information. Once a breach occurs, a synthetic medical identity is developed, and a perpetrator may begin receiving services in another person's name.

■ Conducting data quality assessments of health information in various environments. The authentication of health data associated with an individual and/or organization.

The practice principles on data strategy, analytics, and informatics will enhance the IS work product. Further, the information in this chapter provides an overview of several niche topics that will enhance various sub-specialties. For example, assessing data readiness on behalf of a patient.

The readiness model is applicable within any environment. Specifically, the PCAM model provides an illustrative tool to ensure the patient has the capacity to manage the content of a life care plan. On the concept of data integrity, a review and understanding of identity breaches, theft, and illicit use provides the IS an awareness that data associated with an individual may be flawed. Finally, the ongoing evolution of the cognitive era (based on artificial intelligence) will result in parallel work related adaptions by IS support roles.

Cyber Implication Overview

This chapter provided an overview of the principles of data strategy, analytics, and informatics considerations in a cyber-environment. Additional reading sources are noted within the endnotes.[16]

Data/information roles and managing the risk of misuse of identities were covered. The principles on data readiness have been included as part of assessing the patient's ability to effectively manage their own healthcare data. A detailed assessment model is specified to evaluate patient data readiness. Finally, an effective IS deliverable is enhanced with the intricate use of a data strategy, analytics, and informatics. Once a data strategy is developed and implemented, assurance of the execution of the strategy should be tested.

Endnotes

1 https://ori.hhs.gov/education/products/rcradmin/topics/data/open.shtml accessed August 8, 2018.

2 Johnson, M. (2014, February 13). Udemy *blog: The (Many) Differences Between Data and Information.* Retrieved from https://blog.udemy.com/difference-between-data-and-information.

3 Doyle, A.C. (1891). *A Scandal in Bohemia.* London, UK: G. Newnes; Get it Done (2017, March). *Analytics.* Retrieved from http://instadel.co/services/analytics; https://connect.rehabpro.org/lcp/home.

4 Johnson, M. (2014, February 13). Udemy *blog: The (Many) Differences Between Data and Information.* Retrieved from https://blog.udemy.com/difference-between-data-and-information.

5 Parthun, J. (2013). American Institute of CPAs (AICPA): *An Overview of Data Management.* Retrieved from: http://www.aicpa.org/interestareas/informationtechnology/resources/data-analytics/downloadabledocuments/overview_data_mgmt.pdf.

6 Karim, A.K. (2011). Tecsi Fea Usp. *The Significance of Management Information Systems for Enhancing Strategic and Tactical Planning.* Retrieved from http://www.jistem.fea.usp.br/index.php/jistem/article/view/10.4301%252FS1807-17752011000200011/267.

7 Weinberger, M. (2016). *Why Your Best Digital Strategy Should Be a Human One.* Retrieved from https://betterworkingworld.ey.com/better-questions/digital-strategy-human.

8 Busch, R.M.S. (2016). *Leveraging Data in Healthcare: Best Practices for Controlling, Analyzing, and Using Data.* New York: CRC Press.

9 https://www.isaca.org/Journal/archives/2016/volume-4/Documents/Chief-Cyber-Officer_joa_Eng_0716.pdf.

10 Busch, R. (2017, April). *Preparing for Targeted Third Party Audits/Investigations.* Williamsburg Fraud Conference. Williamsburg, VA.

11 Ibid.

12 Burkhalter, C., and Crittenden, J. (2009). Professional identity theft: What is it? How are we contributing to it? What can we do to stop it? Retrieved from http://www.asha.org/uloadedFiles/asha/publications/cicsd/2009SProfessionalIdentityTheft.pdf.

13 https://www.edmcouncil.org/dcam.
14 Busch, R.M.S. (2017). *Patient's Healthcare Portfolio: A Practitioner's Guide to Providing Tool for Patients.* New York: CRC Press.
15 Busch, R.M.S. (2012). *Healthcare Fraud Auditing and Detection Guide.* Hoboken, NJ: John Wiley & Sons.
16 https://www.wsj.com/articles/SB119565244262500549 accessed August 16, 2018.

Additional Reading

Herland, M., Khoshgoftaar, T.M., and Wald, R. (2014). A review of data mining using big data in health. Retrieved from https://journalofbigdata.springeropen.com/articles/10.1186/2196-1115-1-2.
This paper proposes approaches for analysis of health informatics data gathered at multiple levels, including the molecular, tissue, patient, and population levels and approaches to gain most knowledge in health informatics.
De Gennaro, M. (2016). Big data for supporting low-carbon road transport policies in Europe: Applications, challenges and opportunities. Retrieved from: http://www.sciencedirect.com/science/article/pii/S2214579615300319.
This paper provides the scientific community with a comprehensive overview of the applications of a data processing platform designed to harness the potential of big data in the field of road transport policies in Europe.
Davenport, T. (2013). *Analytics 3.0*, Retrieved from https://hbr.org/2013/12/analytics-30.
Analytics 3.0 is a new resolve to apply powerful data-gathering and analysis methods not just to a company's operations, but also to its offerings—to embed data smartness into the products and services customers buy.
Olavsrud, T. (January 2015). *How Big Data Analytics Can Help Track Money Laundering*, Retrieved from http://www.cio.com/article/2871684/big-data/how-big-data-analytics-can-help-track-money-laundering.html.

Criminal and terrorist organizations are increasingly relying on
   international trade to hide the flow of illicit funds across
   borders. Big data analytics may be the key to tracking these
   financial flows.
HealthIT.gov. Retrieved from https://www.healthit.gov/
Health information technology (health IT) makes it possible for
   healthcare providers to better manage patient care through
   secure use and sharing of health information. Health IT
   includes the use of electronic health records (EHRs) instead of
   paper medical records to maintain people's health information.

Chapter 5

Data in the Cyber Environment

Technology trust is a good thing, but control is
a better one.

Stephane Nappo
*Global Chief Information Security Officer at Société
Générale International Banking. 2018 Global CISO of
the Year*

Introduction

The discussion of personal healthcare portfolio in the last
chapter emphasized the importance of maintaining the integrity of the collected data, but recognized the collection of
management of health data must take place in other healthcare stakeholders also. The capabilities and resources to
ensure integrity are likely to vary with each organization, but
this chapter will lay out a "gold standard" toward which each
organization should strive.

A comprehensive understanding of data and their purpose
provides the framework for auditing any technology-based

infrastructure or exchanges between infrastructures.
A well-defined data dictionary[1] is therefore crucial to the success of cyber data reviews and cyber-health audits. Within a cloud-based environment, it is all about the data contained within technology platforms on the Internet.

This chapter focuses on understanding the concept of data and provides data audit guidelines for behaviors and activities associated with data. Auditing cyber-health data begins with establishing a data dictionary of all the information to be reviewed. Followed by understanding the data flow and the derived data intelligence.

Organizational Audits

The Institute of Internal Auditors (www.theiia.org) is a valuable resource and professional training organization for individuals who would like to expand their audit expertise and capabilities. Likewise, the Association of Certified Fraud Examiners (www.acfe.com) is a valuable resource for individuals who want to develop investigative skills to detect anomalies. Another noteworthy organization is the International Organization for Standardization (www.iso.org) in Geneva, Switzerland, which develops standards for quality control. Its quality standards are recognized worldwide. Infomediary specialists should consider ongoing education from the Health Information and Management Systems Society (www. HIMSS.org), which is a global professional organization focused on better health through information and use of technology.

E-health creates the cyber-infrastructure required for a truly interoperable environment for current and emerging market players within the healthcare continuum. A fragmented data infrastructure transferred into a fragmented digital world will provide little tangible value and merely overwhelm our current system. The key to an effective, data-driven decision-making model is to organize available information and collect other

Checklist	Chapter
Define the current status of e-health within your environment.	1
Define the current status of e-health among your external relationships.	1
Define members within the healthcare continuum (HCC) that impact your organization.	1
Define the market policies with which your organization must be in compliance.	1
Define the current information continuum (IC) infrastructure.	1
Profile public users of your information.	2
Profile private users of your information.	2
Profile e-source data use, data tools, internal controls.	2
Profile current capacity of your IC.	2
Identify IC issues such as development tools, standard open interfaces, inter operability, code reduction, scalability, reliability, and security.	2
Incorporate market professional standards and regulatory requirements.	2
Acquire applicable market certifications.	2
Identify patient clinical decision-making process.	3
Identify patient financial decision-making process.	3
Define appropriate data fields.	4
Define an applicable data library.	4
Define the process to manage new data.	4
Define the process to manage more new data.	4
Define the process to manage processed data.	4
Define the attributes of the data warehouse.	4
Identify current algorithms within the e-health continuum.	5
Identify and separate effective and ineffective algorithms.	5
Identify required algorithms for development.	5
Categorize each algorithm by type.	5

Exhibit 5.1 Organizational audit checklist.

relevant information. Exhibit 5.1 pulls together key subjects discussed thus far to provide the health infomediary with an *organizational audit checklist.* The cyber infomediary perspectives in this chapter have been adapted from the auditor's perspective to that of a cyber-health infomediary specialist.[2]

Internal Controls

As discussed in the previous chapter, a key to the efficacy of health data in a cyber environment is the ability to effectively have control of the cyber data: measure it, manage it, and without question secure it. Audit of cyber-health data can provide reasonable assurance that the cyber infrastructure has sufficient internal controls. Consider the following explanation of *internal control*, and its relation to information systems, provided by the U.S. Office of Budget and Management:

> "Internal controls"… are tools to help program and financial managers achieve results and safeguard the integrity of their programs…. Control activities include policies, procedures, and mechanisms in place to help

ensure that [objectives are met]. Several examples
include: proper segregation of duties (separate personnel with authority to authorize a transaction,
process the transaction, and review the transaction);
physical controls over assets (limited access to
inventories or equipment); proper authorization;
and appropriate documentation and access to that
documentation.

Internal control also needs to be in place over information
systems—general and application control. General control
applies to all information systems such as the mainframe,
network and end-user environments, and includes [security
program] planning, management, control over data center
operations, system software acquisition, and maintenance.
Application control should be designed to ensure that transactions are properly authorized and processed accurately,
and that the data are valid and complete. Controls should be
established at an application's interfaces to verify inputs and
outputs, such as edit checks. General and application control
over information systems are interrelated, both are needed to
ensure complete and accurate information processing. Due to
the rapid changes in information technology, controls must
also adjust to remain effective.[3]

A scope of audit and/or review should be well defined,
with procedures, benchmarks, and a clear understanding of the requirements involved with a specific work flow.
Professional training programs exist to prepare interested
individuals with how to conduct an audit, and it is beyond the
scope of this book to provide those details. However, examples of general questions that may be of interest in the review
of a cyber-health eco-system include:

■ What types of controls are in place to collect and manage
all of the relevant forms of health information used during the course of patient care?

- What types of tests can be conducted to ensure a breach of data has not or will not occur?
- Does the system have adequate controls to prevent inappropriate data use?
- If an issue arises, what are the current mitigation policies and procedures?

Today, recognized industry leaders are formulating market standards for managing cyber-health information (See Chapters 4, 11, and 12 for resources). The market is undergoing rapid change, as a result, staying informed requires vigilant monitoring of evolving standards. As new cyber-health system requirements and market standards evolve, cyber-health information infrastructures will need to implement new controls.

The Data Library

The *data library* consists of the contents of any new or existing data infrastructure, resulting from the organization's collection activities. Regardless of where an internal review occurs within the cyber-health systems environment, data specialists must identify all the data elements used by the particular cyber infrastructure under review.

The first task of a cyber-health internal review is to identify the subject matter of interest and any impacting factors within the cyber environment. This narrowing of the potential areas of review leads to a calling out from the organization's databases an identification of the relevant data to be reviewed, whether or not in electronic format. Identification includes the data element's label and definition as maintained in the data library. The following example illustrates the process of identifying one small operational component involved in the processing of a service claim.

Facilities such as clinics and hospitals submit their claims electronically on a form referred to as a UB-04 (universal billing from the year—2004 format). This form contains up to 86 potential elements of data, each defined by the universal billing committee. A provider might record only a portion of these 86 potential data elements. Those elements captured by a provider arrive at a third-party administrator or insurance company via the UB-04 form. The third-party administrator then decides which of the submitted provider data elements they will decide to keep for processing. At minimum, they tend to keep the data elements associated with the adjudication of the claim and the data points required to respond via a remittance file back to the provider. An employer plan sponsor may receive even less data because a third-party administrator may choose not to store certain data elements that are beyond the adjudication function. Determining why a market player has dropped a particular data element can be important in the identification of any internal control weaknesses. For example, third parties may be using technology tools to ensure the provider is using a current code to represent a service. The altering may be to simply convert an outdated procedure code to a current procedure code.

Data Flow

Once a data specialist obtains from the data library the labels and definitions of each data element being reviewed, they then must note the data element's specific use and delineate multiple uses when appropriate. In defining the "how used" of each data element, data specialists should include how the data may have been used in prior times, as old transactions will otherwise be difficult to reconcile with current ones.
If the data specialists download healthcare claims from insurance companies on behalf of employers, then they should note the appropriate data transactions, which may look similar to the following chain:

(1) Provider *to* (2) Company ABC clearing house *to* (3) Insurance Company DEF *to* (4) Preferred provider organization Network GHI *to* (5) Insurance Company DEF *to* (6) Vendor Check and (7) Explanation of benefits Printing *to* Insurance Company DEF *to* (8) Insured *to* Employer Plan Sponsor *to* (9) Insurance Company DEF

Once the data is mapped to the work flow, with an understanding of what each data element is and how it is used and for what purpose, the control review can uncover serious flaws in the understanding of operational processes taking place in an organization. Consider the following:

A new state-of-the-art specialty hospital announced that it had completely eliminated paper processing in its internal operations. An internal review was conducted to test that all paper processes were in fact eliminated. The review began within the hospital's first point of entry for acute care, the emergency room (ER). Data processing in the ER began with the registration of the patient and included a few other data movements including the documentation of services provided. The first anomaly was discovered when attempting to follow that patient electronically (and physical workflow) to the intensive care unit. The technology-based electronic medical record system lacked the virtual ability to discharge patients from the ER and "admit" them electronically to the intensive care unit. Instead, the ER handed a paper document to the intensive care unit nurse who then inputted the patient information onto the virtual system (electronic health record) to electronically admit the patient into the unit. In this area, then, the hospital had not achieved its goal of elimination of paper and repetitive data entry by people, and had thus not eliminated this potential weakness in data integrity. Data specialists must recognize and understand these types of "missing links" within the provider's cyber-health technology-based eco-system in order to ensure the smooth transition of data throughout the organization.

Dark Matter

The data library in a cyber-health infrastructure enables the activity of *mining for information*. To illustrate, consider the concept of *matter* studied by scientists. Traditionally, *matter* means *mass that occupies space*. Consider electronic data to be equivalent to *mass* in the physical world in that it occupies space within a cyber-infrastructure.

Scientists recently began exploring the concept of "dark matter." Dark matter is all the mass in the universe that cannot be directly observed, but whose gravitational effects can be observed. Scientists currently believe, in fact, that most matter in the universe is either dark matter or dark energy.[4] Consider cyber-health as an opportunity to efficiently find and discern "dark matter." Cyber environments can generate, enhance, and contribute data intelligence by processing previously unattainable information for the healthcare community. In other words, cyber-health presents the opportunity to shed light on virtual "dark matter" data.

Mining data elements to contribute to intelligence is the greatest value proposition in the cyber-health environment. A well-structured data library provides opportunities for understanding and applying data not previously within the reach of the healthcare community. Increasing data intelligence through data mining via comprehensive analytical tools opens the door to derive intelligence from large amounts of quality information.

Data Intelligence

The following is a simple example of a hospital utilizing data analytics to manage nosocomial infections. The hospital noted a high rate of post-bypass patients on a heart bypass unit and gradually discerned a pattern revealing that one surgeon in particular had an unusually high post-operative infection rate. The hospital initiated a study that collected and evaluated defined data from particular medical records. Each medical record required a manual review followed by a manual compilation of findings, additional testing, and, finally, a conclusion. It took a whole year to identify that the surgeon carried the infection and passed it on to his patient during surgery. Had a cyber-health environment been in place, the hospital could have responded in an instant.

Once armed with the information necessary to address the unusually high post-operative infection rates, the hospital could implement a response. It removed the surgeon's surgical privileges pending treatment of his infection. The hospital could have also responded by including the development of better monitoring of etiology for post-operative infections or evaluation of employee and staff health policies.

The concept of collecting outcomes by provider now exists, but measuring outcomes by specific staff members is only beginning to reach the marketplace. In a cyber-health information environment, decision makers can assimilate and process data in a more efficient and timely manner. The virtual world provides the opportunity to analyze outcomes and production at each measurable level and to introduce new data into the healthcare community. Interoperable cyber systems have the potential to integrate the collection of information from multiple environments and create an instantaneous information highway.

New Data

Data, whether in a global cyber system or in manual form, is constantly evolving to meet increased demands for speed, accessibility, and comprehension. Data specialists must keep in mind that although increasing the speed at which information arrives can help deliver optimal results, it can also cause hazardous results at an alarming rate. In a hospital setting, the speed of receiving, processing, and reacting to an abnormal laboratory test (i.e., low blood oxygen levels) can generate an adverse outcome to the patient. In the payer world, if 1,000 fraudulent claims are processed per minute, then money can be long gone before an error is realized.

As the amount of collected data grows, the sophistication of tools to extract information from that data is also growing. *Neural networks* are a set of machine learning algorithms, modeled loosely after the functioning of the human brain. Neural networks recognize patterns within the new data that cannot normally be recognized from structured or unstructured data. They also help group unlabeled data according to similarities among portions of the dataset, as well as help cluster and classify the data. For example, in the provider setting, a neural network can be used to classify the data elements that cause a specific medical error. Any relevant, processed data can be used to prevent this error from happening again.

In the payer setting, a neural network may identify the elements that correlate with a certain type of fraud scheme. Processed data can therefore be used to produce recognizable characteristics of a fraud scheme for a payer to check, prior to paying a claim. A very simple algorithm to detect fraud could involve a neural network with a list of providers with suspended licenses. The neural network could include separate data sources that do not connect. For example, the social security death index, each state licensure data, incarceration data, and data sources with comprehensive listing of legal information. A payer handling a claim submitted by a provider with a suspended license would receive an intermediate response to suspend any further action on the claim. The center point would involve the generation of an exception or error report that demands additional intervention and investigation.

Prior to the implementation of Health Insurance Portability and Accountability Act of 1996's administrative simplification mandate, which called on providers to submit claims electronically in a specified format, claims were generally submitted manually. Therefore, during that time, standardized claims submission did not exist and processors handled each of the $ 3.5 trillion dollars' worth of claims manually. Just imagine the associated transaction costs.

Today's efficiency creates the opportunity to process claims at a rate of thousands per minute. However, the improvement does not come without consequence. Because both legitimate and false claims are now processed at this rate, there is increased opportunity for the ethically challenged to capitalize. Data specialists need to ensure a complete understanding of all electronic data in a cyber environment to define the unethical uses of data and recognize potential areas for breach.

More New Data

The ongoing creation of new data provides even more data outputs and presents even more opportunities for data analysis. Cyber-health opens new doors to detect fraud through effective use of data and its management. The payer claim system provides a simple example of data analytics at work against fraud. For instance, data output may indicate that a particular provider, say, Dr. Speedy, has increased his home visit patient volume from 6 per day to 25 per day. Basic data analysis should recognize 25 patient home visits in 1 day as an anomaly.

Another physician, Dr. Pull, may see a reasonable volume of patients per day, but extract an average of 135 teeth per patient. By profiling Dr. Pull's patients, data analysis should identify 135 teeth pulled per patient as an impossibility.

New data can also improve the quality of healthcare delivery. By measuring and documenting adverse outcomes to medications, for example, providers can make adjustments to treatment protocols.

Processed Data

The generation of an anomaly is the result of analyzing processed data. *Processed data* develops new clusters, neurons, and subsequent etiologies.

Etiology provides the cause and effect of certain sets of data elements. By segmenting clusters by subject matter, neurons acting as the decision tree for processing data elements derive intelligence and lead toward understanding the etiology of anomalies. For example, the etiology of Dr. Speedy could be that he now has an assistant providing service under his license or that he completely fabricates the additional visits.

Data Warehouse

The previous data activities lead us to the data warehouse. A data warehouse retains prior data outputs. Each data output has a data center point that acts as a point of reference for discerning the defined etiology. Within each set of components is the definition of the data elements involved. The final result generates a single or series of algorithms, to be discussed in detail in Chapter 6. One example that is used in Chapter 6 describes the entire admission process into a hospital. One data warehouse item could address the issues involved in the admitting process of a patient. The case study presents the multiple routes with the dependency of outside parties to ensure the accurate admission. This is important because patients associated with any type of insurance could lose the opportunity for coverage secondary to any errors.

Cyber Implication Overview

From the perspective of an infomediary specialist or a health data reviewer, data in cyber-health along with its use in defined algorithms amounts to internal control of information in a virtual environment. The algorithms define what we are doing with the data. Integrating internal control into the data testing process allows for reasonable assurance of data integrity in the financial, operational, and service sectors of health-care environments. The next chapter will generate a more detailed discussion on the use of algorithms with the right question to generate meaningful analytics.

Endnotes

[1] "A Data Dictionary is a collection of names, definitions, and attributes about data elements that are being used or captured in a database, information system, or part of a research project." http://library.ucmerced.edu/node/10249.

[2] Busch, R. (2008). *Electronic Health Records: An Audit and Internal Control Guide*. Hoboken, NJ: John Wiley & Sons.

[3] http://www.whitehouse.gov/OMB/circulars/a123/a123_rev.html.

[4] https://science.nasa.gov/astrophysics/focus-areas/what-is-dark-energy.

Additional Reading

https://www.wsj.com/articles/why-your-doctors-computer-is-soclunky-1521585062 accessed August 16, 2018.

Chapter 6

Algorithms

Effective algorithms make assumptions, show a bias toward a simple solution, trade off the costs of error against the cost of delay, and take chances.

Brian Christian
American nonfiction, science, and philosophy author

Tom Griffiths
Professor of Psychology and Cognitive Science at UC Berkeley and Director, Computational Cognitive Science Lab

Introduction

An algorithm is a constructed set of specifically defined procedures that act upon stored or input data in a specified sequence. An algorithm answers a specific question in response to a hypothesis or to generate intelligence to create a hypothesis for further analysis. The key is to ask the right question that will have a measurable impact on day-to-day health decisions. This chapter provides a fundamental overview of algorithms. These concepts have been applied among all technology platforms.

Understanding Algorithms

Algorithms can execute a process or build models for predictive behavioral analysis. An algorithm could be an informal set of processes or a formal, specifically defined process. Formal processes are required for algorithms managed via the use of a computer programming language that tells the computer what to do. One simple algorithm written for an insurance company's claims adjudication system requires that, for every claim submitted, a patient be a member of the company's insurance program. If the patient is not part of that program, then the algorithm directs the insurance company to deny the claim.

An informal algorithm can be expressed using everyday language. Language coupled with the structure of grammar and use of known references can create a prescribed set of procedures. Consider the following narrative:

> At approximately 8 a.m. the students will arrive at school to register for the final examination. The test will begin at 9 a.m. Late arrivals will not be allowed into the examination room.

The relationships in the narrative are straightforward. The students, the school, the exam room, the final examination, and a set of time sequences comprise the data elements within the relationships. The order of activity is communicated in written form in linear fashion (i.e., students arrive around 8 a.m. to register for a 9 a.m. test; if students are late, then they face the adverse outcome of being excluded from writing the exam).

Flowcharts are often used to illustrate both informal and formal algorithms. We can group algorithms into categories defined by how a process is executed. Consider the simple task of logging on to a domain. Exhibit 6.1 provides a simple flowchart of this process.

Users could experience several different scenarios. When a user enters her login and password, the domain reconciles this information with the master database of users. If the user enters correct information, then the domain allows the user to enter. If the user inadvertently enters incorrect information, then the domain denies entry and typically provides the user a specified number of opportunities to enter correct information. If the user fails to enter the correct information for a specified number of times, then the domain could deactivate the

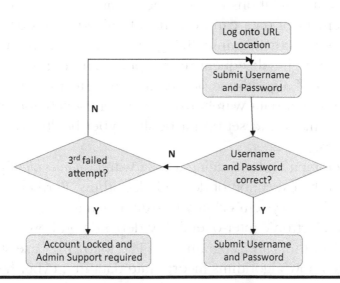

Exhibit 6.1   Sample algorithm execute a process.

central user profile to ensure that only authorized users enter the domain until further mitigation by the system administrator occurs.

We can also group algorithms into categories to solve a problem. Managing patients at the time of registration often causes a problem for hospitals. A hospital must complete a series of tasks to ensure it gathers correct patient information. If it records incorrect information, then the hospital may jeopardize receipt of reimbursement for services performed. Classifying an algorithm by scope is important for efficiency and effectiveness because different algorithms addressing the same problem may confirm a solution or generate new ones.

Data Elements

Algorithms are procedures and tests that act upon individual or groups of data elements, each of which has a meaning and relationships assigned to it. The use and management of data can be conceptualized into four distinct sets of activities: initializing data values, changing data values through subsequent user input, changing data values as a result of algorithmic processing, and storing data in, for example, a data warehouse. Data library activities organize information to set up particular cyber-health workflow processes.

Developing and managing a data warehouse typically relies on the execution of defined algorithms. Furthermore, the healthcare system's ability to truly reach a state of efficient electronic inter-operability depends on how effectively algorithms are programmed. The following case study illustrates how algorithms incorporate data in a cyber-health environment.

Case Study

A 400-bed hospital was experiencing an extraordinarily high volume of claim denials due to the incorrect receipt and processing of patient admission information by registration staff. While some of these problems could be attributed to patients providing incomplete/incorrect information and staff not following proper procedures, the amount of time and labor required for registration staff to properly interview patients played a considerable role. The hospital depended on adequately trained staff to enter complete and accurate patient information at the time of admission, and the impact resulting from errors was causing significant adverse financial results.

Understanding the dynamics associated with this process requires a data library of information. A data library is a reference document containing input-process-output diagrams which capture all of the key business processes in the hospital, the data which are necessary "inputs" to that process and the resulting "output" data which are stored and, in turn, used as input for subsequent business processes. By performing a detailed assessment of how the hospital's business processes work with how the computer algorithms are written, as well as assessing the data required for and resulting from properly executed business processes, with the data the algorithms access and produce, changes can be recommended to improve the current electronic transactions process and develop new electronic transaction models to minimize the amount of direct labor associated with the registration process.

Studying the workflow for registering a patient generated the following patterns:

■ Follow-up admission into the facility
■ Inpatient rollover admission

- Emergency room walk-in visits
- Outpatient admission for services
- Patient-without-insurance admissions
- Role of financial counselors
- Role of insurance verification
- Role of financial arrangements
- Role of condition of admissions—documentation requirements
- Known obstacles
- Role of financial counselors

The flowcharts in Exhibits 6.2 through 6.9 demonstrate the complex patient registration process, functions, and obstacles at different points of entry into a hospital.

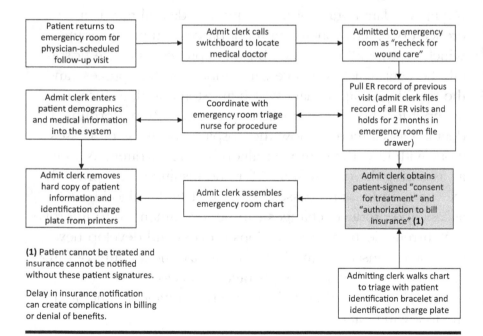

Exhibit 6.2   Data flow for follow-up visit admission.

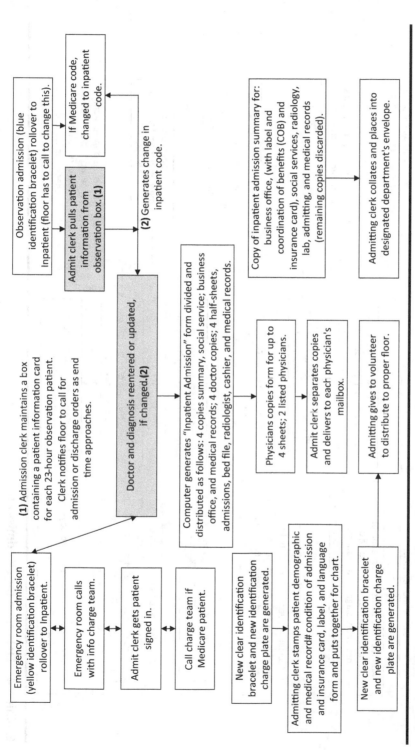

Exhibit 6.3   Data flow for rollover admission.

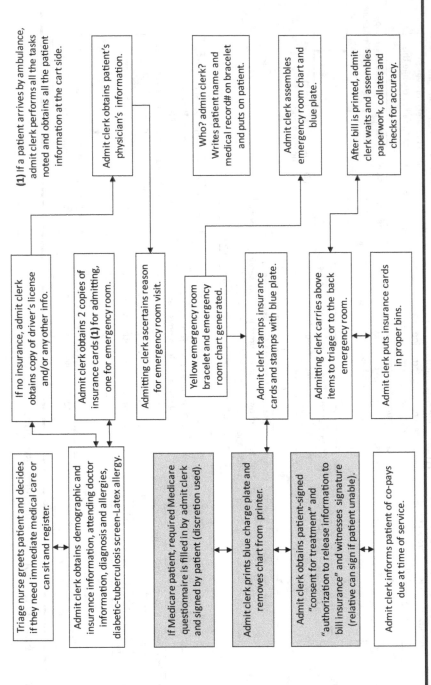

Exhibit 6.4 Data flow for ER admission.

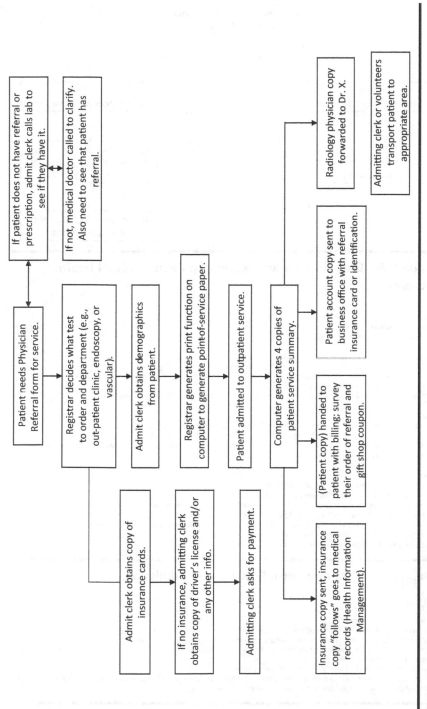

Exhibit 6.5   Data flow for outpatient services admission.

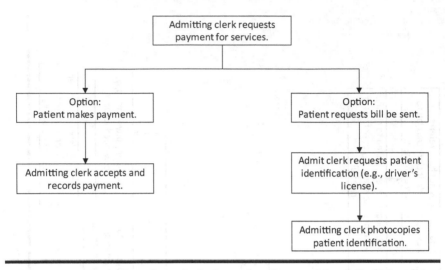

Exhibit 6.6   Data flow for admission of patients without health insurance.

Financial Counselors
❑ Responsible for prompt bill drop.

Medicare
❑ Check Medicare and Medicare days for all Medicare inpatients.
❑ Check for Skilled Nursing Benefits (whether or not admitted to skilled nursing facility; rationale unclear; large volume of work; possibly to assist utilization review case managers).
❑ Enter patient information into Admission Screening Advisor computer for verification of status.

Insurance
❑ Insurance verification and precertification for all observations, same-day surgery, and inpatients.
❑ Notification of patients scheduled for surgery through registration (self-pay is priority).
❑ Notify utilization review and insurance companies when a Health Maintenance Organization (HMO) patient is "out of plan" (patients usually transferred when stable).

Financial
❑ Work self-pay accounts, setting up payment arrangements.
❑ Set up payment schedules before elective procedures or surgery.
❑ Handle collection work for co-pays, deductibles, electives, self-pay, and cosmetic surgeries.
❑ Handle referrals to obtain public aid for eligible patients through outsource corporation.
❑ Verify coding on inpatients so bills drop (check for code specific to insurance, and make sure code noted on chart).
❑ Do case-by-case verifications for billing on clinical screen.
❑ Quote prices for maternity procedures and/or tests.

Exhibit 6.7   Data flow for follow-up visit admission.

Condition of Admission Forms
❑ Verify that all patients have signed "condition of admission" forms.
❑ Without patient signature, hospital has no authorization to contact insurance for precertification.
❑ Admitting staff notifies counselors when patients who entered unresponsive are able to sign. Counselors go to patient bedside to obtain these signatures.
❑ Signature is required to obtain diagnosis and receive benefits.
❑ Form must be completed in order to forward patient information to the billing office; enter patient billing information and insurance contact name and phone number on financial screens.

Exhibit 6.8   Data flow of additional patient registration functions.

Obstacles

☐ Frequently have to make several insurance phone calls per patient folder, at least one to verify precertification and one to verify benefits.

☐ Insurance cards:
1. Patients do not carry them.
2. Cards are outdated.
3. Patients lose or misplace their cards.
(Counselors have learned to keep track of insurance information themselves, on their own Rolodex, to speed up verification process.)

☐ Frequently called upon to handle patients' insurance entanglements.

☐ Frequently called by home care to provide patient benefit information and insurance-contact-person information from counselor's screen.

Exhibit 6.9   Data flow obstacles.

The follow-up admission process involved 10 operational functions performed by different types of hospital staff and two electronic systems (Provider financial system and insurance authorization system) that did not communicate directly. The shaded box in Exhibit 6.3 highlights the fact that patients cannot be treated and insurance companies cannot be notified without appropriate patient signatures and that a delay in insurance notification often creates complications in billing or a denial of benefits.

The rollover admission process, as depicted in Exhibit 6.2, involved 17 operational components. Any errors in the process can impede the financial integrity of that episode. The two shaded areas in Exhibit 6.2 represent specific data actions that, if omitted or incorrectly processed, result in denial of payment for the entire service episode.

The emergency room admission process also involved 17 independent operational functions (see Exhibit 6.3). Any breakdown of information can also lead to lost revenue by the facility. Critical revenue functions are denoted in the shaded boxes (Exhibit 6.4).

The outpatient services admission process depicted in Exhibit 6.5 involved 16 different data processes. Each is labor intensive and requires human interaction with paper documents and electronic entry. The overall impact would facilitate an accurate registration of the patient.

The dataflow depicted in Exhibit 6.6 clearly demonstrates that the admission of a patient without coverage was the least invasive mode of entry for the hospital.

Exhibits 6.7 through 6.10 show data flows that are described in a comprehensive data library and reflect the patient registration process. The collection of initializing data, subsequently input data, and output data resulting from previous operational algorithms facilitates all, in turn, feed new algorithms for the processing of these work functions. As processes become digitized, associated data elements will feed the data warehouse.

This hospital had five different pathways through which it could admit a patient into its facility and a total of 66 distinct operational functions and 23 support functions that required manual interaction and were not electronic. Therefore, before the patient even received any services, the hospital flowchart of people and systems involved 89 operational functions (and four likely obstacles identified in Exhibit 6.10).

Exhibits 6.11 and 6.12 highlight the sample activities that helped identify all the relevant information to develop the hospital's data library. The exhibit lists the audit activities that should be included when evaluating the registration process of a patient. These activities contain algorithms to manage, review, and change processes.

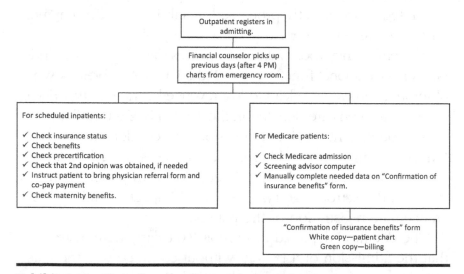

Exhibit 6.10   Data flow for financial counselors.

Data Library	Checklist	Activity	Key Topic
Collect relevant Information	audit	determine scope	high denial rate
	existence	document information	incorrect registration
	identification	label each activity	each mode of admission
	definition	define the activity	flowcharts
	use	define the uses	operational functions
Set benchmarks	source	define route of source	data movement
	value	define (non) & monetary	payment denials $ 15%
	partition	define segmentation	flowcharts
	map	define route of all	flowcharts
	testing	confirm understanding	interviews system review
	redefine	make adjustments	modify flowcharts
	mine	determine intelligence	review outstanding receivables
	modeling	confirm understanding	trend-denial patterns
	output	measure values	measure by source of admission
	response	test values	flowchart error response
	action	measure outcomes	develop internal controls
	implementation	define procedures	measure by source of admission
	next response	reevaluate infrastructure	test system changes
	consequence	measure adverse outcomes	trend-denial patterns
	solutions	redefine scope	adjust process

New Data	Checklist	Activity	Key Topic
Management reports	neural network	subject matter segmentation	measure by source of admission
	hidden patterns	data processing	changes in denials
	deductive	output intelligence	process issues
	predictive	output intelligence	system issues
	information	new audit scope	data-driven decisions

Exhibit 6.11 Data behavioral analysis: route of patient admission.

More New Data	Checklist	Activity	Key Topic
Collect relevant Information	Output Analysis	Measure Values Information	Monitoring Activity
Processed Data	**Checklist**	**Activity**	**Key Topic**
Management Reports	Clustering Neuronsetiology	Information segments Information details Information intelligence	
Data Warehouse	**Checklist**	**Activity**	**Key Topic**
Cyclical patterns feed data Library	Outputs Center points Components Elements Algorithm	Measure values Benchmarks Dataflow Data dictionary Data methodology	Monitoring Activity

Exhibit 6.12   Data behavioral analysis: route of patient admission.

Once patients were admitted, they received service. Exhibit 6.13 illustrates the accounts receivable pipeline for the hospital and provides the key operational components that typically mark patient movement through a facility. Accounts

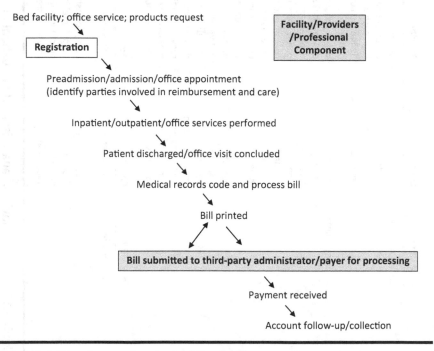

Exhibit 6.13   Accounts receivable pipeline.

receivable data analysis should proceed throughout the entire business cycle of a hospital.

When auditing and assuring the internal control of a cyber-health environment, the first step is to use the input-process-output flowcharts resident in the data library, thereby identifying how one process leads to the next. The format of the output data must be compatible with the expected format of a subsequent process utilizing that data. This is particularly true when output data may be transmitted to external third parties. Professional organizations (described in Chapter 2) developed standards detailing how these electronic communications should occur. For example, it is very common that hospitals continuously communicate with payers. One example of an external communication between hospitals and payers involves the certification of patient stay with an insurance company.

Exhibit 6.13 represents typical operational movement of information and activity. During patient registration, a provider works with claims agents for precertification of services and verification of benefits. In a non-interoperable marketplace, this function typically involves multiple phone calls, facsimile transactions, and manual entry into a registration system. In a cyber-health environment, this function morphs into an electronic communication. Today, some payers provide online patient verification, thus eliminating follow-up phone calls and facsimile activity.

During each of the hospital's five patient registration pathways, hospital staff needed to communicate with the precertification and utilization review components of the appropriate payers system. If the payer denied the service prior to providing the care, the patient and/or the provider could initiate an appeal.

Algorithm Selection

Several basic types of algorithms are commonly taught in computer science programs. The first is a simple recursive algorithm. Recursive refers to a characteristic in the formula or configuration that defines a series of steps that can be applied repeatedly. At times, the simple recursive algorithm will have a loop-like effect. An algorithm of this type can be linear in nature, having a loop effect within one set of procedures. Recursive algorithms can also have a branch-like effect as well, in which the algorithm's rules involve a series of loops.

Within a hospital patient registration process, one would apply a recursive algorithm if only one mode of registration existed. When more than one mode of registration exists, as in the above case study, the *recursive algorithms* would involve a branch-like format due to the complexity and variety of the patient admission process. However, programming solely based on recursive algorithms becomes inefficient when the design involves multiple recursive loops that may limit the ability to gather conclusive information (Exhibit 6.14).

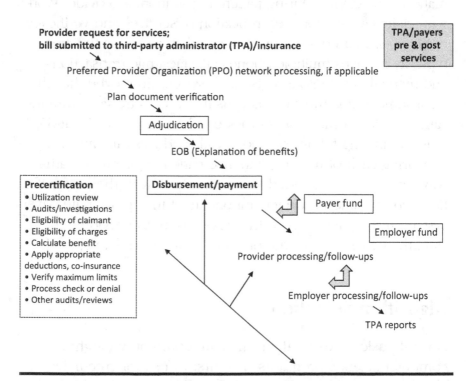

Exhibit 6.14 Payer accounts receivable pipeline.

Therefore, this type of algorithm is more useful as a conceptual tool than as a computational tool.[1]

A second type of algorithm is called *backtracking*. The backtracking methodology walks through a series of decisions until the correct one is found.[2]

This type of algorithm is most commonly used in situations where a series of decisions are made without necessarily having enough information to make an informed selection. As decisions and selections occur, the algorithm generates new information that impacts subsequent decisions. The algorithm eventually might provide one or more solutions.

Exhibit 6.5 illustrates the use of a backtracking algorithm during the course of patient admission for outpatient services. When patients attempt to register for services at a hospital, the first decision determines what type of service they require. Although patients may have a clear understanding of what type of service a doctor has ordered for them, if they forget to bring their prescription with them, a hospital cannot proceed because it lacks written confirmation. The registration process therefore redirects to search for written confirmation. The outcome may be denial of services if documentation cannot be obtained. Upon completing documentation of services ordered from the treating physician, the registrar then gathers health insurance information. Exhibit 6.7 also illustrates decision-making scenarios for obtaining insurance information. The incremental movement within the 16 workflows presented leads closer to obtaining a solution to the problem presented or the workflow task.

A third algorithm is called *divide and conquer*. A *divide-and-conquer algorithm* includes the following dynamics:

■ Deriving output directly from incremental components
■ Dividing large instances into smaller ones, and (recursively) applying the algorithm to the smaller instances
■ Combining solutions for the sub-instances, to produce a solution for the original instance.[3]

This type of algorithm is programmed with two or more recursive commands of the data elements. As its name suggests, this algorithm divides "a given problem into two sub-problems (ideally of approximately equal size)" and conquers "each sub-problem (directly or recursively)." It then aggregates the solutions from the two sub-problems into one global solution. The art of this algorithm lies in this last step of the process.[4] In a very simplified application of patient registration, a presenting question could be, "Why does a hospital have denials from registering patients incorrectly?" This question is initially broken down into the various avenues in which patient registration occurs. The strengths and weakness from each route are then compared to generate global solutions to the problem. In my case study, the solution involved improving both personnel and computerized processes.

A fourth algorithm is called *dynamic programming*. This algorithm type focuses on understanding past results and using them to find new results. They have three general characteristics. The first is that sub-problems overlap; the second is that optimal substructures are used; and the third is that the characters of the algorithm use memorization. The memorization or "memo" function "remembers which arguments it has been called with and the result returned and, if called with the same arguments again, returns the result from its memory rather than recalculating it."[5]

The dynamic programming algorithm can be illustrated with patients who have had prior admissions to a hospital. Regardless of avenue of admission, once hospital staff enters unique patient identification, all prior personal information is retrieved and the need to re-enter all such information would dissipate. Each hospital then can retrieve all episodes of care for that patient upon admission and eliminate the problem of patients with multiple identification numbers.

Within the payer system, a dynamic programming algorithm could recognize when a claim is submitted more than once to ensure that insurance companies do not make multiple payments for the same episode of care. During an initial run of this type of algorithm, the process may recognize that on a particular date, an amount was paid for a specific service. Programming then stops any further processing of this claim and would deny a duplicate claim.

A fifth type of algorithm, the *greedy algorithm*, involves optimization. This type of algorithm finds the best solution based on available data and has several phases. The first phase involves taking the best information available at a certain point in time without consideration of a future consequence. The algorithm results in the optimal solution based on the available data.

A good example to illustrate a greedy algorithm is the patient registration process for the ER, which uses a process called "triage." Hospitals rely on this process to select patients for treatment based on the level of acuity rather than order of arrival. A patient with a minor flu may have to wait behind a patient who subsequently arrives with multiple internal injuries from an auto accident. Triage, however, does not always produce optimal results. For instance, a patient who initially was thought to have merely the flu may in fact have a life-threatening clot that is causing a lethargic, general malaise condition.

Another optimization algorithm is called *branch and bound*. This type of algorithm is useful when a root problem exists and an incremental approach to the data produces subproblems to further delineate issues. As the data are processed, results tie back to the presenting problem (a node). If a result does not relate to the node, the algorithm identifies a new issue and creates a new node.

For example, when auditing a group of pharmacy claims, an original root problem could involve isolating prescriptions dispensed more than once in a given day. Data output could demonstrate patterns where the same pharmacy dispenses more than one prescription per day (node A) or multiple pharmacies are dispensing the same medication to the same patient more than once per day (node B). Additional analysis (or branches) evaluate whether the complicating issue lies directly with the pharmacy claim processing system (node A) or whether resolving the issue requires a better understanding of the patient involved (node B) (i.e., how is a patient able to obtain the same prescription at more than one pharmacy?). The antithesis of the branch-and-bound approach is the *brute force* algorithm. This type of algorithm is also optimizing in nature, combining all data elements into the analytical process until it obtains a satisfactory result. For example, imagine an audit that requires the identification of the top ten medications dispensed in the pharmaceutical claim file on a Friday night. Although the prescribed medications may in fact have an appropriate diagnosis, further audits of highly abused drugs may lead to further discovery. In evaluating these highly abused drugs, an audit question of why they are frequently dispensed on a Friday night versus any other night of the week may be worthy of consideration.

Finally, an auditor can use a *randomized algorithm* to process data elements that lack a definite aim or particular pattern. Using the pharmaceutical claim audit cited above as an example, one algorithm could run a query on the top ten medications dispensed on a Friday. Another data question might involve the average amount spent per month per employee on medication. For example, Xanax and Vicodin are commonly abused medications to treat anxiety and pain. Would it be coincidental that people need to fill a prescription on a Friday night? Would it be coincidental that one pharmacy in particular has a disproportionate share of patients seeking relief on a Friday night? The aggregation of this data can generate the information necessary to conduct more focused audits for specific findings.

Cyber Implication Overview

Which specific algorithm auditors use to solve a problem will depend on the information available to them and will often change in scope or procedure when new data are generated.

Algorithms can drive cyber-health infrastructures to answer the who, what, where, why, and how of a healthcare episode at any given time. As a recap (and an auditor's checklist), thus far we have explored the market background of cyber-health initiatives, cyber-health industry applications between and among public and private users, market standards and compliance requirements, clinical and financial case management, data element activity, and algorithms.

Endnotes

[1] Ivan S., *Recursive Algorithms in Computer Science Courses: Fibonacci Numbers and Binomial Coefficients*, 1999, Department of Computer Science, University of Ottawa, Ottawa, ON.

[2] http://www.cis.upenn.edu/~matuszek/cit594-2006/Lectures/27-backtracking. ppt #276,2,A short list of categories accessed August 2018.

[3] http://www.cse.ohio-state.edu/~gurari/course/cis680/cis680Ch18.html accessed August 2018.

[4] http://www.cs.ust.hk/faculty/golin/COMP271Sp03/Notes/L03.pdf accessed August 2018.

[5] Denis H., "Memo function," The Free On-line Dictionary of Computing, January 21, 2008, <Dictionary.com http://dictionary.reference.com/browse/memo function>.

Chapter 7

Cyber Data-Driven Health Decisions

Most of the world will make decisions by either guessing or using their gut. They will be either lucky or wrong.

Suhail Doshi
Entrepreneur CEO, Mixpanel, a business analytics service company

Introduction

Data-driven decision-making models are emerging in almost every industry sector. Cyber-health infomediary specialists should have a foundational understanding of these models. This chapter will provide examples of the types of models used in healthcare.

Knowledge Models

The following knowledge models are described in detail below. These are:

1. The primary healthcare continuum
2. The secondary healthcare continuum
3. The information continuum
4. Knowledge models

Effective electronic data-driven decisions require well-defined data elements and algorithms, as described in Chapter 6. Several types of *ladders* within defined networks are utilized to develop a framework for a specific knowledge model.

The reference to ladders within these knowledge models refers to the incremental graded series of data elements, their positioning within each framework. The graded series and positioning of the data element will impact the outcome analysis. Each ladder begins with the identification of the healthcare stakeholder, the relevant layers of data by ladder type, and concluding with the appropriate data model. The ladders discussed later in the chapter are:

1. Concept ladder data associated with the general idea of health question.
2. Composition ladder securing the relevant data to address the health question.
3. Decision-making ladder confirming the basis for a response to the health question.
4. Process model that encompasses the flow of business processes of each healthcare continuum (HCC) participant and the decisions which need to be made throughout the processes.
5. Data attributes and characteristics ladder needed to be collected so as to enable the business to make decisions as it executes the business process.

Primary Healthcare Continuum

The primary HCC (P-HCC), as depicted in Exhibit 7.1, illustrates the network of key market participants involved in the movement of health and financial information during an episode of care. If all of the relevant stakeholders are not identified, then all other incremental steps to secure relevant data will compromise the final analysis. The P-HCC sets the stage for all other associated data requirements.

Concept Ladder

The first step in determining the data needed for making any particular healthcare decision is to identify the nature of the key market participants. This step is known as the concept ladder and is illustrated in the table below. The concept ladder seeks to answer in a structured fashion the question: "What types of participants exist in the HCC?"

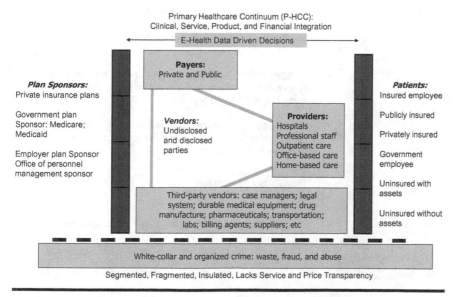

Exhibit 7.1 Primary healthcare continuum.

Developing a knowledge model thus begins by identifying the types of market participants and creating data libraries which specify the potential values the data warehouse must recognize.

The health infomediary specialist must first identify and define all market players within the network to be audited or reviewed. Then the infomediary must isolate each specific player, as illustrated, for the patient, and further break down the segments within that node. A more detailed composition ladder is then required to ensure that a data table exists to process identified variables. Exhibit 7.2 illustrates the patient composition ladder. For each market participant, for each type of participant identified in the concept ladder, such a sub-segmentation should be carried out. For illustrative purposes, though, the detailed analysis is shown for only one participant type in each market participant category.

P-HCC Participant	Concept Model -What types of participants exist within the Health Care Continuum?
Patient	• Active or retired insured private or government employee • Publicly insured or privately insured • Uninsured with or without assets
Provider	• <u>Facilities</u>, such as acute care inpatient, outpatient, same-day surgical center, nursing home, long-term care, rehabilitation, home-based care, and psychiatric • <u>Professionals</u>, such as doctors of medicine (MDs),osteopathy (DOs), dental surgery (DDSs), and chiropractic (DCs), in addition to nurses and physical therapists
Payer	• <u>Third-Party Administrator</u> • Insurance company
Plan Sponsor	• Private insurance, self-insurance, employer, or government
Third-Party Vendor	• Professionals, medical and legal, durable equipment, pharma, transportation, and billing agents

Exhibit 7.2   Concept ladder.

P-HCC Participant	Concept Model - *What types of participants exist within the Health Care Continuum?*	Composition Model – *What is the composition of this group?*
Patient	• Active or retired insured private or government employee	• Type of insurance –Employee Retirement Income Security Act (ERISA) or state regulated? • Medicare, Medicaid, contracted carrier? • Coverage limitations?
Provider	• Professionals, such as doctors of medicine (MDs), osteopathy (DOs), dental surgery (DDSs), and chiropractic (DCs), in addition to nurses and physical therapists	• Professional credentials? • Customer mix and type of patients?
Payer	• Third-party administrator	• Government programs or sponsored programs or self-insured employers?
Plan Sponsor	• Private insurance, employer	• Private employer with >20 full-time equivalents (FTEs), private employer with <20 FTEs, or collective group of individually insured participants?
Third-Party Vendor	• Professionals	• Case managers? Attorneys? Outsourced staff support (e.g., renal dialysis)?

Exhibit 7.3   Integrated collection of data used in a data library or data warehouse.

Composition Ladder

Of course, the need for information about market participants goes beyond what is illustrated in the concept model. Exhibit 7.3 provides more details that a data library might define and a data warehouse might store.

Decision-Making Ladder

Next, the infomediary must consider the patient's decision-making process and test an algorithm to ensure that the electronically defined process proceeds analogously to the actual. Exhibit 7.4 illustrates the typical flow of the patient decision-making ladder. The shaded grey box illustrates a typical decision that will need to be made and which, therefore, requires the accumulation of appropriate data to make it.

Insured patients, for instance, are covered for services under the plan and must pay out-of-pocket

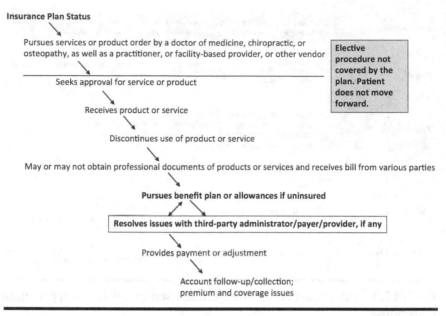

Insurance Plan Status

Pursues services or product order by a doctor of medicine, chiropractic, or osteopathy, as well as a practitioner, or facility-based provider, or other vendor

Seeks approval for service or product

Receives product or service

Elective procedure not covered by the plan. Patient does not move forward.

Discontinues use of product or service

May or may not obtain professional documents of products or services and receives bill from various parties

Pursues benefit plan or allowances if uninsured

Resolves issues with third-party administrator/payer/provider, if any

Provides payment or adjustment

Account follow-up/collection; premium and coverage issues

Exhibit 7.4   Patient decision-making ladder: attributes and process.

for services not covered. Plan provisions must therefore be included in the data library. Similarly, an algorithm must identify services not covered by the plan provisions so that during a request for approval or confirmation, the algorithm triggers the message "no coverage."

The infomediary—particularly in their role as a marketer of health information—may be called upon to mine coverage data to answer questions such as the following questions:

■ How many patients request this service?
■ How many plans do not cover this service?

Cyber-health also provides significant opportunities to exploit the data collected in each process. The infomediary should therefore also review new analytic questions his or her organization are developing interest in, and then analyze each process to determine how relevant data, not currently collected, can be gathered.

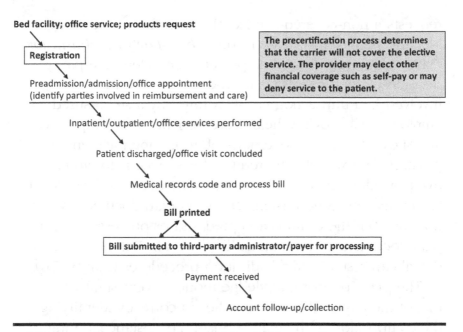

Bed facility; office service; products request

Registration

Preadmission/admission/office appointment
(identify parties involved in reimbursement and care)

The precertification process determines that the carrier will not cover the elective service. The provider may elect other financial coverage such as self-pay or may deny service to the patient.

Inpatient/outpatient/office services performed

Patient discharged/office visit concluded

Medical records code and process bill

Bill printed

Bill submitted to third-party administrator/payer for processing

Payment received

Account follow-up/collection

Exhibit 7.5   Provider decision-making ladder: attributes and process.

Such decision-making models should be created for each of the market participants in the P-HCC. Below are illustrative examples for providers, payers, plan sponsors, and pharmaceuticals.

Exhibit 7.5 illustrates the provider decision-making model. The components listed in the exhibit are typical operational steps in a provider environment. How these components are executed from a technological perspective will vary from one provider entity to another. The infomediary must therefore define the information continuum (IC) for each market entity reviewed or evaluated. Again, the shaded grey box highlights a key decision to be made during the business process.

Generating optimal data intelligence, as noted in the patient model, is the final component of a knowledge model.

As the infomediary specialist identifies additional market players within an e-environment, the general knowledge model will expand.

Exhibit 7.4 illustrates application of the knowledge model profiles to payers. For example, when an insured patient requests a non-covered service, the workflow review might identify the payer involved to be a *third-party administrator* (TPA) with a self-insured employer client. Here, the payer decision-making process is for the case where the payer involved in a transaction is a TPA hired by a self-insured employer that provides healthcare benefits to its employees and shows where key decisions of approving payment take place. If, for example, the request for service is for an elective procedure, then denial can actually occur at three points: (1) during the request itself; (2) during plan document verification; or (3) if the claim is accepted and/or processed during plan document verification as illustrated in Exhibit 7.4, then denial can result from adjudication procedures (Exhibit 7.6).

The plan sponsor knowledge model is very similar to that of the payer. The key issue lies in correctly identifying the composition of the plan sponsor. For instance, during a self-insured employer audit, a review of contract terms brought to light the fact that the employer's particular plan actually intertwined The Employee Retirement Income Security Act of 1974 (ERISA) concepts with insurance provisions.

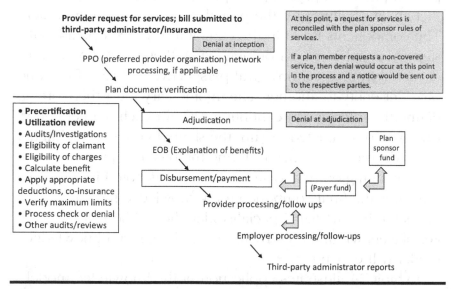

Exhibit 7.6   Payer decision-making ladder: attributes and process.

The employer operated under the assumption of self-insured status (ERISA Plan) when the TPA insurance carrier actually operated as if it offered an insurance program to the employer. Identifying payer composition is important, because compliance requirements and plan rules may vary between state insurance laws and those mandated under ERISA. Exhibit 7.7 illustrates the typical decision-making ladder for plan sponsors.

Plan sponsors should define services to be covered prior to implementing their benefit program (services mandated by legislation, such as obstetrical care, cannot be excluded from any plan). If the TPA uses auto-adjudication processes, the infomediary must verify all electronically programmed inclusions or exclusions. Because requests for services are electronically processed without human intervention, testing the accuracy of those tables is very important.

Third-party vendors refer to the large number of non-professional or facility-based care providers that offer health-related products or services such as durable medical equipment, pharmaceuticals, pharmaceutical benefit managers,

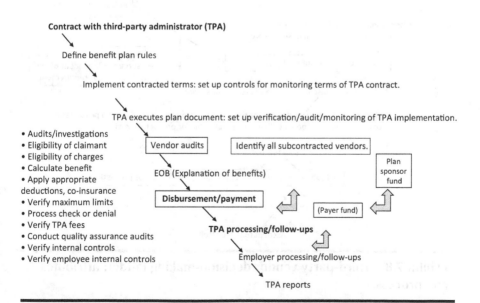

Exhibit 7.7   Plan sponsor decision-making ladder.

ambulances, case managers, and attorneys. The third-party vendor decision-making model illustrated in Exhibit 7.8 recognizes that patients who request a non-covered service might finance the service without plan sponsor approval.

Consider the decision-making ladder for the movement of pharmaceuticals as illustrated Exhibit 7.9. The infomediary would identify the pharmaceutical distribution network and existing nodes within the primary healthcare continuum. A concept ladder and composition ladder would further detail sub-components within the network. The infomediary would then use the secondary healthcare continuum to identify the applicable policies impacting the pharmaceutical industry. Finally, the infomediary would use the information continuum to identify the technological infrastructure in which pharmaceuticals operate.

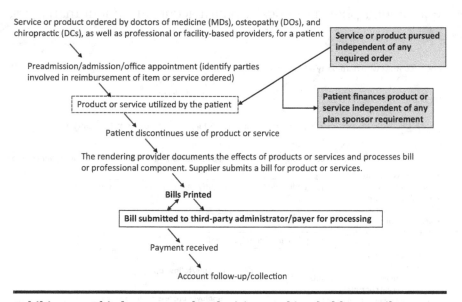

Exhibit 7.8   Third-party vendor decision-making ladder: attributes and process.

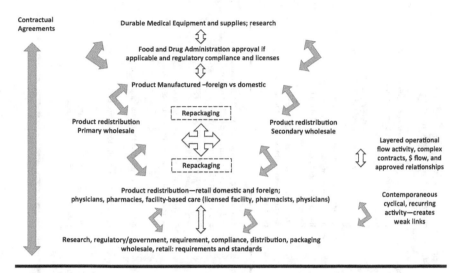

Exhibit 7.9   Pharmaceutical decision-making ladder.

Attributes and Process Ladders

Exhibit 7.10 integrates the decision-making model with the respective attributes ladder. Specifically confirming the characteristics and or logic of the prior ladders that are associated with the presenting question. The process is defined within each continuum understanding the systematic series or increments involved in the response to the presenting question.

We have now completed the identification of the stakeholders in the P-HCC. We have illustrated the concept ladder, the composition ladder, the decision-making ladder, the attribute ladder, the process ladder, and the data models for each. Once stakeholders are identified within the primary healthcare continuum, the identification of benchmarks may be outlined for each stakeholder. Please note, at any time in the process if a new stakeholder is identified, the process should revert back to updating and documenting the primary continuum and repeating each process for that new stakeholder.

P-HCC Participant	Decision-making - confirming the basis for a determination in response to the health question	Attributes - confirming the characteristics/logic of the prior ladders in associated to the health question	Process -defining the systematic series or increments involved in response to the health question
Patient	• Based on orders from doctors/practitioners • Plan coverage or allowances if uninsured	• Patients making decisions based on health plans and services covered by their plan. • Patient making decisions based on choice of service provided by the doctors or facilities.	• Seeks a provider for a service or product. • Selects service or product based on payment options. • Receives service and provides payment or adjustment based on the benefit plan.
Provider	• Capacity of the facility (Number of beds, product request, etc.) • Precertification • Self-pay, payment plan or type of insurance • Type of patient visit • Services offered	• Provider offering services based on the patient's health plan and reimbursement for services provided.	• Receives patient request for service or product. • Provides patients different available options based on benefit plans and availability of services. • Provides requested service and seeks reimbursement from payer for the services provided.
Payer	• Preferred Provider Organization (PPO) In-Network or Out of Network • Plan sponsor contracts • Covered and non-covered services • Explanation of Benefits (EOB)	• Payer including services to a health plan based on contracts with plan sponsors.	• Receives patient request for service or product and evaluates the request based on patients' Explanation of Benefits (EOB). • Provides prior authorization to the patients for service (if qualified). • Receives reimbursement request from providers and sends it to adjudication for processing.
Plan Sponsor	• Benefit plan rules • Covered and non-covered services • Third-Party Administrator (TPA) contracts	• Plan sponsors providing different plans to different hospitals and providers • Plan sponsor negotiating different plans based on type of services required	• Negotiates contracts with payers for patient benefits. • Conducts payer audits to validate EOB.
Third party vendor	• Contractual agreements • Patient finances product or services	• Vendors providing different payment plans and reimbursements based on contracts	• Adjudicates claims based on patient EOB. • Submits bill to payer for processing.

Exhibit 7.10 Pharmaceutical decision-making ladder.

Secondary Healthcare Continuum

Analysis of applicable market and policy issues within the context of the secondary healthcare continuum (S-HCC), depicted in Exhibit 7.11, impacts the knowledge model's framework. When a patient requests a non-covered elective service, S-HCC issues for consideration may include public policy, ERISA requirements, and state insurance requirements. Another consideration may be the case management function, such as payer or provider provision of financial case management services. The process of blending of P-HCC (which involves the identification of all stakeholders) and S-HCC (which involves all the benchmarks which the stakeholders must follow), in addition to distinct market services (each with separate benchmarks of standards to follow), will integrate operational issues that the stakeholder must follow as well. At this point overlaps may be noted, such as the benefit plan design (P-HCC) that may be modified as a result of any relevant policy issues or mandates (S-HCC). For example, a common security requirement under Health Insurance Portability

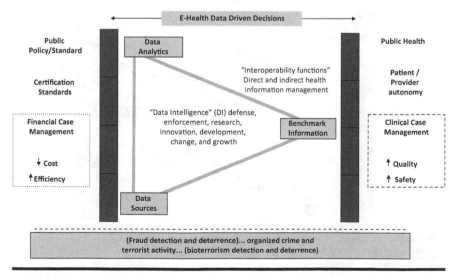

Exhibit 7.11 Secondary healthcare continuum.

and Accountability Act of 1996 is a must for all covered entities (payers, providers, plan sponsors, and their vendors) in healthcare. With respect to the privacy considerations under HIPAA the ladders listed above would include the data associated with privacy as a concept, composition, decision making, attribute, and process.

Information Continuum

The IC, illustrated in Exhibit 7.12, is the third layer to be accounted for and included in the knowledge model. The IC impacts the knowledge network because of the electronic communication tools and infrastructure necessary for handling requests for service.

To recap, the infomediary develops the knowledge model framework by identifying applicable components (based on the presenting task or operational activity) of three networks: the P-HCC, S-HCC, and the IC. They then break down any *information nodes* selected (e.g., patient, provider, payer, and

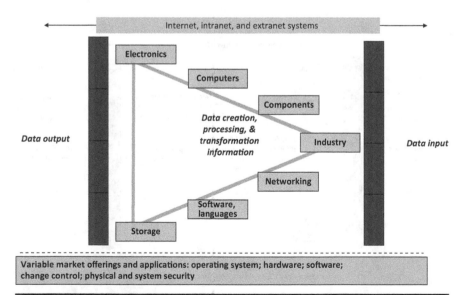

Exhibit 7.12   Information continuum.

plan sponsor). Development of a concept and composition ladder for each node follows. The creation of a decision-making model then highlights the operational activities of each node. Identification of attributes and processes indicates at which point the presenting issue impacts the decision-making model. Finally, the disposition of the task provides a database for future analysis of the defined knowledge network.

Knowledge Models for White-Collar and Organized Crime

White-collar and organized crime share common attributes of deceit and lawlessness. However, each type is distinct with respect to its attributes and components. These attributes and components will be reviewed within the following categories: activity, organization, and system. The attributes of these activities may include:

- Identity theft/medical identity theft
- Sale of medically unnecessary *legitimate* medications, health products, and procedures
- Sale of sub-standard or *counterfeit* medications, health products, and procedures, some of which may be potentially unsafe
- Illegal and unethical marketing and recruitment schemes, including false advertising
- Stealing resources and money from government programs, provider delivery systems, payer systems, and vendor systems
- Misrepresentation of professionals, product, service; false research

The organizational component can simply be one individual or collective group of individuals on behalf of the organization. The system component of the crime can be stand-alone or intermingle with legitimate business activity. Attributes of the system may include banking systems, executive office, licensed professionals, industry-specific vendors, employers, healthcare and payer systems, electronic mediums, laws and regulations by country.

Because the healthcare marketplace generates trillions of dollars, crime must be recognized as a potential issue in any cyber-audit plan. A report published by the FBI entitled *Financial Crimes Report to the Public Fiscal Year 2006*[1] and updated in 2011 noted the following staggering statistics:

- In 2005, 8.3 million cases of identity theft were reported (3.7% of adult population).
- In 2014, the percentage of the population exposed to identity theft has increased to 176.6 million (7% ages 16 or older).[2]
- Increased activity in medical identity theft for false billings or theft of benefits.
- Fraudulent healthcare billing is estimated to involve between 3% and 10% of all claims.
- Significant increase in medical data theft.
- As of 2016, healthcare spending grew 4.3% to $3.3 trillion, or $10,348 per person.[3]
- As of 2016, healthcare spending accounted for 17.9% of the nation's gross domestic product.[4]

Sample Identity Theft Case

The following high-profile FBI case shows how vulnerable healthcare entities are to theft of medical data and the resulting impact:

HAROLD MCCOY, ET AL. (PHILADELPHIA):
Harold McCoy was sentenced to 162 months in prison following a guilty plea to charges of bank

fraud, identity theft, and conspiracy for his role
in a scheme to defraud numerous American Red
Cross (ARC) blood donors in the Philadelphia area.
McCoy obtained the names and personal identifying information of numerous blood donors from
an employee of ARC. He and his co-conspirators,
Karynn Long and Danielle Baker, then used the
stolen information to obtain instant credit loans,
bank loans, and to cash counterfeit checks, causing approximately $800,000 in losses to various
financial institutions. This crime jeopardized the
Philadelphia area blood supply and damaged ARC's
trusted relationship with the public, as many people
stopped donating blood, and two corporate dona-
tion centers ceased their blood drives when the
media reported the crime. For their roles in this
scheme, Long pled guilty to bank fraud and conspiracy and was sentenced to 18 months in prison;
Baker pled guilty to identity theft and conspiracy
and was sentenced to 24 months in prison. All three
defendants were ordered to pay restitution in the
amount of $270,555.[5]

Medical Identity Theft—Definition

Medical identity theft (MIT) is the theft of *individual
identifiable health information*[6] (IIHI) for the purpose of
misrepresentation of health information to obtain access to
property or permanently deprive or harm an individual while
interacting within the healthcare continuum. IIHI are any data
elements that link an individual to a set of health records and
their respective health conditions.

Accordingly, MIT is a type of identity theft relating to the
practice of medicine and matters pertaining to general illness or wellness.[7] In the case of MIT, *property* is defined as

the medical identity of an individual that provides access to healthcare monetary or service benefits. MIT can occur at any point in the healthcare continuum.

MIT has evolved since the inception of healthcare benefit programs and is a matter of urgent attention due to the highly adverse effect it has on individual victims. Healthcare is a high-volume cash industry that goes beyond the commonly discussed patient-provider relationship. To illustrate the magnitude of opportunity for MIT, consider that 3 months of claims data for one Medicare region can create about one terabyte of activity (equivalent to about 40,000 trees shredded into paper). The P-HCC participants who use some form of personal health information in their normal course of business create a source for potential MIT vulnerability with every one of their transactions.

In an electronic health environment, the infomediary will need to be on guard for breaches of IIHI, documented data elements that comprise an individual's identity. Any electronic health record system should secure the following IIHI elements[8]:

1. Names.
2. All geographical sub-divisions smaller than a state, including street address, city, county, precinct, ZIP Code, and their equivalent geographical codes, except for the initial three digits of a ZIP Code if, according to the current publicly available data from the Bureau of the Census:
   a. The geographical unit formed by combining all ZIP Codes with the same three initial digits contains more than 20,000 people.
   b. The initial three digits of a ZIP Code for all such geographical units containing 20,000 or fewer people are changed to 000.
3. All elements of dates (except year) for dates directly related to an individual, including birthdate, admission date, discharge date, date of death; and all ages over

89 and all elements of dates (including year) indicative of such age, except that such ages and elements may be aggregated into a single category of age 90 or older.
4. Telephone numbers.
5. Facsimile numbers.
6. E-mail addresses.
7. Social security numbers.
8. Medical record numbers.
9. Health plan beneficiary numbers.
10. Account numbers.
11. Certificate/license numbers.
12. Vehicle identifiers and serial numbers, including license plate numbers.
13. Device identifiers and serial numbers.
14. Web universal resource locators.
15. Internet protocol address numbers.
16. Biometric identifiers, including fingerprints and voiceprints.
17. Full-face photographic images and any comparable images.
18. Any other unique identifying number, characteristic, or code, unless otherwise permitted by the Privacy laws.

How Medical Identity Theft Occurs

The movement of protected health information within the P-HCC can result in services rendered or products provided and related financial transactions.

Another example includes the case of Katrina Brookes. Ms. Brookes started receiving healthcare bills in the name of her son, which included his middle name. At this point, no one knew her child's middle name except close family and the hospital in which she completed paperwork to obtain her son's social security number.[9] The new paperwork was not placed within her son's medical record. New bills started to arrive from other providers. The mother was suspicious because how could any other new provider know of her son's middle name since she had not shared it with anyone else? The mechanism of the theft was later determined while conducting an identity use work flow since the birth of the child. It was later determined that the independent hospital resource that initiated social security applications had stolen and sold the child's identity. Again, the breach occurred during a non-traditional health service in the healthcare setting. Anyone can be a victim, the elderly, the sick, or the unsuspecting. When it comes to children, however, many of them will not know that their identity has been breached until the age at which they are able to secure credit. With respect to health services, the child will be dependent on the adult to ensure that future providers are not responding to adulterated records.

These examples illustrate exposure to financial issues and medical errors issues, but how about losing your children?

The story of Anndorie Sachs, from Salt Lake City and mother of four children, provides an unimaginable consequence of MIT. Her experience dates back to April 2006, when she was approached by a Utah social worker. The plan was to take away her children. The last time Ms. Sachs had given birth to a child was in 2004. The problem was that Dorothy Bell Moran, a known meth user, gave birth with Ms. Sachs' identification at the hospital. Social Services wanted to take away Ms. Sachs' children because they thought she just delivered a baby with meth in her blood stream. After repeated phone calls for clarification, Ms. Sachs was able to prove that Ms. Moran delivered the baby with meth in her blood stream. Ms. Sachs was then allowed to keep her children. Further consequences were noted when Ms. Sachs was later admitted into a different hospital with a kidney infection. Because Ms. Moran's health records were integrated into Ms. Sachs' record, a critical issue occurred: Ms. Sachs' blood type is different from Ms. Moran's, thus creating an opportunity for Ms. Sachs to be subjected to a medical error due to incorrect information.[10]

Damages to Primary Victims

Primary victims or patients face a variety of threats resulting from MIT. Examples of damages to patients include:

- Denial of access to future healthcare services resulting from exhausted benefits
- Exposure to medical errors due to integration of perpetrator health data into victim's health data
- Unwarranted litigation due to behaviors and activities by the perpetrator during episodes in which the medical identity was assumed by the perpetrator
- Unwarranted financial damage due to behaviors and activities by the perpetrator during episodes in which the medical identity was assumed by the perpetrator

Illustrative Examples of Medical Identity Theft from a Consumer Perspective

When the Consumer Is Not Aware

A woman who was affiliated with a medical facility had access to claim forms and medical records. She submitted claims for heart surgery, gall bladder surgery, finger amputations, a hysterectomy, and more—27 surgeries in all. There were no hospitalizations or claims for anesthesia. The woman utilized protected health information and assumed the identity (on paper) of several patients to collect money.

When the Consumer Is Involved

At an insurance company, all payments of foreign claims are made to the insured and not to the foreign medical provider. An insured submitted $90,000 for fictitious foreign claims from a clinic in South America, indicating that the entire family was in a car accident. A fictitious police report accompanied the medical claims. A telephone call to the clinic revealed that the insured and the dependents were never treated at that clinic.

When an Individual Wants Products or Services

A man stole Medicaid recipient cards that entitled the bearer to medical benefits, including prescription drugs, paid for by the Medicaid program. He also stole written prescriptions, purportedly issued by doctors for various narcotic medicines, for personal use.[11] He was convicted of Medicaid fraud and receipt of stolen property and faced up to 6 years in state prison and a fine of up to $20,000.

Strategies for Preventing Medical Identity Theft

Healthcare consumers have several strategies they can utilize to protect themselves from both identity theft and medical identity theft. These strategies include deterrence methods, detection methods, and defense/mitigation methods.

Deterrence by Consumers[12]
- Shred all explanations of benefits, expired benefit cards, healthcare billing statements, and/or health records prior to discarding them.
- Protect social security numbers, benefit plan identity document cards, and any other document that identifies individuals with any healthcare benefit plan.

- Do not give out personal health information on the phone, through mail, or over the Internet unless the party receiving the disclosed information is known and trusted.
- Never click on links sent in unsolicited e-mails.
- Be mindful of free personal health records programs that offer to track information and free health screenings in which they ask for benefit information.
- Do not use obvious passwords like date of birth, name, mother's maiden name, or the last four digits of social security numbers for electronic communications containing health records or benefit claim information.
- Keep all health information and benefit card information in a safe, secure place.
- If you are admitted into a healthcare setting, leave your credit cards and any other identification information at home.
- Do not have your family bring your personal mail to any inpatient facility.
- Be careful when you do visit any clinic to leave your sensitive information in a locked locker.
- Refuse requests for social security numbers. If absolutely required, request how the information will be stored and monitored. Many carriers are not using social security on their identification card.
- Ask your provider to use your medical record number for identification purposes instead of your social security number.
- From time to time, review the content of your medical records for detailed personal information.
- Most important, never be afraid to ask questions. If you do not understand the response, ask for it again.

Detection by Consumers[13]
- Monitor and review explanations of benefits.
- Look for bills from providers never seen before.
- Look for bills with ambiguous dates of service.

- Look for bills with ambiguous diagnoses on the explanations of benefits.
- Review explanations of review statements in the same manner.
- Review your release of medical records to third parties.
- Check credit reports for any outstanding bills from providers.
- Look for letters from insurance companies regarding denied services for services never requested.

Defense and Mitigation by Consumers[14]

- Place a fraud alert on credit reports. Once perpetrators steal a medical identity, then they may enter into other financial arrangements.
- File a police report and contact providers immediately.
- Obtain copies of medical records and review them for any ambiguous information.
- Work with providers to address any misinformation.
- Report the theft to the Federal Trade Commission.
- Contact your insurance company and request a complete historical claim run. Ask them for a complete listing of any bills submitted in your name with your benefit card.
- Report to your carrier any providers that are on your list that you have never seen before.

Damages to Secondary Victims

Although it is appropriate to view the patient as the central victim in an episode of medical identity theft, secondary victims, including the entities perpetrators breach to gain access to the IIHI, also exist. Examples of damages to secondary victims include:

■ Financial loss by any market player who must write off the theft of goods and services to bad debt

- Risk of litigation by the primary victim resulting from theft within your institution
- Financial loss to the plan sponsor for the cost of goods and services
- Loss of credibility to the institution, which can result in additional financial losses

Medical Identity Theft from an Entity's Perspective

When a provider's employee obtains access to IIHI to submit false claims, the provider may be liable to the patient because of the breach of privacy and information. Vulnerability may be enhanced if the entity does not have the appropriate internal controls that could have prevented such an activity from occurring. Providers are also susceptible to financial loss from the use of unwarranted benefits and fraudulent claims when false diagnosis and procedure codes are generated. This type of breach can also be committed at an insurance company by claims personnel.

Deterrence by Entities
- Implement appropriate infrastructure security measures for all electronic and/or paper transactions.
- Shred all explanations of benefits, expired benefit cards, healthcare billing statements, and/or health records prior to discarding them.
- Use appropriate destruction methods for any electronic storage media prior to discarding them.
- Any systems issues relating to or review of potential security vulnerabilities should meet current market standards and requirements.
- Consider internal control security measures for protected health information access and use from each of the P-HCC participants.

Detection by Entities

- Monitor for data conflict in demographic information of a patient.
- Monitor denials of patient claims based on medical necessity issues.
- Monitor for unusual use or access of the IIHI elements.
- Monitor patient complaints of missing personal items by department.
- Monitor inventory losses of prescription medications by department.

Defense and Mitigation by Entities

- Create internal policies and implement internal controls for verification of patient identity.
- Test controls on a routine schedule.
- Test systems security to ensure appropriate user access.
- Test and review access logs of users who review patient information that is not directly related to their job function.
- Test and review access logs at the time a patient is registered for any activity by users that is not involved in patient registration.

Infomediary Considerations

The infomediary may need to understand how electronic information moves within the healthcare continuum and how data are transferred between market players. *Data integrity of health information* involves internal controls for privacy and security of all IHII elements specifically within the P-HCC and S-HCC. Policies and practices to prevent, detect, and mitigate MIT should be incorporated throughout these healthcare continuums.

Use of stolen IIHI may result in:

- Access to third-party health benefits products or services
- Access to reimbursement funds that result from third-party benefits

■ Access to health data to misrepresent health status for disability employment, and so on
■ Access to health data and assumed medical identity to perpetrate other crimes

Sample Fraud Case

Greed without regard for consequence motivates most fraud schemes. The following case illustrates the ultimate consequence—death:

> JORGE A. MARTINEZ, MD (CLEVELAND): This investigation resulted in the first known prosecution involving a criminal charge of healthcare fraud resulting in death. The case focused on the illegal distribution of pharmaceutical narcotics and billing for unnecessary medical procedures. The investigation revealed that Dr. Martinez provided excessive narcotic prescriptions, including OxyContin, to patients in exchange for the patients enduring unnecessary nerve block injections. Dr. Martinez' actions directly resulted in the death of two of his patients. Over a 6 year period, Martinez submitted more than $59 million in claims to Medicare, Medicaid, and the Ohio Bureau of Worker's Compensation. A jury found Martinez guilty of 56 criminal counts, including distribution of controlled substances, mail fraud, wire fraud, healthcare fraud, and healthcare fraud resulting in death. Martinez was later sentenced to life in prison. This investigation was conducted jointly with the Office of Inspector General, US Department of Health and Human Services (HHS-OIG), Ohio Bureau of Workers Compensation, DEA Diversion, AdvanceMed, Ohio Department of Job and Family Services, Anthem Blue Cross Blue Shield, and Medical Mutual of Ohio.[15]

Sample Pharmaceutical Fraud Case

With the advent of Medicare prescription drug coverage and the high cost of medications, pharmaceutical fraud jumped onto the law enforcement radar screen. The impact, effect, and cost associated with patients receiving medically unnecessary, adulterated, or counterfeit medications are undocumented.

> BANSAL ORGANIZATION (PHILADELPHIA): This investigation was conducted jointly with the Drug Enforcement Administration (DEA) and internal revenue service (IRS) and was focused on a Philadelphia-based Internet pharmacy drug distributor that was smuggling drugs into the United States from India and selling them over the Internet. The criminal organization shipped several thousand packages per week to individuals around the country. Overall, 24 individuals were indicted on charges of distributing controlled substances, importing controlled substances, involvement in a continuing criminal enterprise, introducing misbranded drugs into interstate commerce, and participating in money laundering. Over $8 million has been seized to date as a result of the charges. Within 1 year, 12 suspects have pled guilty, three have been convicted at trial, four are in foreign custody, and five remain fugitives. This investigation was worked jointly with the DEA, IRS, U.S. Immigration and Customs enforcement (ICE), United States Postal Inspection Service (USPIS), and the Lower Merion Police Department.[16]

The knowledge model for white-collar and organized crime also begins with a concept ladder. Both types of criminal activities have evolved significantly with respect to the use of technology and highly skilled professionals. Exhibit 7.13 separates the two types of criminal activity.

What types of crime exist within the healthcare continuum?

White-collar may include:

- Professional misrepresentation
- Facility misrepresentation
- False billings
- False claims
- Unnecessary medical treatment
- Contractual manipulations

Organized crime may include:

- Medical identity theft
- Prescription drug diversion
- Prescription drug counterfeit
- Accident crime rings
- Pill-mill schemes

Exhibit 7.13   Concept ladder.

Exhibit 7.14 addresses the characteristics of white-collar crime activities that tend to be self-dealing in nature. They may occur individually or through collusive behavior among several individuals or entities on behalf of a corporation. The composition of organized crime activity, illustrated in Exhibit 7.15, focuses on the provision of illegal goods and services or the resale of stolen goods or services.

Cyber Implication Overview

This chapter introduced the elements of data-driven decision-making models as defined within the primary and secondary healthcare continuum that overlap with the information continuum. The key points for the cyber infomediary specialist is to understand the implication of data structure, application, and technology associated with the data and their output. Cyber-health exists today but is evolving rapidly. The concepts presented therefore should be used to identify the structure,

What is the composition of illicit behavior noted within while-collar crime?

Key Feature	Characterization of Organized Crime	Modern Technology
Activity	Crimes committed by an affluent person or individuals in position of influence in the normal course of business. These tend to be self-dealing in nature.	Embezzlement, misappropriation of resources; collusion, price-fixing, false advertising; illegal pollution; price fixing; false financials; substandard products; illegal tax avoidance; illegal sale of unsafe products; illegal unsafe working conditions; misrepresentation of professionals, product, service; false research; sale of unnecessary medical services; kickbacks; undisclosed commissions; other financial misrepresentations and/or falsifications.
Organization	Individual or collective on behalf of the organization.	Organization—complex layered, multi-disciplined, multi-professional, and highly skilled.
System	Crime is intermingled with legitimate business activity.	Banking systems, executive office, licensed professionals, industry specific vendors, employers, healthcare and payer systems, electronic mediums, and laws and regulations by country.

Exhibit 7.14   White-collar crime composition ladder.

What is the composition of illicit behavior noted within organized crime?

Key Feature	Characterization of Organized Crime	Modern Technology
Activity	Provision of Illegal and stolen goods and services	Sale of new identities; medical identity theft, sale of medically unnecessary legitimate medications, health products, and procedures. Sale of counterfoil medications, health products, and procedures. Illegal and unethical marketing and recruitment schemes. Stealing resources and money from government programs, provider delivery systems, payer systems, and vendor systems. Intrastate and international theft in all of the above activity. Various schemes include: rent-a-patient, pill mill, and drop box.
Organization	Complex arrangements	Organization—complex layered, multi-disciplined, multi-professional, and highly skilled.
System	Integration of legal and illegal structures	Banking systems, industry-specific vendors, employers, healthcare and payer systems, electronic media, and laws and regulations by country.

Exhibit 7.15   Organized crime composition ladder.

application, and technology of the e-system being reviewed through the knowledge model network diagram process.

The knowledge models in this chapter were illustrated using the behavioral primary, secondary, and information continuum. Additional details of the behavioral continuum model are discussed in Chapters 3, 4, 6 and summarized in the reference guide contained in Chapter 12.

The algorithms in Chapter 6 provide the opportunity for data mining, data-driven decisions, and the development of artificial intelligence through rule-based systems. The market has numerous niche data-driven cyber-health decision offerings. Many of them exist in the form of disease management models to fraud detection systems.

The following examples offer perspectives of cyber-health and e-data-driven model developments outside of the United States. The most significant discussions and focus are on technological infrastructure and complement the discussions of what is occurring within the United States. The next chapter will continue to illustrate analytic tools and review checklists within a series of case studies.

Examples of Worldwide Activity

Australia: Australian Digital Health Agency[17] is tasked with improving health outcomes for Australians through the delivery of digital healthcare systems and the national digital health strategy for Australia. The Australian Digital Health Agency commenced operations on July 1, 2016. The agency is responsible for national digital health services and systems, with a focus on engagement, innovation, and clinical quality and safety.

- *European Union*: European e-health research area is pursuing several objectives "to contribute to the coordination of Member States' e-Health strategy formulation and implementation as well as e-Health-related Research and

Technology Development (RTD)" (http://www.ehealth-era.
org/index.htm).

■ *Africa*: e-Health Africa's mission is to build stronger health
systems through the design and implementation of data-
driven solutions that respond to local needs and provide
underserved communities with tools to lead healthier
lives. e-Health Africa developed the electronic Integrated
Disease Surveillance and Response system to improve
the flow of information within health systems. The tool is
integrated in the national health system through its com-
patibility with the health information system DHIS2 that is
used in over 45 countries, including many with vulnerable
health systems.

■ *Canada*: e-Health initiatives include both administrative and healthcare delivery infrastructures.
The Canadians have initiated the development of
an electronic health record in addition to activities such as teleconsults, for example, remote monitoring of patients in the home setting. eHealth
Ontario,[18] a government-owned independent
agency, has spent in the range of $350 million to
$400 million annually over the past several years
to build a system of electronic medical records for
patients (https://www.cbc.ca/news/canada/toronto/
ehealth-ontario-sale-kathleen-wynne-ed-clark-1.3808734).

■ *Japan*: In 1994, the Japanese Association of Healthcare
Information Systems Industry was established to address
e-Health initiatives. Its mission includes "promoting the
concept of medical information systems, specifically
focusing on the development of electronically processing
medical images, medical records, and receipts." In addition, it focuses on developing standards that will link
health, medical, and welfare services (http://www.itu.int/
itudoc/itu-t/workshop/e-health/s9-02.pdf).

■ *Mexico*: e-Health is integrated into Mexico's e-government
system. The National e-Mexico system focuses on

integrating the efficiency from technology in which its citizens interact with all facets of government programs. The goal of the e-Health initiative is to improve lives, provide access to health information, integrate a digital online dossier, develop a system of epidemiological control, create an electronic information exchange, and communicate on matters of health (https://www.cbc.ca/news/canada/toronto/ehealth-ontario-sale-kathleen-wynne-ed-clark-1.3808734).

■ *World Health Organization* is the directing and coordinating authority for health within the United Nations system. The World Health Organization has developed an e-Health Standardization Coordination Group to develop "a platform to promote stronger coordination among the key players in all technical areas of e-Health standardization. The group is a place for exchange of information and will work towards the creation of cooperation mechanisms to: identify areas where further standardization is required and try to identify responsibilities for such activities; provide guidance for implementations and case studies; consider the requirements for appropriate development paths for health profiles of existing standards from different sources in order to provide functional sets for key health applications; support activities to increase user awareness of the existing standards, and case studies" (http://www.who.int/ehscg/en/).

Endnotes

[1] http://www.fbi.gov/publications/financial/fcs_report2006/financial_crime_2006.htm accessed August 10, 2018.

[2] https://www.bjs.gov/index.cfm?ty=pbdetail&iid=5408 accessed August 10, 2018 accessed August 10, 2018.

[3] https://www.cms.gov/Research-Statistics-Data-and-Systems/Statistics-Trends-and-Reports/NationalHealthExpendData/NationalHealthAccountsHistorical.html accessed August 10, 2018.

4 https://www.cms.gov/Research-Statistics-Data-and-Systems/
   Statistics-Trends-and-Reports/NationalHealthExpendData/
   NationalHealthAccountsHistorical.html accessed August 15, 2018.
5 http://www.fbi.gov/publications/financial/fcs_report2006/
   financial_crime_2006.htm accessed August 15, 2018.
6 https://www.hhs.gov/hipaa/for-professionals/privacy/laws-
   regulations/index.html accessed August 15, 2018.
7 American Psychological Association (APA): "medical" (n.d.),
   Dictionary.com Unabridged (v 1.1), retrieved March 06, 2008,
   website: http://dictionary.reference.com/browse/medical
   accessed August 15, 2018.
8 http://privacyruleandresearch.nih.gov/pr_08.asp#8a accessed
   August 15, 2018.
9 http://www.msnbc.msn.com/id/23392229 accessed August 15,
   2018.
10 Ibid.
11 http://www.nj.gov/oag/newsreleases03/pr20031211a.html
   accessed August 15, 2018.
12 Adapted from Federal Trade Commission www.ftc.gov/idtheft
   accessed August 15, 2018.
13 Ibid.
14 Ibid.
15 http://www.fbi.gov/publications/financial/fcs_report2006/
   financial_crime_2006.htm accessed August 15, 2018.
16 Ibid.
17 https://www.digitalhealth.gov.au/ accessed August 15, 2018.
18 https://ehealthontario.on.ca/en/ accessed August 15, 2018.

Chapter 8

Business Processes and Data Implications

We spend more time shoveling coal than steering the ship. We want to shift our energy to looking at the data and navigating where we are going.

Robert Kagarise
Director of Population Health Informatics and IT for the Delaware Valley Accountable Care Organization[1]

Introduction

Thus far, this book has covered industry applications of cyber-health data, including concepts such as clinical and financial case management. It has also covered the various types of algorithms that can be developed to process data. The previous chapter focused on understanding the models for developing data acquisition strategies to support data-driven health decisions.

Escalating healthcare costs continue to affect the entire marketplace from delivery to the financing of healthcare services.

To be cost competitive, interest focuses on improving business processes and their supporting information technology platforms. Numerous academic institutions, professional associations, and audit techniques can provide infomediary specialists with the deep level of analytical understanding required to keep up with market demands.

The Institute of Internal Auditors (www.theiia.org) is a valuable resource and professional training organization for individuals who would like to expand their audit expertise and capabilities. Likewise, the Association of Certified Fraud Examiners (www.acfe.com) is a valuable resource for individuals who want to develop investigative skills to detect anomalies. Another organization that warrants recognition is the International Organization for Standardization (www.iso.org) in Geneva, Switzerland, which dedicates itself to developing standards for quality control. Its quality standards are recognized worldwide. Infomediary specialists should consider ongoing education from Health Information Management Association (www. HIMSS.org), which is a global professional organization focused on better health through information and use of technology.

Cyber-Health and Healthcare Business Processes

Infomediary specialists have used numerous techniques to review a business process. What is a business process, and what does it involve? A business process is a systematic series of steps to achieve operational objectives and conclusion of a specific trade, service, or product. This chapter outlines business processes for each market player within the primary healthcare continuum and identifies impacting cyber-health initiatives. When healthcare organizations formulate new business processes, infomediary specialists should provide to the team the patient perspectives—e.g., user expectations, available resources, and access to information.

One set of tools which may be used to help understand and improve business process and which has gained widespread acceptance throughout many industries is *total quality management*. Total quality management is an approach that relies on an interactive team to address issues to spur continuous improvement. It includes *benchmarking*, which compares business practices under review with best-in-class practice models. *Gap analysis* is used to understand specific problems and how to mitigate them, in addition to *process flow analysis* or *flowcharting*, which illustrates the operational components of a specific function. (Examples in this book are in flowchart format to illustrate general categories of business functions.) Statistical tools such as *control charts* visually separate variant occurrences from normal occurrences, while *cause-and-effect diagrams* map issues under review. *Histograms* can facilitate the evaluation of the frequency with which a particular set of data elements appear within an activity. Infomediary specialists also use *run charts* to illustrate activity, trends, and variances over time. Another common approach to reviewing quality is the *six sigma* process, which emphasizes data-driven methodology to identify how variation in certain activities causes variation in others. Other general skill sets necessary to develop under a comprehensive audit curriculum include forecasting methods, project management techniques, business process analysis, inventory management concepts, and marketing from a pricing perspective, supply chain management concepts.

Patient Business Process

What types of expectations do patients have? Patients likely expect competent healthcare services and unbiased health recommendations and, in a cyber-health environment, they may demand access to their health information whenever they need it.

What types of resources are available to provide services that meet such patient expectations? Typically, when a health-care episode proceeds smoothly, patients interact with their provider, receive an explanation of benefits, and receive and pay a bill. That's if the patient can make heads or tails out of the various adjustments between what the provider charges and what the patient has to finally pay. If there are issues, the complexity skyrockets, and the patient often is unable to get clarifying information and certainly no relief if he or she perceives any billing errors. Should the patient attempt to determine in advance how much a certain procedure will cost—for the purpose of comparing vendors' prices—well, such a thing is impossible for almost all patients.

What types of information do patients have access to? Current market limitations include a lack of transparency of information and communication between the patient and all other market players within the healthcare continuum. Another important limitation is a lack of interoperable information that makes self-advocacy and the task of obtaining relevant patient information cumbersome. Cyber-health initiatives attempt to create a fluid interoperable environment throughout the entire business process in which patient information is accessible during subsequent requests for service. Let us look at the following financial and clinical problems many patients run into.

PROBLEM 8.1
Financial Case Management Advocacy

"Nora" was an 87-year-old widow. Her husband "Ethan," a Medicaid and Medicare recipient, had died in a nursing home. The nursing home was a Medicaid provider and received a monthly payment of $1,250 from Medicaid. Nora and Ethan's children had been contributing supplemental payments of $1,445 per month.

Two years after Ethan's death, the nursing home hired a new billing agent who went through receivables and initiated billings on accounts in which agreed-on deductions had been made. It then initiated supplemental billing statements during the 3-year period in which Ethan received services and filed a claim against Nora for $21,792 in additional charges.

Nora was aware of neither her own nor her deceased husband's rights and did not understand the concept of balance billing. A lack of transparent reimbursement rules further complicated matters. Cyber-health's ability to create an interoperable environment for billing information among the provider, plan sponsor (Medicaid in this case), and the patient will help alleviate this type of confusion. The couple would have known up-front the potential for balance billing and been able to deal with it before it was too late.

Infomediary Cyber Implication: How will the specialist obtain access to this system and assist the individual to build her own personal healthcare portfolio?

Internal Audit Cyber Implication: How will internal audits test the operations to ensure that the patient can virtually retrieve and authenticate all of this information?

PROBLEM 8.2
Clinical Case Management Advocacy

Recall "Dina" from Chapter 2, our 56-year-old female cancer patient who had never undergone surgery until her cancer diagnosis. Dina had initiated consultations with her family doctor, oncologist, surgeon, pain management specialist, rehabilitation expert, and radiation oncology expert. She received two second opinions and a series of diagnostic and laboratory tests. Each provider initiated his or her consultation and examination without the medical records accumulated from preceding providers and, unfortunately, she ended up experiencing inter-operative awakening.

A lack of real-time access to Dina's entire updated medical record caused providers to make assessments without complete information. Cyber-health's ability to create an interoperable environment for health data will promote complete data-driven decisions that minimize potential for medical errors and provide optimal solutions.

> **Infomediary Cyber Specialist Implication:** Within an interoperable virtual cyber-health environment, the infomediary specialist can ensure that these critical data are available to all of the patients' healthcare providers.
> **Internal Audit Cyber Implication:** Test internal controls utilized by professional staff to ensure they receive outcome measurements for effective population health management.

Provider Business Process

Exhibit 8.1 illustrates a typical provider business process. The provider concept ladder identified two market agents: the facilities where services are provided and the professionals who provide those services. It is important to recognize professionals who bill for their services independent of any facility fee to understand how providers generate fees. For example, a hospital will charge for facility use, but will not charge for the nurse who took care of the patient or the pharmacist who prepared medications.

The physician, however, acting as an outside consultant to the patient's care, bills for the diagnostic or procedural services provided.

The cyber-health infomediary specialists must determine what electronic infrastructures exist that enable providers to communicate internally, externally—both directly and through cloud-hosted applications with other market players during the business process. Beginning with, infomediary specialists must determine how providers obtain registration information and how it connects with third-party audits/reviews and

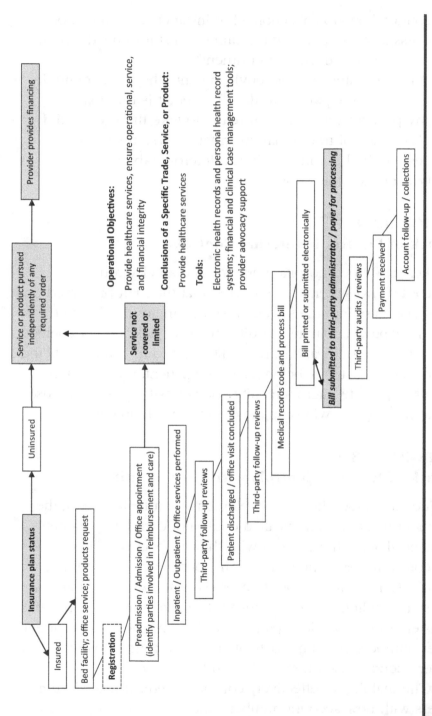

Exhibit 8.1   Business process: providers.

account follow-up/collections. For instance, how much of the process is still dependent on paper and still in need of conversion into an electronic environment?

While an interoperable environment where a community of market participants can fluidly interact is the goal, many providers are far from ready to take that step. Solid performance of traditional information systems must be established before moving to interoperability, as the following example shows.

PROBLEM 8.3
Lack of Electronic Internal Controls

When a 300-bed hospital implemented an electronic health record (EHR) system, it discovered that the EHR preserved only the last entry into the system, resulting in an inability to track user changes, additions, modifications, or deletions of content. Within the modifications, no ability existed to validate whether the changes actually belonged to the patient. Cyber-health's ability to create interoperability coupled with appropriate user internal controls will promote electronic data integrity.

PROBLEM 8.4
Lack of Internal Controls with User Identity

When a 200-bed hospital implemented an EHR system, the patient-tracking tool installed could not correlate patients' financial account numbers with their respective medical record numbers. The result of this deficiency meant that a patient's laboratory would never correlate with the financial system's billing account number. To make matters worse, the system did not retrieve patients' unique medical record identifier numbers. Any time patients returned to the hospital, they were denoted as a new patient in the system.

The inability to effectively correlate medical record numbers with new account numbers and subsequent episodes of care resulted in "missing" patients within the system and non-submitted claims. When claims were submitted, they contained integrity issues, and the selection of diagnostic and procedural information raised the potential for misrepresentation of services rendered by the facility. A medical records department depends on health data to select appropriate diagnostic and procedure codes. When a disruption of aggregating information occurs, a hospital may make incorrect code decisions based on incomplete records. Cyber-health's ability to create interoperability will require strong internal controls and integrity of the health and financial data collected during an episode of care.

   Infomediary Cyber-Health Specialist Implication: Should be able to research the content of an individual's personally identifiable information and correlate to their patient records for any gaps or incorrect data.

   Internal Audit Cyber Implication: Should consider audit testing in reconciling clinical and financial data points by individual identities.

PROBLEM 8.5
Lack of Internal Controls for Services Provided and Charged

When a 450-bed hospital implemented an EHR system, it did not program its charge master (a listing of services and products provided to the patient) with individual unique identifiers. An audit comparing patient final bills to patient medical records could not be completed because generic numbers compromised any tracking of services.

   The hospital therefore was unable to generate prior cost accounting reports by hospital department or post-discharge audit adjustments of over- and undercharges, or measure expenditures by disease category, preventing the evaluation of effective resource utilization. Cyber-health's ability to create interoperability coupled with appropriate internal controls for

individually identifiable service and product charges will be
critical in maintaining financial integrity and disease management accountability.

Infomediary Cyber-Health Specialist Implication:
Should consider medical audit training in order to help
patient validate their hospital charges and utilize virtual
data resources on typical medical billing guidelines.

Internal Audit Cyber Implication: Test internal controls
for managing and maintaining charge data master for
the organization. This should follow testing of the virtual
transfer of the charge data to third parties.

Payer Business Process

Exhibit 8.2 illustrates the typical payer business process. The
business process (revenue cycle) for the payer in Exhibit 8.2
outlines the typical functions involved in processing the services
on behalf of benefit plans and on behalf of their provider
clients. Third-Party Administrators (TPAs) as a courtesy to their
benefit plan customers will process out-of-network claims on
behalf of their beneficiary. Payer processes have a variety of
questions for infomediary specialists to address: What type of
electronic system is used to process claims? What contractual
fee schedules for services and products exist within a network?
Does an entity manage clinical data differently from financial
data? Within an electronic claims environment, for what
percentage of claims does an entity handle claims processing
electronically? Does an entity still receive paper claims?

Infomediary specialists should furthermore ensure that
appropriate communication and exchange of information
among plan sponsors exists. TPAs often process claims on
behalf of a third-party plan sponsor, and defined access to
information and prevention of breaches are important parts
of the business process.

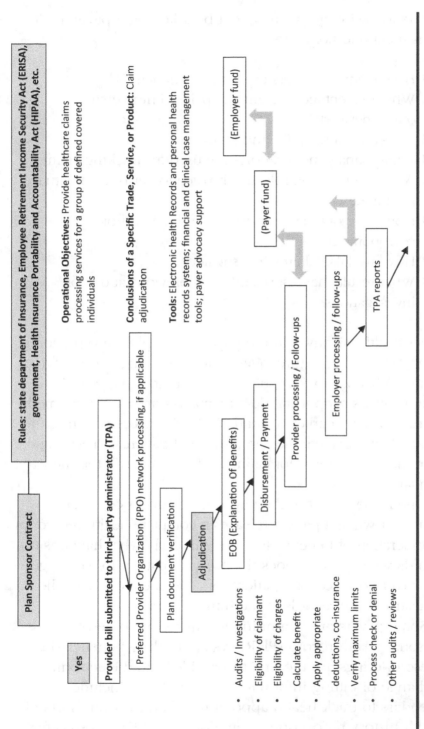

Rules: state department of insurance, Employee Retirement Income Security Act (ERISA), government, Health Insurance Portability and Accountability Act (HIPAA), etc.

Operational Objectives: Provide healthcare claims processing services for a group of defined covered individuals

Conclusions of a Specific Trade, Service, or Product: Claim adjudication

Tools: Electronic health Records and personal health records systems; financial and clinical case management tools; payer advocacy support

Plan Sponsor Contract

Yes

Provider bill submitted to third-party administrator (TPA)

Preferred Provider Organization (PPO) network processing, if applicable

Plan document verification

Adjudication

EOB (Explanation Of Benefits)

Disbursement / Payment

Provider processing / Follow-ups

(Employer fund)

(Payer fund)

Employer processing / follow-ups

TPA reports

- Audits / Investigations
- Eligibility of claimant
- Eligibility of charges
- Calculate benefit
- Apply appropriate deductions, co-insurance
- Verify maximum limits
- Process check or denial
- Other audits / reviews

Exhibit 8.2   Business process: Payer, TPA, or insurance company.

The following questions might be asked on a payer audit assessment questionnaire:

■ How many providers are under contract?
■ What percentage of claims is paid within versus out-of-network?
■ How are claims paid and processed?
■ What management reports are used for tracking claims?
■ What internal controls are in place to verify contractual guarantees?
■ How can contractual terms be audited and/or corroborated?
■ How are false claims investigated?
■ What results have surfaced from previous audits or investigations?

Cyber-health initiatives in the payer marketplace are predominately financial in nature, relating to processing and verifying claims. When a provider submits a claim to a payer, the provider includes supporting documentation from a patient medical record. The market currently lacks the necessary structure to maintain complete files on individual patients. Providing the "minimum necessary" for claim verification is still the industry standard.

One niche aspect in the payer environment considers results for when a patient releases a complete health record for consideration of benefits. It is unclear today what happens to records when a payer does not accept a patient for coverage. If a payer does accept a patient for coverage, how does the payer use those records in the future?

Some payers are beginning to offer some type of personal health record (PHR) system to their beneficiaries. These offerings are the first to provide a fluid electronic exchange of billing information. These PHRs include calendars to track health appointments and various sorts of health history repositories. Some of these PHRs even offer opportunities to scan in actual health records. A challenge facing payer PHRs, however, is consumer confidence in privacy. For example, will non-related health information be secured? In a payer PHR system, if a patient pursues non-covered health services, will privacy and access be controlled?

Following are some problems related to payer information issues.

PROBLEM 8.6
Use and Loss of Health Information—Handling Subcontracted Vendors

National insurance carriers often use brokers to sell insurance coverage and enroll potential beneficiaries into a program by facilitating the enrollment application and obtaining health data. Therefore, brokers collect, store, process, and transfer health information even though they do not typically evaluate any of it. What happens when a broker loses a file containing health information, and what internal controls ensure the integrity of enrollment processes? Cyber-health's ability to create interoperability could create a cyber-health infrastructure for a secure enrollment process, eliminating the unnecessary handling of health information by brokers. Providing patients with direct electronic access to share health information could also provide a cost effective solution.

Infomediary Cyber-Health Specialist Implication: Should consider training on the use of available technology tools that facilitate the medical review of hospital charges and utilize virtual data resources on typical medical billing guidelines.

Internal Audit Cyber Implication: Test internal controls for assurance of interoperability of cloud-based environments.

PROBLEM 8.7
Lack of Insurance—Processing Fraudulent
Claims for Enrolled Beneficiaries

Eligibility verification is a traditional payer function coordinated with plan sponsors that now tends to be done electronically. People who do not hold health insurance may be able to persuade those who are covered to file fraudulent claims for their medications. When a TPA does not reconcile pharmacy benefit managers' medication information with health data, these fraudulent transactions may slip through the system unnoticed and compromise the integrity of the beneficiary file. Cyber-health's ability to create interoperable disease management protocols and medication profiles will provide the optimal environment to ensure claim submission integrity. Interoperability will also help identify patient medication complications, thus preventing and minimizing the impact of medical errors.

> **Infomediary Cyber-Health Specialist Implication:** May assist patient with identity theft self-audits.
> **Internal Audit Cyber Implication:** Test internal controls for managing and maintaining identity proofing procedures.

Plan Sponsor Business Process

The plan sponsor concept ladder details several different categories: self-insured non-governmental employers subject to ERISA guidelines and provisions, government-sponsored programs such as Medicare and Medicaid subject to legislated mandates accompanied by Centers for Medicare and Medicaid Services Manual, and private insurance companies that sell insurance coverage. These private plans are subject to state department of insurance provisions and mandates.

Infomediary specialists should determine what controls are in place to monitor access and use of these data as well as flesh out a comprehensive list of activities when reviewing a particular plan sponsor. The following checklist can be helpful to identify exchanges in cyber-health clinical and financial data within the plan sponsor business process:

- Identify parties involved in the benefit plan management by collecting signed and unsigned contracts. (Do not overlook subcontracted vendors.)
- Identify all fee schedules within each contract.
- Determine sources of data, access parameters, and how data are corroborated.
- Identify right-to-audit provisions and the access level allowed.
- Identify which monetary transactions cannot be audited or corroborated.
- Collect reports that demonstrate adjudication according to the plan document and the source of data that is used for the basis of decisions.
- Identify claims not paid according to plan.
- Identify source of plan information.
- Identify internal controls within the business process.

Plan sponsor cyber-health initiatives relate to the movement of beneficiary health and financial information. Plan sponsors are also initiating PHR offerings for their beneficiaries, which have important implications for the implementation of a cyber-health community. For example, if an employer develops a PHR offering in tandem with a local hospital, how is information that is generated outside the hospital setting handled, and exactly what level of user content control will exist?

Exhibit 8.3 illustrates a basic plan sponsor business process. These operations reflect the receipt of payment for the administration of claims adjudication on behalf of a benefit plan, the execution of provider contracted client

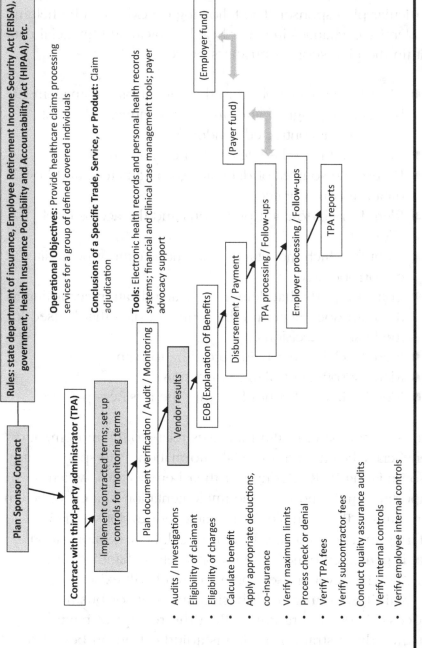

Plan Sponsor Contract

Rules: state department of insurance, Employee Retirement Income Security Act (ERISA), government, Health Insurance Portability and Accountability Act (HIPAA), etc.

Operational Objectives: Provide healthcare claims processing services for a group of defined covered individuals

Conclusions of a Specific Trade, Service, or Product: Claim adjudication

Tools: Electronic health records and personal health records systems; financial and clinical case management tools; payer advocacy support

Contract with third-party administrator (TPA)

Implement contracted terms; set up controls for monitoring terms

Plan document verification / Audit / Monitoring

Vendor results

EOB (Explanation Of Benefits)

Disbursement / Payment

TPA processing / Follow-ups

Employer processing / Follow-ups

TPA reports

(Payer fund)

(Employer fund)

- Audits / Investigations
- Eligibility of claimant
- Eligibility of charges
- Calculate benefit
- Apply appropriate deductions, co-insurance
- Verify maximum limits
- Process check or denial
- Verify TPA fees
- Verify subcontractor fees
- Conduct quality assurance audits
- Verify internal controls
- Verify employee internal controls

Exhibit 8.3   Business process: Payer, TPA, or insurance company.

payments, and the courtesy of processing out-of-network claims on behalf of benefit plan clients.

The following problems relate to plan sponsor information issues.

PROBLEM 8.8
Employee Working Environments

Employers generally initiate periodic quality control reviews of working environments to ensure safety. Assessments often include documenting adverse employee symptoms. For example, hospitals routinely screen and monitor employees with infectious conditions. How is the integrity of the employee health file maintained while an employer tests for potential hazardous exposure? How does an employer ensure that disclosure of any health related information does not impact an employee's work status or subsequent raises and/or promotions? Cyber-health's ability to create interoperable health information will provide opportunities for large-scale analysis and development of effective safety, prevention, and mitigation standards.

Infomediary Cyber-Health Specialist Implication: May assist patient with understanding the root cause of a condition.

Internal Audit Cyber Implication: Test internal controls for managing and maintaining environmental acquired conditions.

PROBLEM 8.9
Employer Increase in Healthcare Expenditures

When an employer discovers a significant increase in health expenditures, it will often audit the plan to analyze the source for increased expenses and identify opportunities for cost reduction. How is the integrity of the employee health file maintained while an employer evaluates expenses? If an audit identifies specific employees as high risk, how will the information be handled? How will the discovery impact their job status? Some employee wellness programs construct specific health goals and consequences.

For example, if employees do not complete a smoking-cessation program, they are terminated. Health policies directly impacting employment status is a new concept, and the implications of such policies are currently being tested in the marketplace. Cyber-health's ability to create interoperable health information will provide opportunities for large-scale analysis and to improve disease management and reduce plan sponsor costs.

> **Infomediary Cyber-Health Specialist Implication:** May assist patient with maintaining wellness goals.
> **Internal Audit Cyber Implication:** Test internal controls for managing and maintaining wellness initiatives.

Third-Party Vendor Business Process

Infomediary specialists should use traditional methodologies to understand process, movement of information, and operational and financial impact as a guide to review any type of third-party vendor. Because the list of types of third-party vendors is as diverse as it is long, this chapter addresses one specific niche third-party vendor: pharmacy benefit managers (PBMs).

The costs associated with the use of prescription medications have been increasing annually, causing PBMs to grow into larger players within the healthcare continuum. An analysis of PBMs also demonstrates how an interoperable cyber-health environment can unite a fragmented business process.

The PBM marketplace is comprised of very complex relationships among business functions and cyber-health communications. Numerous contracts exist among the market players and not all are transparent.

Exhibit 8.4 illustrates typical product and monetary movement within the PBM marketplace.

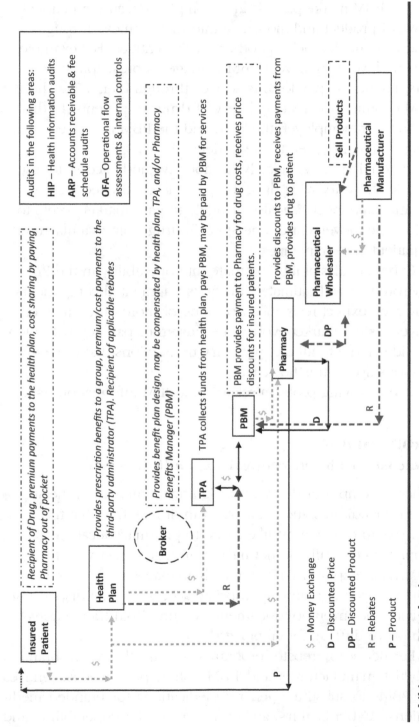

Exhibit 8.4   PBM business process.

The PBM marketplace is also complex because additional flows of product and monetary information move through independent channels via other service entities. For example, the employer may have a PBM manage its prescription benefits. Employers pay for this service through their TPA. The PBM contracts the retail delivery of drugs to patients. In this scenario, the employer, the TPA, and the PBM never see what drug is actually given to the patient.

In addition, they typically do not have audit access to test, sample, or verify what drug the patient actually receives. Infomediary specialists also struggle to gain market access to follow the movement of one specific drug from manufacturer to patient consumption.

Cyber-health's ability to create interoperability in the PBM environment will ultimately unify its fragmented components. However, expect resistance from one or more of the market players as the market evolves, because transparency will often provide clarity to all the monetary transactions that drive the relationships in this flowchart.

The following problem relates to a PBM information issue.

PROBLEM 8.10
Increase in Pharmaceutical Expenditures

When an employer discovers a significant increase in health-care expenditures and audits its plan, it may find that the increase in cost is most likely due to pharmaceuticals. Employers typically do not have a direct contract with their PBM. The employer's TPA typically manages the PBM relationship, therefore, gaining appropriate access to retail dispensing activity and inventory documents to audit PBM transactions can prove difficult for employers.

Furthermore, rebate programs set up between branded product manufacturers and PBMs often provide disincentives for PBMs to substitute generic medications for branded medications. Cyber-health's ability to create interoperability and transparent financial transactions will help employers evaluate PBM activity more accurately.

Cyber Implication Overview

This chapter explored market player business processes and the impact of cyber-health. The bottom line of interoperability and accessibility is the value proposition of a cyber-based platform for any of the functions discussed in this chapter. The next chapter will review a sample of various electronic information infrastructures and look at how data (practice standards) are currently shared and what the future holds.

Endnote

[1] https://www.healthcare-informatics.com/blogs/david-raths/leadership/favorite-health-it-quotes-2017-baker-s-dozen accessed for August 20, 2018.

Chapter 9

Evolving from e-Health Systems

Every Village in Africa now has a Cyber Café.

Patrick Chappatte
A Lebanese Swiss editorial cartoonist, comics
journalism, and animated documentary work
Born 1967 Karachi, Pakistan

Introduction

On January 31, 2006, President George W. Bush declared,
"We will make wider use of electronic records and other health
information technology to help control costs and reduce dangerous medical errors." President Obama's administration furthered
this vision with the implementation of the Affordable Care Act.
The Obama administration's encouragement of creating public use files of government health data has opened the door
to progressive data analytics. Changes are expected within the
President Donald Trump administration. An infomediary specialist should monitor ongoing changes with each new administration. The private sector, likewise, will drive technology innovation

as consumers (in the spirit that every village has an Internet café) increasingly demand access to information off of an Internet connection through a personal computer or mobile device.

The healthcare market will continue to have significant growing pains as it continues to refine its electronic interoperable ecosystems. Imagine the future of healthcare operating within a cyber-virtual cloud-based "health mall." This chapter focuses on providers, who collect and transmit health information, and payers, who receive health information through claims data.

Moving from Independent Health Electronic Systems to a Cyber Platform

Exhibits 9.1 and 9.2 demonstrate the vastness of electronic and cloud-based health vendor offerings in the provider and payer marketplaces. These offerings are not integrated from one provider to another, the patient in today's environment is limited to the self-defined groupings of providers. For example, if a patient chooses a specialist from one set of relationships they will have to independently get hard copy or electronic access to their health information and merge data from the unconnected provider independently. Regardless, the lists in Exhibits 9.1 and 9.2 provide the ideal data points that would be considered when merging into a cyber-based interoperable platform.

As stated, although the lists do not exhaust all possible offerings, they recognize the features and functions commonly advertised by vendors within respective market segments. In addition, depending on the particular vendor, the technology behind each feature and function varies significantly. As a result, future technology should include scrubbing formats into an independent patient-centric system, thereby offering the patient a centralized source for all of their health information.

The goal of a cyber-health provider offering should be to focus heavily on workflow and emphasize aggregation of overall patient health records. Providers fundamentally treat patients and require aggregated comprehensive health information to do so effectively.

• Billing
• Blogging and secure instant messaging
• Charge capture functions
• Claims processing
• Clearing house functions
• Clinical decision-making tools
• Documentation – clinical; annotation; procedures; imaging; management; templates
• Coding rules and support tools
• Compliance tools
• Connectivity – device; internal; external
• Electronic prescribing; refill requests; and responses
• Data storage and technology solutions – market standards
• X-rays, films, scans
• Disease management tools
• Educational tools – staff; patients
• EHR
• – acute care hospital; ambulatory care, cardiology, chiropractic; dermatology; family medicine; gastroenterology; hematology; general surgery; immunology; internal medicine; neurology; obstetrics-gynecology; oncology; ophthalmology; optometry; otolaryngology; orthopedics; pediatrics; podiatry; primary care; psychiatry; radiology; rheumatology; surgery; urology; registration and discharge
• Health information management services
• Maintenance alert systems; adverse alert systems; rules alert system
• Integration interface engines
• Interactive voice response
• Interoperability functions
• Letter and form generation modules
• Vital statistics
• Master Patient Indices (MPI)
• Medical transcription
• Multi-site management
• Networking systems software
• Order entry applications
• Outsourcing components
• Patient portal support
• Performance measurement support tools
• Portability options
• Workflow applications and automation
• Scheduling
• Quality care indicators and assurance tools
• Transcription interface

Exhibit 9.1   e-Health provider offerings.

• Accounting integration	• Data import / export and warehousing
• Regulatory compliance management	• Indemnity
• Medicare / Medicaid, health maintenance organization (HMO), and preferred provider organization (PPO)	• Documentation – case notes; task management; imaging tools; repository
• Assign claims	• Diary and alert / alarm tools
• Automated forms	• Electronic data interchange (EDI) capability and electronic submission
• Case management tools	• Premium billing
• Claims processing – dental; prescription; health; vision	• Self-insured management
• Claim – customer account history; resolution tracking	• Health Insurance Portability and Accountability Act (HIPAA) management
• Consolidated Omnibus Budget Reconciliation Act (COBRA) administration	• Historical access retrieval systems
• Coordination of benefits	• Legacy health systems
• Co-pays and deductible management	• Emerging e-formats
• Workflow management	• Manual entry capability
• Customer relationship management (CRM) integration	• Membership management
• Customer service integration capability	• Mobile access
• Customization - user interface; fields; functionality	• Tools – modeling; cost analysis; edit; actuarial reporting; payment processing; portability; disability management; adjustor analysis
• Federal employee products	
• Claims specialty – auto; life; propertyand casualty (P&C); complex litigation; excess coverage; medical malpractice; public entity; workers' compensation	• Multi-currency and language
• Provider credentialing	• Multiple benefit programs support
• Policy management	• Rules-based adjudication

Exhibit 9.2   e-Health payer offerings.

The final deliverable of any provider of healthcare service or product results in the generation of some type of health notation (a narrative describing some update on the patient, an assessment with new health information, and report findings). Independent cyber-health offerings transfer these health notations into a cloud-based domain. Because each diagnostic category (e.g., oncology, neurology, etc.) possesses unique attributes, health notations vary, and vendors offer different cyber-health solutions for different diagnostic departments. Connectivity and portability of healthcare data are functionalities critical to an interoperable environment. Once they are achieved, the provider should anticipate developing technology to merge the patients' health information into a patient-centric cyber platform. Auditors can use Exhibits 9.1 and 9.2 as a checklist to assess and compare functional offerings between vendors.

Exhibit 9.2 details certain cyber-health payer offerings. Unlike today's situation, the payer market should anticipate the exportation of all claims-related activity to a patient-centric, cyber-based platform. A current gap for patients is this: When a payer sends information to a patient, they often do not include all relevant diagnosis and procedure codes. If the patient is to become a data-driven consumer, they cannot go down this path without knowing what the provider did to them (procedure code) or the reason why the service was performed (diagnosis code).

This gap exists because when a payer adjudicates a claim, validation of the service only requires the minimum necessary health information to confirm the contents of a claim. The need for comprehensive centralized patient records is not a direct workflow requirement. Payers tend to seek comprehensive patient records only when a need arises to investigate an individual patient or provider. Exhibit 9.2 lists claims processing categories such as dental, vision, prescription, and health. The business of processing claims does not typically require attention to subspecialty diagnostic categorization. Claims processing rather requires attention to the form in which a claim is received. For example, providers submit health claims in Centers for Medicare and Medicaid Services (CMS) professional form CMS 1500 and submit health and dental claims on a universal billing form UB04. Prescriptions also use their own type of claim form. Because payers rely on billing information contained on claim forms, they face significantly fewer issues than providers when communicating the services rendered and corresponding fees, in the right format. A cyber-health data strategy should include the transfer of much more data and would not be limited to the data required to do the current task or operation.

Exhibit 9.3 presents a sample of cyber-Health features and functions that provider and payer systems share (by subject, not necessarily by process).

One growing cyber-based platform is billing centralization software. While development in this area is still slow, it remains active due to the utility it has in facilitating

Provider	Functions
Accounting integration	Accounting integration
Billing	Claims processing: dental
Claims processing	Claims processing: prescription
	Claims processing: health
	Claims processing: vision
	Claims specialty: auto, life, property & casualty (P&C)
	Claims specialty: complex litigation
	Claims specialty: excess coverage
	Claims specialty: medical malpractice
	Claims specialty: public entity
	Claims specialty: workers compensation
	Claim and customer account history
	Claim resolution tracking
Clearing house functions	Data import/export
	Payment processing tools
Clinical documentation	Documentation: case notes
Portability options	Portability tools
Workflow applications	Workflow applications
Workflow automation	Workflow automation
Workflow management	Workflow management

Exhibit 9.3   Sample listing of shared vendors' functional offerings.

interactions between providers and payers, given that such
SaaS (Software as a Service) programs help patients move
all of their billing data into one location. Providers thrive on
centralized comprehensive information for the effective delivery of care, payers, in most cases, make do with the minimum
necessary collection of health information to verify presenting
claims. Patients struggle to understand their health condition and the respective billing associated with their providers
and payers. Providers and payers therefore will likely wrestle
over market standards for cyber-health information standards.
We should anticipate continued demands from the patient
for access and centralization of all the informatics generated
by payers and providers, in addition to subsequent changes
within and among all healthcare stakeholders.

If you are a healthcare professional responsible for making
decisions on the choice of technology, it is important to fully
evaluate the current capacity of the technology, and the ability of that technology to integrate easily with the cyber-systems
under development. Choosing a vendor that does not continue
to adapt to the market will require an organization to essentially
start over when the product becomes outdated or obsolete.

Market Evolution on the Content of Data Within Healthcare

The healthcare industry desperately needs more cooperation, commonality, and transparency. The current universal billing form generated by the National Uniform Billing Committee facilitates standardization of claims, developed because of the administrative simplification initiatives outlined in the Health Insurance Portability and Accountability Act of 1996.[1] Exhibit 9.4 lists a sample of common data elements that providers exchange with payers to share information in a consistent manner. Exhibit 9.5

Box #	Description
1	Facility name, address and phone number
2	Facility pay-to name and address
3.a	Patient control# (patient account#) no change
3.b	Medical record # (UB92 box 23)
4	Type of bill
5	Federal tax number
6	Statement covers period —from/through
7	Covered days
8.a	Patient identification
8.b	Patient name (UB92 box 12)
9a, 9b, 9c, 9d	Patient address, city, ZIP code, state (UB92 box 13)
10	Lifetime reserve days
11	Unlabeled
12	Patient name
13	Patient address
14	Patient birthdate
15	Patient sex
16	Patient marital status
17	Admission date
18	Admission hour
19	Type of admission/visit
20	Source of admission
21	Discharge hour
22	Patient status/discharge code
23	Medical record number
24–30	Condition codes
29	Accident state (new field)
31	Unlabeled
32–35	Occurrence code/date
39–41	Value codes

Exhibit 9.4   UB04 data claim elements: First 41 standardized data elements.

Box #	Description
42	Revenue code and line level details
43	Revenue code description
44	Healthcare Common Procedure Coding System (HCPCS)/rates/Health Insurance Prospective Payment System (HIPPS) rate codes
45	Service date creation date
46	Units of service
47	Total charges
48	Non-covered charges
49	Unlabeled
50	Payer name primary, secondary, tertiary
51	Health plan identification (ID)
52	Release of information primary, secondary, tertiary
53	Assignment of benefits primary, secondary, tertiary
54	Prior payments primary, secondary, tertiary
55	Estimated amount due primary, secondary, tertiary
56	National provider identifier (NPI)
57	Other physician ID primary, secondary, tertiary
58	Insured name primary, secondary, tertiary
59	Patients relationship primary, secondary, tertiary
60	Insured unique ID primary, secondary, tertiary
61	Insured group name primary, secondary, tertiary
62	Insured groups number primary, secondary, tertiary
63	Treatment authorization code primary, secondary, tertiary
64	Document control number
65	Employer name primary, secondary, tertiary
66	Diagnosis qualifier
67	Diagnosis
68	Unlabeled
69	Admit diagnosis
70	Patient reason for visit
71	Prospective payment system (PPS) code
72	External cause of injury
74a–e	Principal procedure code
75	Unlabeled
76	Attending—NPI/qual/ID
77	Operating—NPI/qual/ID
78	Other ID
79	Other ID
80	Remarks
81	Code to code field

Exhibit 9.5   UB04 data claim elements: Remaining standardized data elements.

lists the remaining data elements. Overall, 81 categories of information have been standardized. In comparison with a medical record on an individual patient, the number of elements to be defined would be in the thousands.

A similar list of shared fundamental data elements exists for processing professional fees. Laboratory result names have also been standardized to facilitate clear communication. Initial laboratory result communication standards did not include recommendations for the name of the services ordered or the lab result values, but simply focused on the standardization of the result names.[2] Exhibit 9.6 illustrates operational components for which commonality standards could be defined. Laboratory services fit into the category within the shaded box.

Exhibit 9.7 isolates the inpatient business process category that is found midstream in the provider business process (Exhibit 9.6) and illustrates key operational components in greater detail.

Each operational component within each business process requires a specific market standard if healthcare is to achieve true interoperability. Every hospital has a charge master that numerically lists all products and services that can be provided to patients, including the services identified in Exhibit 9.7. Charge masters can easily have 8,000 individual charge items and each individual charge item can easily have up to 50 data elements documented to reflect service. As illustrated in Exhibit 9.7, inpatient services break down into another 11 categories with 56 additional sublayers. The following is a list of other processes auditors need to consider to develop a complete picture of data element fields:

- Selection of room and board
- Provision of office services preadmission
- Products request
- Registration
- Payer certification
- Preadmission

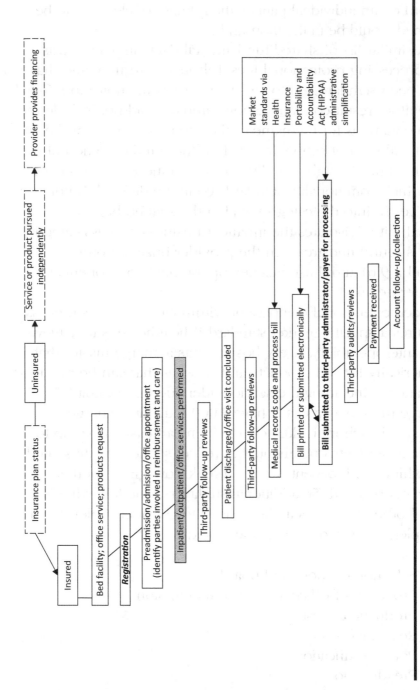

Exhibit 9.6   Business process: Provider facility-global category of operations.

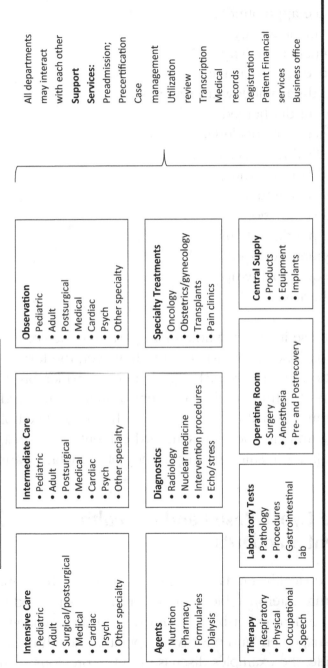

Inpatient Acute Services Performed

Intensive Care
- Pediatric
- Adult
- Surgical/postsurgical
- Medical
- Cardiac
- Psych
- Other specialty

Intermediate Care
- Pediatric
- Adult
- Postsurgical
- Medical
- Cardiac
- Psych
- Other specialty

Observation
- Pediatric
- Adult
- Postsurgical
- Medical
- Cardiac
- Psych
- Other specialty

Agents
- Nutrition
- Pharmacy
- Formularies
- Dialysis

Diagnostics
- Radiology
- Nuclear medicine
- Intervention procedures
- Echo/stress

Specialty Treatments
- Oncology
- Obstetrics/gynecology
- Transplants
- Pain clinics

Therapy
- Respiratory
- Physical
- Occupational
- Speech

Laboratory Tests
- Pathology
- Procedures
- Gastrointestinal lab

Operating Room
- Surgery
- Anesthesia
- Pre- and Postrecovery

Central Supply
- Products
- Equipment
- Implants

All departments may interact with each other

Support Services:
Preadmission; Precertification
Case management
Utilization review
Transcription
Medical records
Registration
Patient Financial services
Business office

Exhibit 9.7   Business focus inpatient acute care facility.

- Admission
- Office appointment
- Inpatient activity
- Outpatient activity
- Office service activity
- Third-party follow-up reviews
- Patient discharged
- Office visit concluded
- Medical records assembly
- Code of procedures
- Bill preparation
- Bill submission
- Bill pending status
- Payment received
- Account follow-up
- Collection

Today, these items, in whole or in part, may be communicated from one facility to another, however, the format and description of what is exchanged varies considerably. Common concerns affecting the development of market standards are the cost and availability of proven technology, stakeholders reaching an agreement on standard content, and, most important of all, the resulting transparency of monetary transactions.

Future Cyber-Based and e-Health Content Standards

Current e-Health standards can easily serve as the framework for a future interoperable, patient-centric, cyber-based platform. Imagine similar cyber-based platforms for the exchange of disease management and effective population health management. That aside, the examples discussed in the previous section focus on the format and structure of electronic function offerings with two examples of standardized communications of billing data, such as the UB04 form. Another area of the market to watch out for includes specific standards on clinical record content. One example includes the efforts of an organization started in 2003 known as Continuity of Care Record (CCR) standards.[3] This is an organization that any auditor involved in analyzing or testing internal controls in the collection, organization, and movement of health data, should monitor for developments. Currently, the standards are evolving into two segments, the first being the CCR record and the second in the Continuity of Care Document. The ultimate goal is to improve the continuity of care provided to the patient, thereby reducing medical errors resulting from misinformation and to improve the transportability of the information between providers.[4]

The organization describes a sample of data objects that should be included in a CCR transaction between one provider and another in their respective patient record. The three components include the "header" of the electronic file; the "body" which is the content of the transmission; and the "footer" which describes authorship.

The content for the header includes:

- Patient
- To
- From
- Purpose
- Date

The content for the body includes:

- Adverse Directives
- Alerts
- Encounters
- Family History
- Functional Status
- Insurance
- Immunizations

- Medications
- Medical Equipment
- Plan of Care
- Problems
- Providers
- Results
- Social History
- Support
- Vital Signs

The content for the footer includes:

- Actors
- Comments
- Signatures

The universal billing committee provided consistent market structure for all providers to submit billing data in the same format. Conceptually, this organization is moving in the same direction by initiating content standards. The CCR standards target continuity of care and patient safety by communicating core data elements via electronic transmissions. This cannot be done without setting standards for the organization of the content of health information.

Cyber-Based Opportunity

Market offerings are currently being offered to individual consumers to manage their protected health information. Offerings may be weighted toward financial information versus clinical data. Some offerings include both. Healthcare professionals should be following another set of standards that are developing and referred to as Personal Health Record System Functional Model. The focus of these standards is to establish the criteria for features and functions that will allow the patient to effectively manage their health history. Expect to see these standards developed within SaaS-type cloud-based offerings.

Cyber Cloud-Based Technology Offering Vulnerabilities

Healthcare's most significant vulnerability, as it migrates into an e-health environment (putting aside the well-documented concerns over security and privacy), is ensuring that the vendor offerings actually perform as advertised. Many references and consultants are available to help facilitate e-health initiatives. It is important to establish a team that has operational understanding and know-how of each business process. Before a conversion to a new e-health system takes place, it is important to prepare backup plans for functions that appear not to work. Many entities have experienced pain because of provisions overlooked during the design of the e-health infrastructure. In addition to being a burden on staff, the cost of corrections can easily reach the seven and eight-figure range.

The following case study presents what can go wrong during a systems conversion.

Case Study Summary

During a post-implementation audit of a hospital's electronic health record (EHR) system, significant functionality issues were experienced in the following departments:

■ Admissions
■ Patient Billing Financial Services
■ Collection Accounts Receivable
■ Central Services Inventory Control

- Health Info Management (Medical Records)
- Insurance Verification
- Management

Over a period of 14 months, the listed departments remained non-functional, resulting in a "no-confidence level" by the hospital in its ability to generate and submit accurate patient claims. The dysfunction noted in the audit resulted in significant revenue and labor damages reaching multimillion-dollar figures. After significant revenue losses and compliance exposure, the hospital's chief executive officer made a determination to discontinue EHR services. It was less expensive for the hospital to start over with an entirely new system than to fix problems with the current one.

Case Study Audit Activity

The following items were reviewed and analyzed for preparation to re-start non-functional modules:

- Operational analysis of the request for proposal
- Analysis of items categorized as "must have," "highly desirable," and "desirable"
- Analysis of manual versus automatic functions
- Impact of attempted implementation
- Review of business office functions
- Design/implementation of employee interviews
- Impact of damage to the hospital
- Analysis of fluctuations in hospital revenues
- Analysis of fluctuations in census data
- Analysis of compliance and revenue impact
- Analysis of inefficiency impact
- Analysis of labor impact
- Financial damages

Case Study: Data Profile 1—Contracted Functions

The EHR vendor contract pertained to 1,012 different hospital business functions in 27 different departments. Each function was assigned a priority level. Within each department listed in Exhibit 9.8, the vendor contract provided for items that were categorized as (1) desirable, (2) highly desirable, and (3) must have.

Exhibit 9.9 provides a sample listing of "must have" contracted items that the EHR vendor indicated it could already accommodate within the admissions department.

Exhibit 9.9 illustrates the format in which the information was organized in an auditor worksheet. The first audit objective was to identify the functions that were actually implemented. The next objective was to determine if the function required manual user activity. Later analysis determined the impact on operations, financials, and compliance for each department in the hospital. Gathering this data is an extensive and time-consuming process.

#	Hospital Department	#	Hospital Department
1	Admissions	15	Laboratory
2	Billing Patient Financial Services	16	Management
3	Collections Accounts Receivable	17	Marketing
4	Accounts Payable	18	Medical Staff Coordination
5	Case Management	19	Neurology (electrocardiogram, electromyography, electroencephalogram)
6	Central Services Inventory Control	20	Nursing Order Entry
7	Communications	21	Payroll
8	Education Patient	22	Pharmacy
9	Emergency Room	23	Physical Therapy
10	General Ledger	24	Podiatry
11	Golden Clinic Kedzie Avenue	25	Radiology
12	Health Information Management	26	Renal Dialysis
13	Information Systems	27	General
14	Insurance Verification		

Exhibit 9.8 Hospital departments with EHR functions proposed.

#	Function	Vendor Responsible	Priority	Implemented	Manual/Auto
1	Supports inpatient and outpatient registrations, including emergency room	Yes	3	Yes	Manual
2	Supports online ability to manually add, edit, or delete inpatient and locations:	Yes	3	Yes	Manual
	* Business—admitting				
	* Emergency room—admitting				
	* #1 Clinic				
3	When adding a new patient registration, the system should default the discharge date to be the same as the admission date if the admitting disposition is outpatient.	Yes	3	No	Manual
18	The admissions, pharmacy, order entry, and billing functions should use the Physician Master List for validation purposes.	Yes	3	No	
19	Provide security that only the medical staff coordinator or other authorized personnel may add or edit physicians on the Physician Master List.	Yes	3	No	
20	Keep audit trail of who originally created the physician record and when.	Yes	3	No	

Exhibit 9.9   Electronic health record (EHR) admissions functions.

The EHR vendor listed 69 total functions in its offering for admissions, which the hospital rated based on priority. The plan and contract categorized 55 of the 69 functions as, "must haves." "Highly desirable functions" totaled 5 and "desirable functions" totaled 7 of the 69. Two items were not categorized. The audit within admissions found that the EHR vendor implemented 36 functions, while 33 items were not installed or demonstrated no capability. Out of all of the functions implemented, 9 resulted in automation and 27 still required manual user activity to complete the function. The remaining functions did not work in any capacity.

Exhibit 9.9 illustrates audit results for 6 of the 69 functions reviewed within the admissions department. When a specific function did not work at all, the level of risk was assessed. Functions #18 and #19 were critical non-functioning items. Imagine being a patient in a facility that did not have the ability to verify the legitimacy of a physician prescribing medications? Function #20 was also very significant, the EHR system implemented did not have an audit trail function to track entries. This issue surfaced in every department in which the EHR system was implemented. As a result, the audit identified that no security existed to protect or monitor user activity.

Case Study: Data Profile 2—Analysis of Business Functions by Hospital Department

The proposal included a listing of functions to be delivered. Each function had a rating associated and designated by the provider. For example, the rating "must have" indicated that this was a mandatory requirement of the system and the vendor responding that they in fact do have the function available. The list continues with two other designations of "highly desirable" and "desirable" with respect to availability by the vendor in addition to the priority ranking of the function. The must have items were mandatory functions requested by the provider and committed to by the vendor. The following list is a summary break down of the number of functions that fell into each category.

- 1,015 functions were presented in the e-health vendor proposal.
- 830 (82%) functions were designated by hospital as "must have."
- 114 (11%) functions were designated by hospital as "highly desirable."
- 55 (5%) functions were designated by hospital as "desirable."

Case Study: Data Profile 3—Audit Result of Functionality

Overall, 55 percent of the functions were never implemented because of significant issues with the ability to resolve non-working functions across several departments. The system failed in very critical operating areas of the hospital, including admissions. The issues noted included the inability to track the patient from the time of admission and onward, along with any financial management of the care provided. The audit of the items implemented noted the following statistics:

- 19 percent of the functions implemented overall did not work.
- 51 percent of the admission functions did not work.
- 41 percent of the billing and patient financial services functions did not work.
- 63 percent of the accounts payable functions did not work.

An interview matrix was created to consistently evaluate the employee response to the implemented functions. Some of the functions had two or more issues identified. The results of those interviews are noted in Exhibit 9.10.

Exhibit 9.11 is a subcategory of items designated in the contract as "must have."

Exhibit 9.12 breaks down the response by category "highly desirable."

Category of Issues Identified During Employee Interviews			
Issue Found	**Issue Description**	**# of Business Functions with this Issue**	**% of Business Functions with this Issue**
No Issues	No issues identified (not applicable)	57	5.64%
Issue 1	Never implemented due to contract issues	563	55.74%
Issue 2	Electronic record never provided	255	25.25%
Issue 3	Not part of financial system	18	1.78%
Issue 4	Never reviewed, tested, trained	232	22.97%
Issue 5	Interface issues	206	20.40%
Issue 6	No audit trail	406	40.20%
Issue 7	Never worked	108	10.69%
Issue 8	Data integrity	386	38.22%
	Total Activity	2231	
	Total with No Issue	−57	
	Total Never Implemented	−563	
	Total Activity with Issues	1611	72.21%

Exhibit 9.10   Category of issues identified during employee interviews.

Analysis of Level 3 Must Have Criteria				
Priority	Type of Issue	Description	# of Functions	%
3	No Issues	Functions with no issued identified	36	1.98%
3	Issue 1	Never implemented due to contract issues	448	24.64%
3	Issue 2	Electronic record never provided	179	9.85%
3	Issue 3	Not part of financial system	0	0.00%
3	Issue 4	Never reviewed, tested, trained	177	9.74%
3	Issue 5	Interface issues	191	10.51%
3	Issue 6	No audit trail	356	19.58%
3	Issue 7	Never worked	95	5.23%
3	Issue 8	Data integrity	336	18.48%
	Total		1818	
	No Issue		−36	
	Issue 1		−448	
	Total with Issues		1334	73.38%
	Level 3 Functions	**Total Request for Proposal Functions**	827	
	Average	**Average Number of Issues per Level 3**	1.61	

Exhibit 9.11   Analysis of level 3–must have criteria.

Category of Issues Identified During Employee Interviews				
Priority	Type of Issue	Description	# of Functions	%
2	No Issues	Functions with no issued identified	21	8.20%
2	Issue 1	Never implemented due to contract issues	64	25.00%
2	Issue 2	Electronic record never provided	59	23.05%
2	Issue 3	Not part of financial system	18	7.03%
2	Issue 4	Never reviewed, tested, trained	26	10.16%
2	Issue 5	Interface issues	4	1.56%
2	Issue 6	No audit trail	29	11.33%
2	Issue 7	Never worked	6	2.34%
2	Issue 8	Data integrity	29	11.33%
	Total Items		256	
	No Issue		−21	
	Issue 1		−64	
			171	66.80%
		Total Request for Proposal Functions	114	
		Average Number of Issues per Level 2	1.50	

Exhibit 9.12   Analysis of level 2–highly desirable criteria.

Exhibit 9.13 breaks down the response by category "desirable."

Exhibit 9.14 illustrates that 83 percent of the issues and unresolved problems fell into the "must have" category.

Analysis of Level 1 Desirable Criteria				
Priority	Type of Issue	Description	# of Functions	%
1	No Issues	Functions with no issued identified	0	0.00
1	Issue 1	Never implemented due to contract issues	43	34.96
1	Issue 2	Electronic record never provided	17	13.82
1	Issue 3	Not part of financial system	0	0.00
1	Issue 4	Never reviewed, tested, trained	22	17.89
1	Issue 5	Interface issues	10	8.13
1	Issue 6	No audit trail	13	10.57
1	Issue 7	Never worked	5	4.07
1	Issue 8	Data integrity	13	10.57
	Total Items		123	
	No Issue		0	
	Issue 1		−43	
	Total with Issues		80	65.04%
		Total Request for Proposal Functions	55	
		Average Number of Issues per Level 2	1.45	

Exhibit 9.13   Analysis of level 1–desirable criteria.

Distribution of Issues Identified by Level Criteria			
Level	Description	# of Issues	%
3	Must Have	1782	83.27%
2	Highly Desirable	235	10.98%
1	Desirable	123	5.75%
	Total	2140	

Exhibit 9.14   Distribution of issues identified by level criteria.

In addition, the functions' status as automatic versus manual attribute was also evaluated. Exhibit 9.15 illustrates that, of the implemented EHR functions, 36 percent are classified as manual. Manual is defined as an employee having to do the same number of "paper steps" as "computer steps." Only 9 percent of the functions provided automated execution. Finally, 55 percent of the functions remained unchanged. Therefore, the progress of efficiency within the EHR system was not realized.

Exhibit 9.16 illustrates impact by job function. The review did not address all of management (or senior management) who did involve themselves in resolving many of the issues that are raised by the audit, including that the EHR system generated incorrect claim information. The focus of the "jobs" was on those positions that are on the front line. The impact is noted

Analysis of the Quality of Functions		
Implemented Manual vs. Automatic		
Function	# of Functions	% of Total
Manual	361	35.57%
Automatic	91	8.97%
Unchanged	563	55.47%
	1015	

Exhibit 9.15   Data profile: Automatic versus manual functions.

in the last column. The function of admitting the patient into the system is critical from a compliance and financial integrity perspective. The initial designation of the patient is what determines the system's ability to track the electronic information of that patient. If the patient is mislabeled, numerous issues from patient safety to financial integrity are compromised.

When an error or malfunction in the EHR software occurred, employees that held the job functions listed in Exhibit 9.16 faced the resulting problems during each patient care episode. The impact was significant unanticipated labor costs. Exhibit 9.17 provides additional critical highlights from the audit.

The Diagnosis Related Group system, which is dependent on health information and updated coding information, is the reimbursement formula for how the hospital gets paid from Medicare. If this is not done correctly, the hospital could face significant compliance repercussions. The system's malfunction in this area placed the hospital in a vulnerable position.

Case Study Observations

Errors that occur while the patient is still in-house results in inefficiency, increased expenditures, and lost revenue. Once the patient is discharged and a bill leaves the hospital, the hospital faces increased exposure to compliance and potential false claim issues with both public and private payers simply because the provider is generating claims with the wrong

Example #1:				
Job function	**Department**	**RFP#**	**Description**	**Impact**
Registration	Admissions	10	Enforces Medicare benefits prequalification via advance beneficiary notice for all Medicare outpatients during the registration process.	Patient admitted without proper registration
Utilization Review				Will have to respond to denials or other issue as a result of improper registration
Medical Coder				Should be able to code
Biller				Will have to resubmit bills after any corrections
Utilization Review				May have to get involved with errors, communicate with registration health information management, collector
Collector				Will have to communicate with above parties
Registration/Patient Accounts Director				Will have to communicate with above parties may get involved with any party above / Provide approval for write-offs and/or adjustments
Registration	Admissions	7	Batch interface	Data integrity & manual changes
Utilization Review				Data integrity & manual changes
Medical Coder				Data integrity & manual changes / Potential for lost records
Biller				Data integrity & manual changes / Potential for lost records
Utilization Review				Data integrity & manual changes / Follow-up payer calls / Follow-up surgical department calls
Collector				Data integrity & manual changes / Follow-up payer calls / Follow-up surgical department calls
Registration/Patient Accounts Director				Data integrity & manual changes / Follow-up payer calls / Follow-up surgical department calls / Management of lost records and or write-off decisions

Exhibit 9.16   Data profile: Job impact.

Example #1:				
Job function	**Department**	**RFP#**	**Description**	**Impact**
Registration	Billing Patient Financial Services	60	Supports ability to manually update the Medicare Diagnosis-Related Group (DRG) Reimbursements table. This must include the ability to add, edit, and inactivate DRG codes descriptions, the Basic DRG dollars, allowance, Medicare DRG weighting and disproportionate share dollars.	Patient will be registered properly if all items under admissions were working properly.
Utilization Review			Supports ability to manually update the Medicaid (Public Aid) DRG Reimbursements table. This must include the ability to add, edit and inactivate DRG codes, descriptions, the Basic DRG Dollars, allowance, Medicaid DRG weighting and daily disproportionate.	Data integrity and manual changes Follow-up payer calls Follow-up surgical department calls Office of the Inspector General compliance issues
		61	Supports ability to manually update the Medicaid (Public Aid) DRG. Reimbursements table. This must include the ability to add, edit, and inactivate DRG codes, descriptions, the Basic DRG dollars, allowance, Medicaid DRG weighting and daily disproportionate.	Work with management
Medical Coder				Data integrity and manual changes Follow-up payer calls Follow-up surgical department calls OIG compliance issues Work with management
Biller				If errors not caught, incorrect bills will be sent
Utilization Review				Follow-up as above if problem unresolved after discharge
Collector				Data integrity and manual changes OIG issues in pursuing collections on bills incorrectly submitted
Registration/Patient Accounts Director				In addition to above, chief executive officer involvement Significant risk exposure for false claims

Exhibit 9.17   Diagnosis Related Group impact.

patient information. The wrong information can result in a higher payment or lower patient reimbursement. Continuity of care would be compromised because case management activity is driven by claims and clinical data, for example, listing a blood test on the wrong patient. The real patient may be denied that test because, in the system, the patient is viewed as if they just had one when in fact they did not.

Interface issues, no audit trail, and data integrity were the problems most frequently found in the area of revenue and compliance.

An audit of the EHR system's impact on compliance and revenue revealed the following audit integrity issues impacting the representation of accurate revenue postings:

- Medicare Bad Debt Report requirement for CMS/Medicare.
- Inpatient and Outpatient Illinois Healthcare Cost Containment Council Reporting for State was compromised.
- Medicare benefits prequalification screening via advanced beneficiary notice for all outpatients, at registration.
- Provide same screening activity for all other payers.
- Interface issues.

The resulting non-functional operations, along with the compromised functional areas that were implemented, created additional labor hours to determine and correct problems. As a result, the audit included a measurement of efficiency issues.

With respect to hospital efficiency, the audit found that the key implementation problems were "EHR system never provided," "Never reviewed, tested, or trained," and "Never worked."

An audit of the EHR system's impact on operations efficiency revealed the following audit integrity issues that resulted in manual processes (i.e., electronic steps taken that did not result in automated functions). Two key issues were identified. The first is that insurance verification capabilities not provided or compromised and significant interface issues were not addressed.

Case Study: OIG Compliance Issues

The following key items specifically addressed compliance issues and high-risk exposure. The most significant impact was that the chief executive officer of the hospital reported after initiating implementation of the software that he was unable to verify financial accuracy.

■ The contracted services called for a total of 1,012 functions; 452 were implemented or involved attempted implementation. The remaining functions were never initiated due to numerous issues.

■ As a whole, 38 percent had no audit trail. The significance of no audit trail would directly impact OIG's compliance guidance of internal controls. The system implemented by the e-health vendor will only document the last individual who made a change in the system. This is a significant system issue because an audit trail of any financial or clinical activity cannot be tracked appropriately for any type of investigation or quality control activity.

■ As a whole, 36 percent had data integrity issues. Again, this presents significant internal control issues with respect to accurately representing an episode of care from a reimbursement perspective.

Case Study: General Audit Findings

Information that is required for a complete evaluation was obtained. Specifically, it is important to obtain information on the components of the operational software along with workflows associating it with implementation schedules. Additionally, specific deficiencies were noted along with an analysis of the damages to the hospital. The following is an example of issues that were addressed within the audit report:

1. During the analysis of any type of operational software, a process flowchart of design/implementation areas should be completed prior to designing and implementing a new system. The auditor never received any preliminary analysis from the EHR vendor. Exhibit 9.18 illustrates the accounts receivable pipeline for a provider.
2. EHR systems must be prepared to handle complex potential reimbursement methodologies to process accounts receivable. EHR vendors should analyze reimbursement methodology diversity by performing a payer mix analysis. In other words, providers must understand the diversity of payer activity that occurs at their facility. The auditor never received any payer mix analysis from the EHR vendor.
3. Exhibit 9.19 illustrates a sample data identification map, typically produced during the assessment phase prior to the implementation of a new software system. At minimum, a data map of the hospital should have been prepared for the EHR functions that correlated to the request

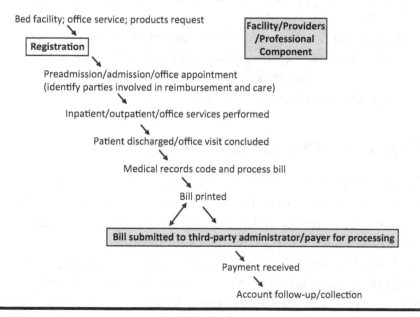

Exhibit 9.18   Accounts receivable pipeline.

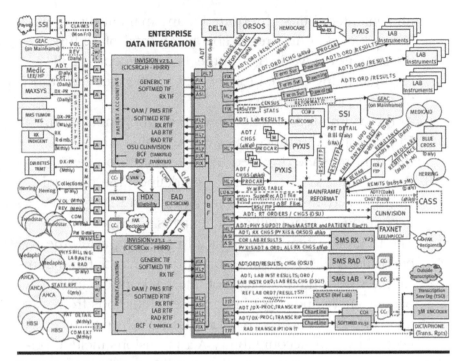

Exhibit 9.19 Sample data map.

for proposal. The auditor never received any analysis of the hospital's data layout from the EHR vendor.

4. Implementation of new software without consideration for operational pipelines often leads to clinical and financial data integrity issues that may impact both quality of care and revenue. A lack of data integrity might also impact management of the business infrastructure and the staff associated with the delivery of that business function, including direct and indirect patient care. Implementation of new software without consideration for reimbursement methodologies can result in compliance and lost revenue issues. Implementation of new software without consideration of activities within a data map can cause significant interface issues.

5. In totality, the EHR contract called for 837 "must have" functions. Of these, the billing patient financial services had a total of 86 functions, 42 never worked, and 44 were

implemented, but still required many manual functions. Collections accounts receivable had a total of 32 functions, 16 never worked, and the 14 implemented still required many manual functions. On average, each function experienced 1.55 issues.

6. At the committed completion date of implementation, 55 percent of the functions were not initiated.
7. Inpatient revenue dropped by more than 5 percent.
8. Based on the OIG compliance guidelines, the hospital appropriately disengaged from a program that was not generating accurate billing statements.
9. The lack of system audit trails adversely impacted the hospital's ability to initiate appropriate financial and clinical internal controls. A lack of internal control can impact patient safety and carry financial repercussions from third-party payers. The most recent Health Insurance Portability and Accountability Act provisions include private payer programs as well as public programs.
10. A lack of data integrity adversely impacted the hospital's ability to maintain quality of care and accurate charge capture. A lack of data quality can impact patient safety as well as generate over- and under-charges to third-party payers.

Case Study Damages

During the course of the audit, a methodology was outlined to measure actual damages, and the following assessment was incorporated into the audit:

1. The hospital suffered a multimillion-dollar loss in net inpatient revenues as a result of the agreed upon, nonfunctional "must have" processes.
2. The hospital suffered more than a quarter of a million dollars in labor costs associated with inpatient activity to mitigate non-functional aspects of the EHR system.

3. The hospital suffered a loss of over a million dollars in net outpatient revenues as a result of the agreed upon, non-functional "must have" processes.
4. The hospital suffered almost half a million dollars in labor costs associated with outpatient activity to mitigate non-functional aspects of version 4 software.
5. Total operational damages were noted at almost $5 million dollars.

Cyber Implication Overview

Buyers beware! EHR offerings in the marketplace are numerous and sophistication varies significantly among vendors. Within one entity, the transfer and modification of an e-health environment was costly and compromised an organization significantly because careful planning and testing did not occur. The transition of that e-health data into cloud-based platforms such as a patient's personal health record has even a great exposure to adverse complications. The internal auditor's role is to ensure reliability of the offering, benchmark against market standards, and continue ongoing testing of internal controls to preserve defined functionality.

How a truly interoperable cyber-health environment comes into being is unknown and will only manifest itself as market participants each take their own incremental steps toward it. As discussed in earlier chapters, this level of interoperability has been achieved in other industries, where user and provider communities can post advice, ask questions, rate each other, and share details of their experiences. In healthcare, there are additional challenges:

■ Will there be a way for a patient to sit at one location, fire up his or her computer, and gain immediate access in a single place to all prior health records? If so, implementation will require either: (1) real-time access to all prior health provider systems by a program which knows where to look or (2) a periodic downloading to a third-party data host by all providers whenever they have an interaction with the patient. In both cases, the challenges for standardization of formats and migration from e-health systems to cyber-health systems are going to be immense.

■ Who will perform the role of "hosting" the accumulation of data and creating access? Will the patient buy a service (like tax preparation software) in which he or she can download from various providers and payers the info which the user can then manipulate on their desktop, or will there emerge a regulated entity (like an insurance company) who takes all the claims info they get and create a window for the patient to see everything. They could be compelled to do it via regulation and they could recover the cost via premiums.

■ Who will employ the infomediary specialist? As discussed in the Introduction, this term encompasses a wide range of activities. Some will be unique to the patient, and the patient may retain such a specialist. Other activities will take place inside a corporate entity. More and more tasks once under the purview of a chief information officer will become the areas of expertise for a corporate infomediary specialist.

Endnotes

[1] http://www.nubc.org/ accessed August 30, 2018.
[2] http://www.whitehouse.gov/omb/egov/documents/domain1.doc accessed August 30, 2018.
[3] http://www.ccrstandard.com accessed August 30, 2018.
[4] https://aspe.hhs.gov/report/literature-review-and-environmental-scan/continuity-care-record-versus-continuity-care-document-basis-interoperable-information accessed August 15, 2018.

Chapter 10

The Data-Driven Cyber Patient

There are risks and costs to a program of action—
but they are far less than the long range cost of
comfortable inaction.

John F. Kennedy
35th President of the United States (1917–1963)

Introduction

A healthcare portfolio contains a file of patient health
information or an individual personal health record. Market
offerings for individual personal healthcare record systems
are rapidly emerging. They vary in scope, format, structure,
and delivery. The Centers for Medicare and Medicaid Services
(CMS) has initiated its own pilot of a personal health record
for Medicare beneficiaries:

In June 2007, CMS initiated a new pilot project to
encourage Medicare beneficiaries to take advantage of
Internet-based tools to track their healthcare services

and provide them with other resources to better communicate with their providers. The project is expected to run for 18 months and will enable certain beneficiaries to access and use a personal health record (PHR) provided through participating health plans and accessible through www.Mymedicare.gov. CMS will collect data to assess the use, usability, and feature preferences of the tools.[1]

In addition, CMS has released the following comments regarding PHRs:

> The Personal Health Record (PHR) is an adjunct tool related to the provider based electronic medical record. In its ideal form, it would be a lifelong resource of health information used by individuals to make Healthcare decisions, and to enable them to share information with their providers. While a uniform, standard definition does not yet exist of a PHR, consistent applications for PHRs are beginning to emerge. The ideal is for a PHR to provide a complete summary of an individual's health and medical history with information gathered from many sources, including self-entries. Personal Health Records will have stringent controls to protect the privacy and security of the information, and individuals will have control over who has access to the information. Today, Personal Health Records are offered by health plans, providers, and independent vendors. Standards are being developed and the tools will continue to evolve along with all of the health information technologies under way.[2]

PHRs are the first stepping stone toward empowering individual patient-consumers. Current market offerings mainly act as data repositories versus an interactive tool for self-advocacy.

Portfolio Case Study

Portfolia™ is a patient electronic health system[3] that provides health information when patients need it. Inadequate access to accurate health information causes problems for patients. Why is access such a problem? First, let us quickly review the healthcare continuum from a slightly different perspective. Numerous challenges in managing patient health information exist because of the fragmented nature of our healthcare system. Exhibit 10.1 illustrates the lack of interoperability within healthcare.

Fragmentation occurs because patients see multiple providers. Providers are not equipped with a centralized database to help them organize comprehensive patient health information and therefore face the cumbersome challenge of exchanging healthcare information among themselves. Difficulty in exchanging patient health information also subjects patients to a higher risk of medical errors, financial errors, and delayed treatment.

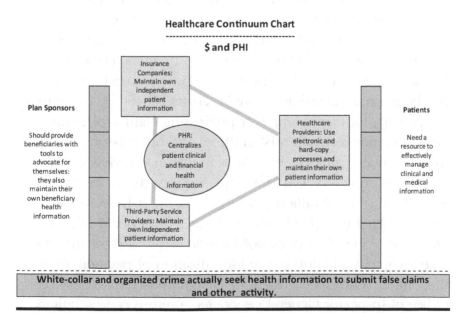

Exhibit 10.1   Healthcare continuum—PHR perspective.

The payer is not, at present, a solution for a centralized database with comprehensive patient information either. Although it is often the case that health information from fragmented providers will pass through a single payer, this is not always the case and, moreover, much important health information needed for self-advocacy is retained only by providers and not passed on with the claims to payers.

Healthcare providers continue to use hybrid solutions for their medical records, blending paper and electronic information formats. Insurance companies tend to collect their own files on patients for information relevant to their business needs. Employer plan sponsors similarly maintain only relevant health information on their employees. Numerous third-party players within the healthcare continuum also keep patient files of one sort or another.

As illustrated in the audit guidelines and market discussion throughout this book, healthcare has significant issues to address outside of access to information and the delivery of healthcare services. First, we must recognize that medical errors do occur. According to the Agency for Healthcare Research and Quality, the price tag for medical errors is about $37.6 billion or about $4.3 million per hour.[4] Financial errors also occur. Much of public research on financial errors is limited to those generated by providers. Little research, however, has been done regarding financial errors caused by other market players, for example, payer processing claims, pharmacy benefit manager rebate mishandling, and other issues recognizable under employer benefit plan expense reviews. With respect to providers, CMS has released reports noting that $36 billion of $390 billion paid in claims in 2017 were paid in error.[5] That is $4.1 million per hour 7 days per week for Medicare alone. This does not include error rates for the private sector. In addition to the identification of payment errors, the United States Department of Health and Human Services, Office of Inspector General negotiated a return of $2.4 billion in healthcare fraud judgments. Healthcare fraud schemes' annual price range according to the National Healthcare Anti-Fraud Association estimates 3%[6] of healthcare's $3 trillion-dollar market contains fraudulent claims. That is $90 billion dollars per year or $10 million per hour.

Note: Health Insurance Portability and Accountability Act of 1996 (HIPAA) is not clear on protecting self-insured or uninsured individuals from healthcare fraud. HIPAA statute Section 18 U.S.C., Ch. 63, sec. 1347[7] defines fraud this way:

1. Whoever knowingly and willfully executes, or attempts to execute, a scheme or artifice
   a. To defraud any Healthcare benefit program
   or
   b. To obtain, by means of false or fraudulent pretenses, representations, or promises, any of the money or property owned by, or under the custody or control of, any healthcare benefit program.

In other words, HIPAA protects against defrauding a benefit plan, not individuals in the benefit plan or individuals who are not in a benefit plan.

How to fix: Change the law UNDER 1 (a) to READ as follows:

1. To defraud any healthcare benefit program OR INDIVIDUAL OF ANY HEALTHCARE PLAN, SELF INSURED INDIVIDUAL, OR UNINSURED INDIVIDUAL.

Portfolia provides a retrospective, concurrent, and prospective tool for analytics and patient self-advocacy. MBA's[8] PHR originated out of MBA's pro bono services to individual consumers stuck in the healthcare system. Long before any market discussion of a PHR or active cyber-health initiatives, MBA used its audit tools to help individual patients organize and utilize health information for a purpose defined by the patient. Information was organized to mitigate a current issue and prevent future errors. MBA's Portfolia has developed into a comprehensive, action-driven, private, portable, personal diary and blueprint of health and related financial information. The following are key Portfolia system functions:

- Collect a patient's complete medical records and health, insurance, and financially related information—all the materials involved in a patient's healthcare experience—in one central, easily accessible, secure resource.
- Enable patients to determine access levels of their data to share health information with providers to enhance the quality and consistency of care.
- Prepare customizable reports explaining the *who, what, when, where, why,* and *how* of a healthcare episode at any given time.
- Include manual and electronic management and analysis of clinical and health financial information.
- Alert patients to any anomalies with respect to healthcare and financial episodes.

In 20 years of advocating for individual consumers, MBA has found that, even with the advent of well-crafted patient tools, patients need some type of ongoing resource support. Because of healthcare's continuous dynamic changes, it can be difficult for patients to stay current with market issues. Furthermore, once a patient becomes afflicted with extensive health issues, the volume and magnitude of information can be overwhelming. The way the healthcare marketplace is structured, it is prohibitively difficult for some patients to obtain, understand, and use the meaningful information needed to make sound healthcare choices. Therefore, there is an active need in the healthcare market for a role that fills this void. Some refer to such a position as an infomediary specialist.[9]

Health Infomediary Support

As cyber-health evolves, the health infomediary specialist will play an important role as a dedicated, clear-thinking advocate for the patient. These individuals should be trained and certified to provide support to patients who have difficulty obtaining, understanding, and using meaningful information in such a way that facilitates sound healthcare choices. Health infomediary specialists might help patients identify the necessary information to:

■ Interpret medical and related financial documents.
■ Prepare insurance appeals and fight denials.
■ Choose between care alternatives.
■ Interact with providers, insurance companies, and benefit plan managers.
■ Protect patient interests under the Patient Bill of Rights.

A common and openly discussed concern among patients is how to handle claims denied by the insurance company. Providers do not effectively track patient employer types and many patients and providers waste time appealing claims incorrectly. For example, a patient covered by a self-insured employer is subject to the Employee Retirement Income Security Act,[10] while a patient who is employed by an employer buying health insurance is subject to the state department of insurance. An effective infomediary specialist would need a thorough understanding of the dynamics of each market player from operational, functional, reimbursement, and clinical perspectives.

PHR Attributes

The market will continue to evolve content, privacy, functionality, and security standards for PHRs. PHR usability, however, is also important. PHRs that act solely as data repositories miss fundamental usability opportunities. The standards discussed in this chapter complement basic marketplace initiatives and are driven from an audit perspective and understanding of the healthcare continuum. Prevention and mitigation should be functional components of every PHR. PHRs should also contain a comprehensive patient medical history which would allow providers to offer treatment suggestions with access to the whole story. A comprehensive patient medical history includes personal health information, personal healthcare financial management information, and personal documents and research information. Most current data repository systems are not structured to achieve this goal.

PHRs should also demonstrate tangible proof of patient health status and prior health services and allow providers the opportunity to obtain information that patients may not think relevant. A common misconception is that patients have the skill set to obtain and document all relevant information. Patient advocates often observe firsthand the patient frustration and confusion with their advocacy patients. For instance, "Dina," the 56-year-old cancer survivor referred to throughout this book, revealed to her patient advocate that at least three other family members had also experienced inter-operative awakening in the past. In all of her family discussions, it never occurred to her that this would be relevant to her situation.

Exhibit 10.2 illustrates the original intent of the Portfolia program and a simple infomediary specialist checklist for patient advocacy:

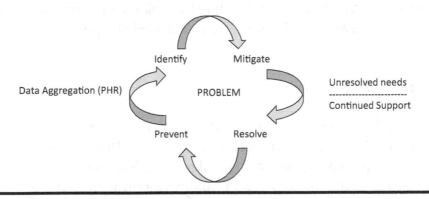

Exhibit 10.2   Original PHR mission.

The process of data aggregation collects all patient health information into one secure place, creating a data repository. Exhibit 10.2 illustrates how to structure the preparation of a patient to address and handle ongoing issues. Patient access to health information requires managing consumption on a timely basis.

Having an option for provider access and transfer of patient health information is another important attribute for an effective PHR. This function breaches new technological territories, but will ultimately facilitate interoperability. Nevertheless, patients with information in hand who actually point things out to their providers such as: "Wait—my last doctor already did that test on me!" are valuable commodities.

In time, PHRs should include the following attributes:

■ Collect a patient's complete medical records and health, insurance, and financially related information—all the materials involved in a patient's healthcare experience—in one central, easily accessible, secure resource.
■ Enable patients to allow restricted access to share health information with providers to enhance the quality and consistency of care.
■ Explain the *who, what, when, where, why,* and *how* of a healthcare episode at any given time.
■ Include manual and electronic management and analysis of clinical and health financial information.
■ Alert parties of any anomaly with respect to healthcare and financial episodes.
■ Demonstrate tangible proof of patient health status and prior health services and allow providers the opportunity to obtain information that patients may not think relevant.
■ Allow providers access to secure patient healthcare information to support patient visits.
■ Facilitate home accommodations and other decisions like exercise regimen and eating habits.

- Facilitate measurable metrics such as blood pressure reading, sugar levels, medication compliance.
- General behavioral health metrics especially for those undergoing psychiatric or general behavioral healthcare support.

Major Market Activity

Several major players have taken the initiative to develop PHRs. Employer groups are driven by the ever-increasing cost of providing benefits and are actively seeking online solutions through various avenues. Insurance companies are also exploring their own answers, but tend to offer limited solutions. Providers are developing programs that tend to be limited by their internal infrastructure and their own scope of service offerings. They seem to address only financial and technical constraints in their electronic health record systems. A number of cottage-industry market players are also launching various forms of data repository tools. These PHR offerings do not include interactive tools that make the PHR a usable and productive self-empowerment tool. Exhibit 10.3 highlights the status of the marketplace.[11]

Cyber Implication Overview

Health infomediary specialists should appreciate the development of electronic health record business solutions throughout the healthcare continuum and how many market players are attempting to offer various forms of patient PHR tools. For the time being, many electronic health record offerings should be classified as "hybrid solutions," in the sense that some part will be electronic and some will be paper. As a result, patients will continue to struggle to aggregate data. That aside, in an

PHR Capability Analysis	Data Repository	Health Research	Clinical Case Management	Financial Case Management	Error and Fraud Detection Training	Market Expertise	Patient Centric	Certified Advocate Specialist Support
Ideal PHR	x	x	x	x	x	x	x	x
Government	TBD	TBD	TBD			Developing		
Employers	TBD	TBD	TBD					
Insurance Companies	X	Limited	Limited	Limited		Developing		
Providers	X	x	X			Developing		
E-Health Information resources	X	X	X	X		Developing	x	
Cottage industry	x		x			Developing	X	

Exhibit 10.3   PHR market activity.

environment without content standards, the key operative audit issue remains the interoperability of any of these independent system offerings.

Endnotes

1 http://www.cms.hhs.gov/PerHealthRecords/ accessed August 15, 2018.

2 Ibid.

3 Medical Business Associates. (MBA) 580 Oakmont Lane Westmont IL 60559 www.mbaaudit.com accessed August 15, 2018. White paper case study electronic PHR.

4 http://www.ahrq.gov/qual/errback.htm accessed August 15, 2018.

5 https://www.racmonitor.com/cms-paid-390-billion-in-claims-36-billion-paid-in-error-2017-cert-report accessed August 16, 2018

6 https://www.bcbsm.com/health-care-fraud/fraud-statistics.html accessed August 16, 2018.

7 https://www.law.cornell.edu/uscode/text/18/1347 accessed August 16, 2018.

8 MBA. Medical Business Associates. 2017 www.mbaaudit.com accessed August 20, 2018.

9 Jim A, Healthcare 2015 and U.S. Health Plans (New York: IBM Corporation, 2007), p. 24.

10 https://www.dol.gov/general/topic/retirement/erisa accessed August 20, 2018.

11 www.ahima.org has a list of PHR offerings.

Chapter 11

Summary of Key Points in the Book

> I've never found it hard to hack most people. If you listen to them, watch them, their vulnerabilities are like a neon sign screwed into their heads.

Elliot Anderson (Rami Malek) from Mr. Robot

Summary

The e-health market standards developed by Centers for Medicare and Medicaid Services and other independent organizations for healthcare stakeholders are progressing. The progression and use of technology beyond the minimum requirements does vary. Patients are encountering different technologies. To illustrate, the patient work flow of Ms. Smith, with health maintenance organization (HMO) coverage, is illustrative of the segmented flow that is still common patient experience.

Case Vignette

Ms. Smith enrolled into an HMO benefit plan whose provider system is within 5 minutes of her home. She selected a primary care provider (PCP) as required by the policy. Upon her initial attempt to schedule her wellness appointment visit with the PCP (Dr. P), the frustrated registration clerk, knowing the HMO status of Dr. P's practice, bantered with the patient. The registration clerk presented several reasons as to why Ms. Smith should select another PCP. The argument was that Dr. P had too many patients to accept another HMO patient. Further, their sister office had younger, more inexperienced doctors who needed to increase their patient volume. Eventually Ms. Smith received her appointment.

Ms. Smith arrived with her healthcare portfolio in hand, a written detailed health history, which the doctor copied. But, even with online research of wellness diagnostics that are recommended for females from the ages of 50 to 60, Ms. Smith could not get Dr. P to perform any of the wellness diagnostics Ms. Smith reviewed. The following pattern was illustrative with each inquiry.

> Ms. Smith: "I have never had a bone density exam, should I have one?"
> Dr. P: "That is only for women who are menopausal."
> Ms. Smith: "I am 54 and have been menopausal."
> Dr. P: "Well then," and she writes the script.

During the series of wellness diagnostics and subsequent referrals, Ms. Smith collected all the resulting reports and placed them in her personal health record. She brought her personal electronic health record (PHR) with her for every appointment with a new doctor. Each doctor asked to photocopy the test results from other providers. Further, the patient had access to this hospital's patient portal. What became obvious is that the doctors who were employees could access the patient portal, while doctors who were independent practitioners could not. Therefore, the patient can log in, receive reports, send an email with a question only to providers who were employed with the hospital. To further illustrate, within this scenario, Ms. Smith was referred to an allergist.

Ms. Smith had to fill out the similar hard copy paper work for consents. The patient/provider portal did not have the capability to send the referral electronically. The patient had to physically bring the paper referral. Further, the referred allergist is an independent provider so was not part of the hospital patient portal. The patient had to telephone the provider and/or go in person to address follow-up questions.

The above vignette demonstrates the desperate need for the development of a patient-centric cyber personal health record with the means for providers to transfer their data as accumulated directly to the patient. The standards of practice raised throughout this publication within a cyber-based platform will transform healthcare delivery and healthcare informatics. Key standards simplify networking, interoperability, system infrastructure, content, and security capabilities. For instance, providers must take into account related payer industry standards when developing any internal system changes. The following list highlights the resources that infomediary specialists should use as a base when developing a market standard reference list:

- Agency for Healthcare Research and Quality, www.ahrq. gov
- National Resource Center for Health Information Technology, healthit.ahrq.gov
- The Office of the National Coordinator for Health Information Technology, www.hhs.gov/healthit/
- "Recommended Requirement for Enhancing Data Quality in Electronic Health Records," www.hhs.gov/healthit/
- Health Level Seven, www.hl7.org
- American National Standards Institute, www.ansi.org
- Certification Commission for Healthcare Information Technology, www.cchit.org
- Department of Defense Records Management Program (DOD Directive 5015.2), www.defenselink.mil/webmasters/
- Association of Records Managers and Administrators, www.amra.org

E-health/cyber cloud-based initiatives are not limited to the United States. In today's healthcare community, we have international employers, employees, and travelers. Infomediary specialists should also appreciate evolving standards worldwide. How will we effectively manage a patient working 1 week in the United States and the next week in India? The PHR will become a significant tool in helping this type of patient.

Cyber-health continues to develop and transform at a swift pace. Infomediary specialists should expect today's environment to become obsolete within the next 10 years. The audit process in cyber-health requires management of current infrastructure while preparing for ongoing changes to the environment. Infomediary specialists therefore should also expect to invest heavily in research in preparation for auditing cyber-health system infrastructures and resources. The following is a recap of key concepts addressed in the previous chapters.

Chapter 1 Navigating Health Informatics within the Cyberspace

- **Objectives:**
  - Introduce and recognize the cyber patient and evolving needs.
  - Understand the evolution of a self-service economy in healthcare.
  - Review of informatics in healthcare.
  - Review concepts in patient engagement.
  - Provide overview of cyber-health management data activity.
- **Chapter Abstract:** Individuals need to maintain their healthy selves and selves in illness, and, to do that, they need information. This chapter introduces the cyber patient and recognizes their role as an informatics consumer. The informatics cyber-based consumer is adapting to a self-service economy in the management of their health informatics. To support this progression, this chapter reviews the current state of informatics. An understanding of patient engagement should be included in any technology strategy, followed by an understanding of how providers will utilize cyber analytic tools to manage health data. The cyber challenge is to innovate beyond our current capabilities and in a cyber environment where opportunities appear truly limitless, it can be done.
- **Cyber Implication:** The future of healthcare analytics is dynamic and rapidly changing. With rapid advancements in the field of healthcare analytics, we have more and more tools that have predictive and prescriptive functionalities based on advanced technologies such as artificial intelligence, machine learning, and deep learning. These technologies enable usage of data more effectively to establish a 360-degree view of the patient. This view can be utilized by providers to deliver the highest

quality care possible, as well as by patients to increase awareness of the current state of their health and wellness. As technology continues to advance, managing this information will become easier, increasing patient/provider engagement and perhaps increasing population health in general. How does the practitioner even begin to help patients manage their healthcare data within a cyber environment? It is important in the cyber environment to know and understand the categories of data to e-search within provider electronic eco-systems and to be prepared to transition into a patient-centric, interoperable, cloud-based platform.

Chapter 2 Transcending Case Management within a Cyber-Based Environment

■ **Objectives:**
  – Demonstrate how the emergence of health information and computer technology will profoundly change case management and the roles (and required skills) of case managers.
  – Provide an overview on the concepts of Virtual Case Management, Financial Case Management, and Clinical Case Management.
  – Explain how isolation of Financial Case Management from Clinical Case Management necessitates controlling potential conflicts-of-interest.
  – Provide an outline for clinical decision-making strategies independent of financial decisions.
  – Provide tools to assist patients within virtual case management programs.
  – Illustrate the role of informatics education and training.

■ **Chapter Abstract:** This chapter continues the discussion of the cyber patient navigating health informatics in the context of case management. A summary of case management is provided as it exists today focusing on differentiating the management of patient care from a financial versus clinical perspective. The financial issues and opportunities consumers with a personal healthcare portfolio face are presented. The chapter continues with an overview of virtual case management with patient, payer, hospital, physician, allied health services, and non-traditional health service models. The cyber implication is presented within each case. The role of the medical auditor involved in supporting internal audit functions is demonstrated in the case study. Further, the infomediary specialist (IS) should have training and a level of understanding on access limitations associated with any provider technology. Overall, securing our future within a cyber-based environment is dependent on the integration of professional and consumer training and education at all levels.

■ **Cyber Implication:** Clinical decisions should be made independently of financial decisions. Healthcare professionals should provide reasonable assurance that current procedures do not allow financially driven conflicts-of-interest to affect clinical decisions. Separating Financial Case Management from Clinical Case Management in the Virtual Case Management model will set the stage for developing conflict-of-interest controls throughout the healthcare continuum. Further, tools to assist patients in a virtual environment is the next wave of informatics. This chapter has outlined those roles within various types of virtual case management programs. The next chapter will introduce the role of the cyber nurse case manager, review current case management practices, the process of case management, and the subject matter expertise relevant to perform the function. The next chapter will also include virtual world implications of case management.

Chapter 3 The Cyber-Nurse Case Manager

- ■ **Objectives:**
  - Define the role of the cyber nurse case manager.
  - Review what case management is and provide an overview of current practice standards.
  - Share considerations for virtual case management.
  - Summarize the qualifications needed for a virtual case manager.
- ■ **Chapter Abstract:** The chapter introduces the role of cyber nurse case manager, reviews current case management practices, the process of case management, and the subject matter expertise relevant to perform the function. The chapter also includes a virtual world case illustration. Finally, ideal qualities that define a passionate qualified case manager. The essence of the patient experience is at the heart of understanding what is optimal in managing a healthy self and self in illness. The progression of electronic tools in provider settings has not been quick, efficient, or easily accessible. In the absence of organized, accessible informatics, patients and healthcare professionals often jump to a browser to quickly search for information. Provider tools have not even come close to the breadth and depth of online browser search engine capability. Without standards on content in the cyberworld, discerning credible information will be the ultimate consumer challenge. During this transition stage, the case management function is in the prime role to be an IS to help patients navigate what is or is not real. The demand for online tools has accelerated the pace of provider production of cloud-based technologies.
- ■ **Cyber Implication:** The practice standards established within traditional settings established the foundation for practice standards within a virtual setting. The cyber nurse role in a virtual environment can support the information overload and foreign territory that patients will continue to experience. The push for cloud-based

technology has saturated healthcare, setting the stage for the cyber nurse to also become proficient as an IS. The cyber nurse case manager is the ideal role to facilitate the coordination and continuity of care for patients in an environment where health functions, information, and support continue to move into the cloud. The cyber nurse in addition to the patient will increasingly be exposed to new technologies. At every stage, the opportunity for becoming a data driven consumer will increase. Specifically, the data driven patient will increase the use of analytics in managing their healthy self and their self in illness. The cyber nurse, as a case manager, will continue to support the patient with the use of analytics.

Chapter 4 Cyber Data Strategy, Analytics, and Informatics

■ **Objectives:**
  - Provide an overview on the role of an IS.
  - Introduce a general framework for understanding data strategy, analytics, and informatics.
  - Describe the current and future state of managing data.
  - Predict the emerging roles needed to facilitate the management of data.
  - Assess the risks and vulnerabilities.
■ **Chapter Abstract:** Materials in this book progress from the discipline of case management, to the roles of the case manager, and now for the needs of the IS working within case management to support the analytics required to effectively manage health. The change in the management of data can be found in the emerging roles within the C-suite. An overview of key cloud-based system risks are included, specifically the exposure of the various forms of identity theft. Within the running theme of the emerging needs of the cyber patient, a data management capability assessment model is presented and applied

from a patient perspective. If the expectation is for the cyber patient to become technically savvy, it is important for the Infomediary Specialist to have the ability to assess a patient's current skills. An additional behavioral assessment framework is also presented—a healthcare continuum model that the IS may use when implementing a data and information strategy.

■ **Cyber Implication:** This chapter provided an overview of the principles of data strategy, analytics, and informatics/cyber environment considerations. Further, the information must be accurate, informative, productive, measurable, and support the strategic objectives set by the IS on behalf of the receiving party. Furthermore, ensure the analytics performed are scientifically based and the authenticity of data is validated and protected. Key internal control management questions, which must be answered, are considered.

Data/information roles and managing the risk of misuse of identities are covered. The hybrid of identities by types is provided to more effectively evaluate the sources of data and the integrity of those data. The principles of data readiness are included as part of assessing the patient's ability to effectively manage their own healthcare data. A detailed assessment model is specified to evaluate patient data readiness. Finally, an effective IS deliverable is enhanced with the intricate use of a data strategy, analytics, and informatics. Once a data strategy is developed and implemented, assurance of the execution of the strategy should be tested.

Chapter 5 Data in the Cyber Environment

■ **Objectives:**
- Understand the opportunities of healthcare data audit.
- Explain the roles of an auditor/IS in creating and managing a data library.

- Explore stakeholder cyber-based business processes and internal control requirements.
- Develop a framework and checklist for data specialists' data assessment strategy.
- Introduce internal control concepts regarding processed data.

■ **Chapter Abstract:** The continued progression of materials in the book began with perspective of the cyber patient navigating a cloud-based interoperable health mall. Discussions included case management broken down from traditional brick and mortar, to case management within a virtual environment. Within the domain of case management, a breakdown by discipline. The need for a data strategy and a tool to assess data strategy, its implementation, and ongoing use require an internal audit discussion on assurance that the data strategy is operating as established. This chapter provides the internal audit perspective on providing assurance of the implemented operation of the data strategy. This begins with an overview of asking the right audit question. The key principles discussed include activities associated with a data library, data flow, and data intelligence. The chapter illustrates audit checklists which help in managing the review. Further is a discussion in managing new data and ongoing additions of new data. Once this is achieved, considerations for processed data, processed data audit checklists, and categories on how to classify data are included.

■ **Cyber Implication:** To an auditor or an IS, data in cyber-health along with its use in defined algorithms amounts to internal control of information in a virtual environment. The algorithms define what we are doing with the data. Integrating internal control into the data testing process allows for reasonable assurance of data integrity in the financial, operational, and service sectors of healthcare environments. This chapter's explanation of data behaviors and elements should provide auditors with the necessary checklist to review the global cyber, electronic eco-system infrastructure of any player within any healthcare stakeholder environment.

Chapter 6 Algorithms

- ■ **Objectives:**
  - – Provide a clear understanding about algorithms and how they are used to resolve business problems.
  - – Explore the various data elements that can be identified and utilized by these algorithms.
  - – Illustrate with a practical case how algorithms can be implemented in a cyber-health environment.
  - – Explain how algorithms can drive cyber-health infrastructures to answer the who, what, where, why, and how of a healthcare episode at any given time.
  - – Explain briefly the most common algorithms used in the industry for providing solutions.
- ■ **Chapter Abstract:** This chapter is focused on "the ask" that is converted to an appropriate algorithm based on validated, simple assumptions. Simplifying the ask will increase the likelihood of achieving a response from the analytics that will be useful, measurable, and responsive to a patient's specific need for information. Such a data-driven system will require its own checkups in the form of routine internal audits to provide assurance of its optimal performance. As such, this chapter will discuss the attributes needed to write the right algorithm in response to the right queries on behalf of the user. This chapter will also review the definition and components of the algorithm, including data elements and their behaviors. A hospital case study will demonstrate the use of algorithms in understanding

denial of claims. Applications of the case study include the use of algorithms and the use of a previously discussed behavioral analytics tool. Finally, the case study will illustrate the selection of algorithms used and the general categories of the types of algorithms by type and their purpose.

■ **Cyber Implication:** Which specific algorithm auditors use to solve a problem will depend on the information available to them and will often change in scope or procedure when new data are generated. Algorithms can drive cyber-health infrastructures to answer the who, what, where, why, and how of a healthcare episode at any given time. As a recap (and an auditor's checklist), thus far we have explored the market background of cyber-health initiatives, cyber-health industry applications between and among public and private users, market standards and compliance requirements, clinical and financial case management, data element activity, and algorithms.

Chapter 7 Cyber Data-Driven Health Decisions

■ **Objectives:**
   – Provide an overview of the elements of data driven decision-making models.
   – Review the data-driven decision-making models within the context of primary healthcare continuum, secondary healthcare continuum, and information continuum.
   – Explain the health decision model to capture relevant data incrementally that will help impact outcomes— from patient, payer, and provider perspectives.
   – Explain the implications of data structure, application, and technology associated with the data and their output.

- Illustrate these principles through case studies that
clearly explain medical identity theft and provide
insights into an effective data driven process for health
decisions.

▪ **Chapter Abstract:** The vision behind this book reflects
the following: The cyber data driven patient, alongside
a well-trained cyber infomediary/nurse case manager,
armed with productive data analytics driven by appropriately prepared algorithms and the right technology, has
everything he or she needs to navigate the cyber-health
world. This chapter further explores the data driven
process with an overview of data driven decision-making
models.

Knowledge models are reviewed within the previously
discussed healthcare continuums—primary, secondary,
and information. The health decision model is detailed
within a set of incremental steps of data and process
accumulation which capture relevant data and impact
outcomes. Illustrations of this model are presented from a
provider, payer, and plan sponsor perspective. An illustration of the knowledge model is also presented from a
white-collar and organized crime perspective. The illicit
examples include a deeper discussion and application
on medical identity theft and a review of the individually identifiable health information data components. The
case study illustrated a multi-layered damage impact from
all identified stakeholders. A second illicit case study will
illustrate the application of the data driven analytics on a
pharmaceutical case.

▪ **Cyber Implication:** The key points for the cyber IS to
understand the implication of data structure, application,
and technology associated with the data and their output.
e-health exists today, but is evolving rapidly. The concepts
presented therefore should be used to identify the structure, application, and technology of the e-system being
reviewed through the knowledge model network diagram

process. The algorithms in Chapter 6 provide the opportunity for data mining, data driven decisions, and the development of artificial intelligence through rule-based systems. The market has numerous niche data driven e-health decision offerings. Many of them exist in the form of disease management models to fraud detection systems. The chapter also provides perspectives of e-health and e-data driven model developments outside of the United States.

Chapter 8 Business Processes and Data Implications

- **Objectives:**
  - Explore the market player business processes and the impact of cyber-health.
  - Explain how the role of the internal audit and cyber-health IS expands as market participants migrate toward true interoperability.
  - Highlight the business processes in which data driven decisions occur.
  - Provide an overview of the market factors and cyber-health infrastructures that impact healthcare.
- **Chapter Abstract:** This chapter explores market player business processes and the impact of cyber-health. This chapter highlights the business processes in which data driven decisions occur. The chapter walks through several case studies to illustrate post electronic implementations, the steps involved, and the adverse risks that can occur with improper planning and the failure of a technology purchased.
- **Cyber Implication:** The evolution toward interoperable communities of patients, providers, payers, plan sponsors, and other market participants will take significant investment in information technology capabilities. Entities that have not demonstrated capability with current levels of technology must do so in order for cyber activities to be built upon a strong foundation.

Chapter 9: Evolving from e-Health Systems

- ■ **Objectives:**
  - Understand the capabilities of e-health vendor offerings.
  - Explain the evolution and transition of different e-health to cyber-health offerings.
  - Explain the roles of an auditor in assessing the various e-health and cyber-health vendor offerings.
  - Identify the potential pitfalls of implementing/ upgrading e-health software.
  - Suggest considerations for moving technology to a cyber-based platform.
- ■ **Chapter Abstract:** The race is on to move all paper platforms into an electronic, cloud-based infrastructure. The groundwork for making this move is presented by reviewing key data elements that are in active use. All provider offerings specify the data elements needed for their promised functionality. Those data offer analysis beyond the software's basic functionality. The standardization of widely used data elements is necessary for cyber-health interoperability. Examples of those standards are reviewed, and their movement into cloud-based platforms is discussed.

  Implementation of major information systems is never easy, and cyber-health systems are no exception. This chapter conducts an extensive case study post mortem demonstrating the mistakes that can occur with the aim of offering lessons learned for future implementations.
- ■ **Cyber Implication:** Buyers beware! Electronic health record offerings in the marketplace are numerous and sophistication varies significantly among vendors. The implications of errors that occurred within this implementation were serious and significant in just one eco-system. Imagine the complexity of executing a similar task within a cloud-based system, where auditors, infomediary specialists, and other healthcare stakeholders interact with

each other. Within one entity, the transfer and modification of an e-health environment can be costly and compromise an organization significantly if careful planning and testing does not occur. The transition of that e-health data into cloud-based platforms such as a patient's personal health record have even a great exposure to adverse complications. The internal auditor's role is to ensure reliability of the offering, benchmark against market standards, and continue ongoing testing of internal controls to preserve defined functionality. The e-health systems in this chapter are discussed from the perspective of the business using the software.

Chapter 10 The Data-Driven Cyber Patient

- **Objectives:**
  - Provide an historical overview of personal health record system.
  - Provide an overview application of a patient-centric personal health record system.
  - Present a case study of the application of a healthcare portfolio.
  - Present the role of health IS to support PHR efforts.
  - Provide an overview of PHR attributes and current state of the marketplace for PHR systems.
- **Chapter Abstract:** Leading up to this chapter, the cyber patient is presented as an individual who needs to maintain his or her health self and self in illness. The cyber patient and the professionals supporting the patient cannot do so without information. In the cognitive era, the patient, along with the provider, is on information overload and technological transition. Thus the need for understanding the science driving professional and consumer-based informatics. The cyber nurse case manager with expertise as an IS is the ideal person to support the cyber patient and will need to understand the current

state of managing data, information, and analytics. The IS will benefit from a data strategy and a tool to assess data strategy. Its implementation and ongoing support from internal audit function to ensure the integrity of informatics utilized. The use of data analytics is effective when they have measurable simple algorithms to support analytics and data driven decisions.

This chapter focuses on personal healthcare record data sets. As all professional healthcare stakeholders continue to evolve in their use of technology, a parallel movement is occurring with individuals. A series of offerings are developing independent of professional stakeholders that are patient driven. It is anticipated that these offerings will be deployed at a faster rate than what is occurring with large institutional providers and payers. This chapter illustrates the framework of one patient-centric approach to a personal health record system.

■ **Cyber Implication:** Health infomediary specialists should appreciate the development of electronic health record business solutions throughout the healthcare continuum and how many market players are attempting to offer various forms of patient PHR tools. For the time being, many electronic health record offerings should be classified as electronic/paper hybrid solutions. As a result, patients will continue to struggle to aggregate data. That aside, in an environment without content standards, the key operative audit issue remains the interoperability of any of these independent system offerings.

Consumer Survey

The Wall Street Journal released a survey finding of consumer responses to the benefits of electronic health records. They included 2,153 United States adults in their 2007 study, which noted some of the following statistics:

- 75 percent of respondents believe that patients would receive better care if doctors and researchers were able to share information more easily via electronic transactions.
- 63 percent believed medical errors would be reduced.
- 55 percent believed it would reduce healthcare costs.
- 25 percent use some type of electronic medical record.

Congress allocated $37 billion dollars in 2009 to help providers upgrade from paper files. The reality is that efficiencies have not materialized. As the patient vignette on Ms. Smith demonstrates, the disjointed process has become more cumbersome.

It is inferred from this study that if healthcare providers, researchers, and the end user (patient/family members) had access to the patient's aggregated health, market informatics errors and efficiencies should have improved significantly. However, this has not been confirmed. Please note the following responses from a health survey.

The respondents included a range of professionals and stay-home parents. The free-form narrative responses provided the greatest insight. The process generated some very interesting comments. One response from a healthcare professional read as follows "URGENT—Now that I answered your survey, tell me if the average Joe, not working in healthcare, knows what you are talking about!" The response is a gentle reminder to industry professionals to not forget the most important stakeholder—the patient.

Among attorneys who represent clients in worker's compensation and personal injury cases, one attorney's first response to the idea of cyber-health reflected his experience with his clients: "I cannot tell you the number of times in which I have clients shocked at what is contained within their medical records. The reality of what is written and documented within their records comes to them as a shock. In particular, when sensitive, very personal, emotionally intimate items are discussed. The first question they ask is if they can block that information." In fact, the survey revealed that not one person owned a complete copy of their medical records to review. Another interesting commentary about the legal system is the notion that once patients become involved in litigation, their rights to privacy are "waived" or lost. The concept that an individual who needs to utilize the civil or criminal process to self-advocate must relinquish his or her privilege to privacy should put a privacy activist on alert.

The following survey questions are followed by particular responses that well represent the range of responses or raise one or more significant insights not addressed in other responses:

1. Do you know what a personal electronic health record is?
   - A record of a person's history of health kept on a computer. It can track if something changes dramatically so that you can become more aware of a problem quicker.
   - I don't know for sure. I'm assuming it's a disk/ electronic device or something that would hold all your health information.
   - An online format of your health records that has everything available for a doctor to view in case of emergency.
   - I have no idea.
   - Electronic health records are stored on the computer and can be shared with other health professionals and insurance companies if need be. They are a more efficient way to store records, but the concern as always is patient privacy.
   - It is a repository in electronic form of all relevant health information related to an individual, including diagnoses, allergies, medications, surgeries, physician notes, radiology and lab results, and other relevant medical information.

- A record of a person's medical history kept on a computer file. It would be kept up to date and available to a healthcare provider if the patient consents.
- The "flip" answer would be that it computerizes healthcare records, speeding the ability to document badly and spread the errors more broadly, rapidly, and efficiently for the benefit of all parties except the patient.
- It enables ambulatory care physicians and clinical staff to document patient encounters, streamline clinical workflow, and securely exchange clinical data with other providers, patients, and information systems.
- An electronic health record allows people to keep track of their own records.
- The Veterans Administration (VA) hospitals are on top of that. A computerized record that enables each specialist to cross check treatment and medications in a patient.
- One-stop shopping for my medical history.
- It is an electronic record of my healthcare activity provided by the doctor, laboratory, etc., to be used instead of just a paper chart.

2. Whom would you want to host your personal health record and why? (Sample options of insurance company, hospital, professional, and Third-party were provided.)
   - I would prefer to have my personal physician host it and allow it to change with personal care physicians because the track record is personal. If something changes, I would rather know from a doctor, not an insurance company.
   - Certainly not my insurance company or a hospital. Seeing that many people have different doctors, I would believe a Third-party/professional or myself. I don't trust insurance companies at all. People see different doctors and go to different hospitals for different

things, so it wouldn't make sense for them to manage the information. The best host, I would guess, is me.

■ Insurance company.

■ Never the insurance company, because they may use the information to weed out unhealthy patients. I would want the records held by my doctor or the hospital as they are using the information to help care for me.

■ I would prefer that my electronic personal health record be hosted by my hospital. I know that the hospital has to comply with Health Insurance Portability and Accountability Act of 1996 (HIPAA) and the Office of Inspector General (OIG) is looking at intrusion. In addition, most hospitals have disaster recovery plans and backup plans in emergency situations. I would be more comfortable knowing that my hospital has controls in place than a Third-party that is more susceptible to intrusion from the outside.

■ A Third-party that could communicate with hospitals, doctors, insurance companies.

■ Would prefer the doctor to host it due to privacy issues.

■ Third-party—so that I can truly administer.

■ I believe physicians should have a database where they could enter information easily with each visit, the same way they write in your chart or record when you visit them. Also, with each inpatient or outpatient hospital visit, the hospital could also forward your medical records to that common database. I can see potential for error in any system that would organize medical records.

■ I prefer to host it myself. All others have incentives to use it for their purposes, which may not align with my best interests.

■ Doctor only, with restrictions on whom he or she can share information with and only with my oral or written permission to do so.

- Third-party and available to those who need it.
- Providers and payers for systematic data management and exchanges.
- If my insurance company hosted the info, then it would be the most accessible. If you happened to be a party to an incident anywhere in the world, you would most likely have your insurance card on hand and the health provider can look up the info on a database.
- I am not sure, but I imagine it's just a matter of time before they all have access to it, especially if someone can make a buck doing it.

3. Do you keep track of your information now?

- I go to the doctor once a year for a checkup and that's all the tracking I do. If I need to watch cholesterol, I exercise more. I am fairly healthy!
- Yes. I have it all filed and recorded.
- Not really.
- I keep all the billing information.
- I have kept some important x-ray reports or lab work in a file at home.
- I keep track of my health information that is provided to me manually in a file.
- No—I rely on my hospital and doctor.
- Yes—paper file.
- Not really; I have some lab reports, etc., from the past. I do not have a personal medical record.
- Kind of. I have hardcopy files for each family member. Within each file are folders for each illness they had along with the bills for that illness and one general folder for miscellaneous doctor visits. An example: My son had a broken leg and a shoulder injury 2 years ago. So in his file for 2 years ago, he would have a folder for "shoulder injury," one for "leg injury," and one for miscellaneous doctor visits (like sinus infections or minor medical problems). I also keep a folder in each of our files for eye care

and dental visits. Though the explanation of benefits
(EOBs) mostly make up what is in the folders, I also
add medical information that pertains to that particular illness.

■ No (thankfully, still simple enough healthcare issues).

■ Yes, as a diabetic I monitor my sugar regularly.

■ I just keep the RX records on my computer.

■ I keep track in my head.

4. How confident are you that when you go to see a doctor/
healthcare professional, he or she always has an accurate
and complete picture of your prior medical history?

■ I am not confident. My doctor of over 20 years needed
to move to Wisconsin because of malpractice insurance. I trusted her. Now I belong to a family community group in which the doctors change every 2 or
3 years after they graduate and move on. I know my
previous medical history and thank God that I am
healthy and not that concerned!

■ I'm pretty confident that they have a clear picture
because I tell them exactly what I have. But I don't
believe every doctor/healthcare professional/hospital
always listens.

■ Not confident—recently went to the doctor, who
couldn't remember all of my dates, immunizations,
etc., especially for my children.

■ Not at all. That is why I try to present a summary of
my case or that of my loved ones in addition to important previous test results and lab data.

■ I only see one doctor, so I am confident the information is complete and accurate.

■ Have gone to the same doctor for 14 years, so I feel like
he personally knows me, but he could still forget some
things unless he really digs deep or I remind him.

■ Fairly confident if in network—not confident at all if
out.

■ I am not. I try to stay with the same doctors and/or I try to be as accurate as possible with my medical history. However, mine is not that extensive so it is not so difficult.

■ I have had the same medical doctor (MD) for 25 years, so she knows our family pretty well, but perhaps a quick access to a database would be beneficial for the primary MD along with any consulting MDs a patient may need.

■ Every year when I have my annual physical, I get a set of forms from my PCP, one of which is a Review of Systems. Every year I include some new finding in the Review of Systems, and I vary it from year to year. To date my PCP has never asked me a single question about the Review of Systems findings, suggesting he's never read it.

■ Not much confidence. I always have my own entire history. My experience is, don't assume your doctor knows you that well.

■ I am confident that my PCP has a reasonably accurate picture of the important aspects of my personal medical history. However, when assisting in the care of my aged parents (before they died), my brother and I learned we could not be confident that physicians had an accurate picture of important aspects. When they were hospitalized, my brother and I took turns making certain one or the other of us were there in order to make certain that mistakes (sometimes life-threatening mistakes) were not made in their care. We learned from experience that doctors tended to treat the simple basic picture and had difficulty incorporating important variant information and it was nearly impossible to correct erroneous information mistakenly documented. (Example: Somewhere along the line, my mother's PCP entered into her record that she had had a heart attack. He never removed that from his record despite my mother, myself, and her cardiologist all providing documentation demonstrating that the information was wrong.)

■ To the degree I am alert, I can tell them. If I arrived unconscious, then it could be a different story. They need to be updated on major stuff.

■ I assume they know nothing because that's what I am used to. But lately, they can relay to me exact dates I was last in with the same symptoms, and that's kind of cool, as far as seeing trends.

5. Do you think an electronic PHR can reduce the number of redundant or unnecessary procedures and improve healthcare quality?

■ Absolutely.

■ No.

■ Possibly, because other professionals could see when the individual last had a test done.

■ Don't know—wouldn't think people didn't know what they've had before and could control that.

■ Yes, I could see how they would streamline all different doctors' info and past procedures together.

■ Perhaps, if it was set up in an organized way where the healthcare providers could quickly get the information they were looking for.

■ Possibly, provided that docs use the medical record and really look at all notations made by all docs, RNs, etc.

■ Have not seen the real outcome yet. Theoretically, it should.

■ In theory—assuming accuracy and accessibility it should help. Records are only as good as the record keeper. The concept is a good one. Just like computers can keep track of your taxes, your music, your e-mails, your stock trades—why not all your medical records? I would be interested in software to store this for myself in my house on my computer.

■ Definitely, as long as those results from those procedures are entered into the database in a timely and

accurate manner. That would mean that it would be
necessary to have a system in place to automatically
enter that info into the files for folks who are involved
in an electronic health record program. It would
improve the quality and the continuity of care for
those involved.

6. Do you think an electronic PHR can significantly decrease
the frequency of medical errors and reduce healthcare
costs?

- Yes to the first, because reading the electronic record
  is easier than some handwriting. No to the second,
  because e-PHR is not cheap.
- Errors will occur because humans are running the
  tests. Incorrectly inputted information can mislead the
  patient. I think it may decrease, but I think it will raise
  healthcare costs because of the cost to implement the
  system.
- Yes.
- No.
- Not necessarily, unless the medications or tests are
  being reviewed by a Third-party.
- Probably.
- Yes, it seems that they would. Also, I think it would
  really help those patients who face numerous procedures and illness or who can't speak the language,
  and/or cannot take care of themselves.
- I am not sure. It may help with medical errors and
  healthcare costs, but I personally do not believe having PHRs would have a significant effect on costs. I
  think other factors influence healthcare costs more.
- It's one way, but not the only means, and I don't think
  it would significantly reduce errors.
- I don't know how many medical errors come from
  inaccurate medical records.
- As long as the e-PHRs are utilized adequately. (You
  know how the healthcare system is!) With any

providers going electronic, I would imagine this would make it easier for providers to comply with getting all the info into the profile in a timely manner.

7. Do you think patients should have direct access to their own medical record maintained by their physician?

■ Yes. I already know that the orthodontist allows you to view your personal information online.

■ I think everyone should have access to their own medical records.

■ Yes.

■ This may not be a good idea.

■ Yes and no—I would like to see my medical record. However, I do think that if doctors knew that patients would see what they wrote after each visit it would affect what they would write. It may be less objective.

■ I think patients should have read-only access to their medical records.

■ The system should not be for providers only. The patients should have equal access.

8. Do you think an electronic PHR will make it more difficult to ensure patient privacy? Why?

■ Anything online is subject to scams and to vulnerability of information being released without knowledge. I still do not trust the online security system. Therefore, I do not use it.

■ Depends on how the information is managed. If I care for my own records, I think that the information is kept mostly private, but I could lose them. That's not to say that some other Third-party couldn't lose them. Things are lost all the time. Problem is that when things are lost, sometimes they are found by others and what they do with that information is of concern. Also, I think people are finding more ways to break through electronic codes and that could put someone at risk for exposure. I also think it leaves your whole healthcare open to be viewed by whatever person you're seeing—who may not need to know certain information.

■ People try to hide stuff and it might be dangerous, like the types of medicines they may be taking and then getting a procedure, and people forget!

■ No.

■ Not really. I don't know how secure the paper copies are.

■ Yes, depending on how it is maintained. If it is maintained by a third-party vendor online, there can be intrusion and backup issues. If maintained by your hospital electronically, I feel it can be more secure.

■ No; someone would have to work pretty hard to get to the information.

■ No; this stuff is transmitted all over the Internet now.

■ Yes; I would just be afraid that someone could hack into a computer and find out another's personal info. With so much identity theft out there, this could potentially become another form.

■ Yes; whenever more people are entering information somewhere, privacy becomes an issue.

■ There is always the issue of judgment errors by those who maintain and release information.

■ No. Anyway, the benefits far exceed.

■ It could result in privacy concerns because more people will access them, even IT supporting staff for the system.

■ Probably, because over time the databases will be sold, acquired, and/or merged by larger groups, first local, then community, then regional, and then national.

9. What frustrations do you have with managing your health or that of a loved one? What would help alleviate these frustrations?

■ Frustration occurs only if you do not have a physician whom you can trust or rely on. If you have a good physician, you should not worry about your health.

I think people want to micromanage everything and that causes too much stress on the individual. If you have a physician or group of physicians that you trust, then I believe that you will be okay. My aunt recently did not trust any Illinois physicians and went to the Mayo clinic in Minnesota. She found comfort and was taken care of there. Her trust in the Mayo clinic was encompassing and she went back for the checkup there. Yes, it was expensive, but for peace of mind it was worth it. If the doctors don't know how to read the medical information provided, they still won't be able to help the patient. The doctors have to be knowledgeable and honest.

■ I have no real frustrations with the management. My frustration is that when I see a new physician, very seldom do they look at me as a person who understands my own healthcare. They also, all too frequently, will rerun a test that has been performed before. As if their test will yield something different, which in my case it never has. It would be helpful if the government would make it illegal for insurance/drug companies to give a doctor anything in exchange for "recommending" medicine or doing any other "favor."

■ Remembering dates and names of medicines.

■ Frustration is with the insurance companies, bad service, billing mistakes, etc.

■ There are not enough services for the elderly and there is not enough coverage for drug expenses. We need better home care.

■ No.

■ Communicating with physicians.

■ I am frustrated with my mother's healthcare professionals; they aren't thorough or that familiar with her past medical history.

■ Insurance companies—what's covered, what's not, etc.

■ At this time, I have no major frustrations—I have more issues with insurance companies. It would be nice, though, to be able to have my whole family's health records streamlined. It would have helped when I lived out of the country.

■ You know how a light goes on in your car when it is time for a tune-up? A reminder on a PHR would be helpful. Also, I think it would be helpful for patients to have an area where they could print up helpful forms, for example, a standard form for the medications they are on. That way they could keep it up to date, use it as a tool.

■ Other countries, like Israel, are very successful in centralizing the data with access for the patient and health providers.

■ Expensive. Can't get appointments.

■ Lack of access to the medical records. Lack of continuity of care. Repetition of all the same information (some people have very lengthy healthcare histories). When I worked in Ambulatory Care and I would begin asking all the health history questions, the patients would get very frustrated and ask "Don't you have all this information already?" I of course would have to answer "no" because unless they were with us previously, there is no continuity of care. The patients would have to repeat all of their info over again, including all of their drug info. I would have to make several phone calls trying to get recent EKG results, labs, etc. If I could go to one database that included all of their health information and their testing results, this would save so much time and frustration, both for the health provider and the patients. We wouldn't have to bother them as much as we do.

10. Would you pay an expert to manage or help manage your healthcare experience to ensure optimal healthcare service?

■ Not sure if I could manage it myself—maybe a software program would help.

■ No, we need to let doctors do their job and stop adding another layer of professional healthcare service.
■ Yes.
■ Yes, if I had complete confidence in them; they would have to convince me that my info could not be misused, and I would want to have access to it.
■ At the present time, I do not think I would pay someone to manage my family's healthcare information. I am capable of doing that for us. With the high costs of healthcare, I don't know if the consumer would want to spend one more dollar on healthcare. I also believe that the consumer believes it is the healthcare providers' obligation to provide some of these services.
■ No, but some seniors who are without family or without active involvement by their families could benefit from such a service.
■ It should be a part of the insurance program that you are on.
■ In this squeezed generation, taking care of old folks is crazy. I could see people paying someone to get that off their backs. Sift through the mess of all the specialists. Plus, if you have a sick person, just the emotional release of feeling they have someone on their side would probably work.
■ No. Too many conflicts of interest. Healthcare concierge—would be just like a hotel concierge—you get sent somewhere by who pays the most, who refers back the most, etc.
■ I think it would be an option for an individual to pay for this. As an individual (being an registered nurse [RN]), I would pay for this only if I was certain that the providers would use it. If I were not an RN, I might use it (pay for it) solely to get everything in order. I would think it more reasonable to have a provider, mainly an insurance company or a physician's office, pay for the service. Someone would have to get all of

the patient's data in the file after obtaining the info/ records, which seems to be the hard part these days. Since the physicians (and nobody else) receive reports on the patient's testing, they seem to be the most obvious folks to keep track of the e-file. I think this would be a nice service for either the insurance companies (they would have to receive all the testing results, though) or really the patient's physician's office to provide for their clients.

Cyber Implication Overview

As stated in the Introduction, the objective of this book is to recognize the current state of segmented use of e-health technologies within and among healthcare stakeholders, and how it will evolve to a full-blown cyber cloud-based environment. The concepts set forth within this publication are current active frameworks and in the future how we manage and look at healthcare delivery and the informatics that are derived will not look like anything we see today.

The survey presented in this chapter is intentionally structured as free-form narrative. The traditional yes/no response may facilitate statistical analysis, but the tone of the original statements provides for a different kind of understanding. As the market evolves and standards are developed, I hope we do not lose sight of the ultimate stakeholders. The ultimate goal behind the development of an interoperable, cost effective, transparent, and optimal healthcare environment is to provide market players with effective tools so that they can effectively and reliably service the ultimate customer— the patient. What does the cyber-based platform ultimately have to offer, the ability to go back to our roots in healthcare or our motto of doing no harm? The route to this path is to ensure that we do not lose our abilities as practitioners to lose our human bonds of healthy self and self in illness with our patients and ourselves as practitioners. As stated earlier, the essence of bonding which creates the optimal environment for effective communication between patient and provider needs to improve and formally be recognized. The key ingredient toward developing that bond necessitates active listening. This is why understanding how we interact with patients is critical toward an optimal interpersonal relationship between provider and patient. Thank you for reading!

Chapter 12

Reference Guide

Principles and rules are intended to provide a thinking man with a frame of reference.

Carl Von Clausewitz
Prussian general and military theorist who stressed the "moral" (meaning, in modern terms, psychological) and political aspects of war (1780–1831)

Introduction

This chapter provides a series of graphics and tables to illustrate key points within this book. They are intended to support academic instruction. The appendix also provides a listing of professional associations and credentials that would support the technical development of an infomediary specialist, in addition to staying current on emerging trends and ongoing continuing education.

Healthcare Infomediary Specialist

The healthcare continuum model serves as a framework for addressing the questions an infomediary specialist may face when implementing a data and information strategy. Infomediary specialists provide services including patient advocacy, data analysis (including market research), and case management while using his or her knowledge of clinical health sciences, health finances, the science of informatics, and the science of human capital.

A typical health infomediary specialist is often skilled in teaching, managing a patient health portfolio, cyber navigation, and electronic health. A skilled infomediary specialist starts with data that have been aggregated (in conformance with an organization's data strategy) and analyzes those data through, converting them into useable information (via the science of informatics). Research followed by critical review is a fundamental component of the work of an infomediary specialist. The infomediary specialist may be involved in assisting the individual patient (or case review of an individual's set of health records) in organizing personal healthcare records (Exhibit 12.1).

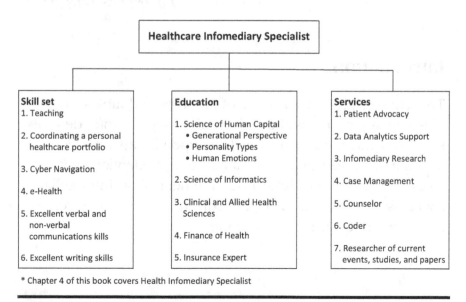

Exhibit 12.1 Healthcare infomediary.

Cyber Case Management

Financial case management enables accurate and complete reimbursement for patient services delivered while proactively monitoring the accounts receivable pipeline during the time of patient service to prevent or correct errors before discharge. Financial case management also ensures both the correct application of all payer criteria and a thorough understanding of clinical diagnoses, procedures, and options. Clinical case management at hospitals and other providers ensures adequate and timely monitoring of patient care. Data management plays a crucial role in helping patients and advocates identify key data elements of virtual case management.

Patients and advocates have often found it difficult to switch between their provider's cyber-health tools and their own personal use of the cyber environment when navigating their own healthcare needs. Managing the personal healthcare by understanding the financial and clinical aspects of healthcare helps a patient make more informed decisions. A virtual case management patient model will support a new healthcare environment, where patients acting like customers will drive the treatment selection process using an intelligent electronic web-based application, equipped with tools for comparative analysis and interactive decision making.

The market is responding to these patient needs. Managing the patient in the cyber environment will also require the use of electronic health tools. Adapting the discipline of case management to the electronic health environment, followed by the cyber virtual environment, encourages a case to be viewed in two separate categories: financial case management and clinical case management. Virtual case management is case management where the communication of information and provision of services function in a true state of interoperability. Virtual case management will automate the decision-making process, facilitate recommendations, and communicate personalized information and advice. It will create the infrastructure desperately needed to manage healthcare services in a defined-contribution or managed-care environment. It is critical to understand the importance of case management and integration of informatics into case management (Exhibit 12.2).

Personal Healthcare Portfolio

The personal healthcare portfolio (PHP) allows patients to aggregate critical data to improve self-advocacy. It helps the patient make informed decisions, avoid adverse health events, and manage ongoing healthcare and health-care costs, while allowing the patient to plan for future healthcare.

The PHP contains data that are standardized so as to provide consistency as to meaning and how each data element relates to others in the PHP. The critical topics of health management, wellness management, financial management, and personal health assessments each contain such data.[1]

Advocacy for patients can be improved by using tools and practices like the personal healthcare portfolio. All stakeholders—providers, advocates, and, most importantly, patients—can create, manage, validate, and update patient-centric health information in the PHP to help meet an individual's health objectives.

A patient advocate as a navigator, story teller, infomediary specialist, or an educator plays a huge role in empowering a patient to take control of their healthcare. A patient advocate can be an attorney, a friend, a nurse, an ombudsman, a physician, or anyone depending upon the level and type of care the patient requires (Exhibit 12.3).

	PATIENT IDENTIFICATION	PROBLEM IDENTIFICATION	PLANNING	IMPLEMENTING	MONITORING	EVALUATING OUTCOMES
CURRENT STATE	**Patient Identification – Current Trends**	**Problem Identification – Current Trends**	**Planning – Current Trends**	**Implementation – Current Trends**	**Patient Monitoring – Current Trends**	**Evaluating Outcomes – Current Trends**
● ACTIVITIES - Clinical Case Management - Life Care Planning - Discharge Planning	●Use a confirmation process to help match the patient and the documentation ●Use a standard display of patient attributes across the various systems ●Implement monitoring systems to readily detect identification errors ●Include high-specificity active alerts and notifications to facilitate patient identification	Clinical decision support systems provide: ●Evidence-based guidance, response to clinical need ●To entire care team–including the patient ●Through the right channels (e.g., EHR, mobile device, patient portal) ●At the right points in workflow for decision-making.	●Patient diagnosis and treatment summary ●Best schedule for follow-up tests ●Information on late- and long-term effects of cancer treatment ●List of symptoms to look for ●List of support resources	**CPOE - Computerized provider order entry** ●Facilitates healthcare tracking and healthcare progress ●Decreases medical error, improve quality **EHR - Electronic Health Records** ●Provides patients with necessary information required for optimal care ●Help patients understand the complexity of medical care and participate in clinical decision-making.	●Enhance provider communication with remotely monitored patients ●Utilize enhanced healthcare metrics, patient messaging, mobile device integration, and in-home–focused monitoring solutions	●Assessing Readiness To Change ●Identifying Priorities for Quality Improvement ●Implementing Evidence-Based Strategies To Improve Clinical Care ●Monitoring Progress and Sustainability of Improvements ●Analyzing Return on Investment
- Financial Case Management			Does not provide cost estimate			
			CYBER WORLD			
PROVIDER-CENTRIC TOOLS	●TeamSTEPPS® 2.0 for Long-Term Care – Agency for Healthcare Research & Quality	● First Databank ● Troven ● Cerner	● Siemens Healthineers ● Philips Pinnacle 3 ● RayStation	●Cerner Millenium ●Eclipsys Knowledge-Based CPOE ●GE Centricity CPOE	● ApexPro, GE ● Honeywell, Genesis ● Philips Healthcare, EncorePro 2	● Change Healthcare ● Greenway Health
	Opportunity to bridge cost and clinical care		Opportunity to bridge cost and clinical care	Opportunity to bridge cost and clinical care		
PATIENT-CENTRIC TOOLS	Opportunity to bridge cost and clinical care	● HumanDx	Opportunity to bridge cost and clinical care	Opportunity to bridge cost and clinical care	● Healow, eClinicalWorks ● MyChart, Epic Systems ● Follow My Health, All scripts	Opportunity to bridge cost and clinical care

Exhibit 12.2   Case management perspective.

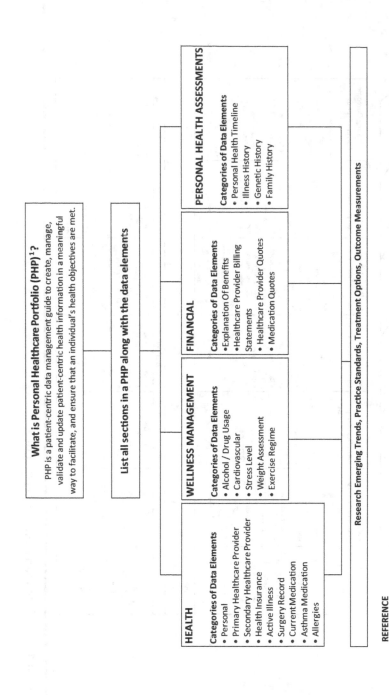

What is Personal Healthcare Portfolio (PHP)[1]?

PHP is a patient-centric data management guide to create, manage, validate and update patient-centric health information in a meaningful way to facilitate, and ensure that an individual's health objectives are met.

List all sections in a PHP along with the data elements

HEALTH

Categories of Data Elements
• Personal
• Primary Healthcare Provider
• Secondary Healthcare Provider
• Health Insurance
• Active Illness
• Surgery Record
• Current Medication
• Asthma Medication
• Allergies

WELLNESS MANAGEMENT

Categories of Data Elements
• Alcohol / Drug Usage
• Cardiovascular
• Stress Level
• Weight Assessment
• Exercise Regime

FINANCIAL

Categories of Data Elements
• Explanation Of Benefits
• Healthcare Provider Billing Statements
• Healthcare Provider Quotes
• Medication Quotes

PERSONAL HEALTH ASSESSMENTS

Categories of Data Elements
• Personal Health Timeline
• Illness History
• Genetic History
• Family History

Research Emerging Trends, Practice Standards, Treatment Options, Outcome Measurements

REFERENCE
1. *Patient's Healthcare Portfolio: A Practitioner's Guide to Providing Tools for Patients* (CRC Press: Boca Raton, FL) by Rebecca Busch, 2009

Exhibit 12.3   Personal healthcare portfolio.

Data as an Asset: Framework and Analytic Roadmap

Data are an asset that, like other assets, should be inventoried, measured, valued, and accounted for. A comprehensive understanding of data as an asset and their purpose provides the framework for auditing and testing the analytics generated between any electronic infrastructure or exchanges between infrastructures.

Entities responsible of production of data often create data that might not be consumed by other healthcare players during an episode of care. However, all data, when properly collected, organized, and utilized, provide an avenue to improve the management of population health at reduced cost. Any inventory and management of data by various players are part of a well-defined data strategy. Various continuums, tools, and models provide a framework for data strategy. Data collected are often classified by the types, characteristics, purpose, or components of data.

The data managed by healthcare entities are often leveraged to gain insights, identify patterns, and forecast consequences in a healthcare episode. Metrics are defined in order to help verify success. If the data are not found to be useful, one should always go back and update the strategy to meet the goals (Exhibit 12.4).

Cyber Data Strategy: Internal Audit Framework

Cyber data strategy is an internal audit roadmap which provides assurance of the operations and execution of an organization's strategy. A comprehensive understanding of the data strategy and the purpose provides the framework for assurance testing of the cyber data strategy for any electronic infrastructure or exchanges between infrastructures. A well-defined data dictionary is therefore crucial to the success of cyber data reviews.

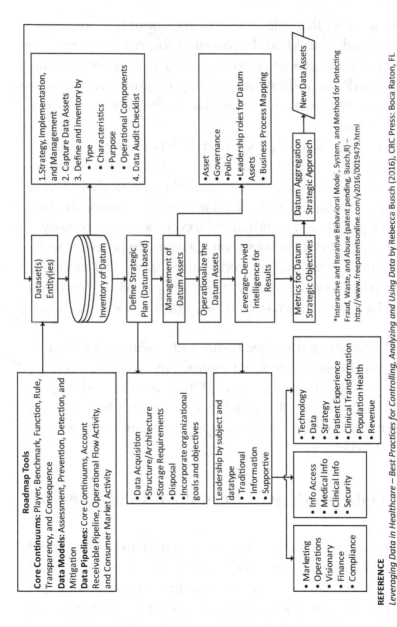

Roadmap Tools

Core Continuums: Player, Benchmark, Function, Rule, Transparency, and Consequence

Data Models: Assessment, Prevention, Detection, and Mitigation

Data Pipelines: Core Continuums, Account Receivable Pipeline, Operational Flow Activity, and Consumer Market Activity

Dataset(s) Entity(ies)

Inventory of Datum

Define Strategic Plan (Datum based)

Management of Datum Assets

Operationalize the Datum Assets

Leverage-Derived intelligence for Results

Metrics for Datum Strategic Objectives

1. Strategy, Implementation, and Management
2. Capture Data Assets
3. Define and inventory by
   • Type
   • Characteristics
   • Purpose
   • Operational Components
4. Data Audit Checklist

• Asset
• Governance
• Policy
• Leadership roles for Datum Assets
• Business Process Mapping

Datum Aggregation Strategic Approach

New Data Assets

• Data Acquisition
• Structure/Architecture
• Storage Requirements
• Disposal
• Incorporate organizational goals and objectives

Leadership by subject and datatype
   • Traditional
   • Information
   • Supportive

• Technology
• Data
• Strategy
• Patient Experience
• Clinical Transformation
• Population Health
• Revenue

• Info Access
• Medical Info
• Clinical Info
• Security

• Marketing
• Operations
• Visionary
• Finance
• Compliance

*Interactive and Iterative Behavioral Model, System, and Method for Detecting Fraud, Waste, and Abuse (patent pending. Busch,R) – http://www.freepatentsonline.com/y2016/0019479.html

REFERENCE
Leveraging Data in Healthcare – Best Practices for Controlling, Analyzing and Using Data by Rebecca Busch (2016), CRC Press: Boca Raton, FL

Exhibit 12.4 Datum as an asset—Interactive and Iterative Behavioral Model, framework, and analytic roadmap.

Data attributes and well-crafted algorithms help patients make informed decisions. Patient advocates, auditors, and infomediary specialists must consider the patient's decision-making process and test an algorithm to ensure that the electronically defined process proceeds analogously to the actual process. Organizational checklists for patient, provider, plan sponsors, and other players in the healthcare industry help manage the key data elements useful for decision making.

Auditors and cyber-health infomediary specialists serving as subject matter experts can use analytics to break down information into data elements and extract basic principles to understand the interrelationships among those data elements and their impact on a specific task or subject. These analytics help a patient understand the healthcare decision making process from both clinical and financial perspectives. Although there are various cyber-health solutions, it is always a good practice to study the gaps in current process and the complete impact of implementing a solution (Exhibit 12.5).

Behavioral Continuum Model

The behavioral continuum model helps patients/advocates identify the relevant parties in an episode of care and their relationship. The continuum model can be further categorized in terms of primary healthcare continuum, secondary healthcare continuum, information continuum, consequences continuum, transparency continuum, and rules continuum. These continuums can help identify various data elements that need to be managed effectively to improve the quality of care.

Patient self-advocacy can help manage their care and reduce the associated costs. Patients can create, manage, validate, and update their health information so as to help meet their health objectives. There are various tools and processes that improve the efficiency of self-advocacy (Exhibit 12.6).

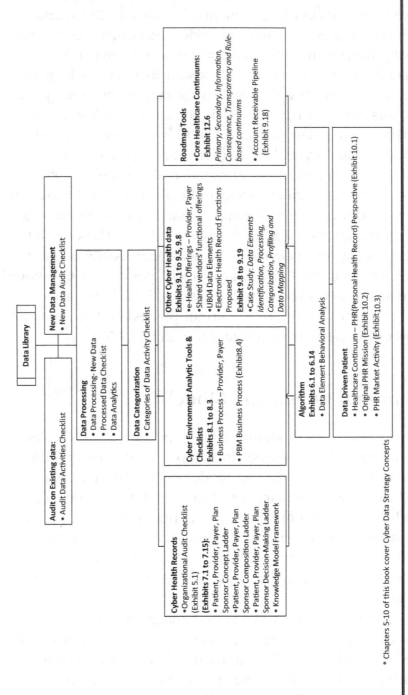

Data Library

New Data Management
• New Data Audit Checklist

Audit on Existing data:
• Audit Data Activities Checklist

Data Processing
• Data Processing- New Data
• Processed Data Checklist
• Data Analytics

Data Categorization
• Categories of Data Activity Checklist

Roadmap Tools
•**Core Healthcare Continuums:**
Exhibit 12.6
Primary, Secondary, Information,
Consequence, Transparency and Rule-
based continuums
• Account Receivable Pipeline
(Exhibit 9.18)

Other Cyber Health data
Exhibits 9.1 to 9.5, 9.8
•e-Health Offerings – Provider, Payer
•Shared vendors' functional offerings
•UB04 Data Elements
•Electronic Health Record Functions
Proposed
Exhibit 9.8 to 9.19
•Case Study: *Data Elements*
Identification, Processing,
Categorization, Profiling and
Data Mapping

Cyber Environment Analytic Tools &
Checklists
Exhibits 8.1 to 8.3
• Business Process – Provider, Payer
• PBM Business Process (Exhibit8.4)

Cyber Health Records
•Organizational Audit Checklist
(Exhibit 5.1)
(Exhibits 7.1 to 7.15):
• Patient, Provider, Payer, Plan
Sponsor Concept Ladder
• Patient, Provider, Payer, Plan
Sponsor Composition Ladder
• Patient, Provider, Payer, Plan
Sponsor Decision-Making Ladder
• Knowledge Model Framework

Algorithm
Exhibits 6.1 to 6.14
• Data Element Behavioral Analysis

Data Driven Patient
• Healthcare Continuum – PHR(Personal Health Record) Perspective (Exhibit 10.1)
• Original PHR Mission (Exhibit 10.2)
• PHR Market Activity (Exhibit10.3)

* Chapters 5-10 of this book cover Cyber Data Strategy Concepts

Exhibit 12.5   Cyber data strategy: Internal audit framework.

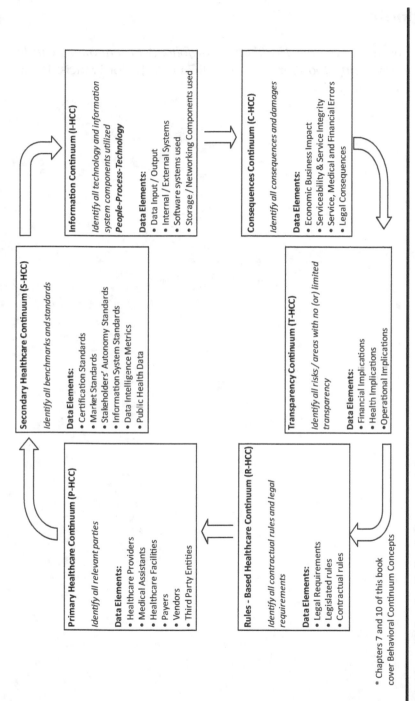

Primary Healthcare Continuum (P-HCC)

Identify all relevant parties

Data Elements:
• Healthcare Providers
• Medical Assistants
• Healthcare Facilities
• Payers
• Vendors
• Third Party Entities

Secondary Healthcare Continuum (S-HCC)

Identify all benchmarks and standards

Data Elements:
• Certification Standards
• Market Standards
• Stakeholders' Autonomy Standards
• Information System Standards
• Data Intelligence Metrics
• Public Health Data

Information Continuum (I-HCC)

Identify all technology and information system components utilized
People-Process-Technology

Data Elements:
• Data Input / Output
• Internal / External Systems
• Software systems used
• Storage / Networking Components used

Rules - Based Healthcare Continuum (R-HCC)

Identify all contractual rules and legal requirements

Data Elements:
• Legal Requirements
• Legislated rules
• Contractual rules

Transparency Continuum (T-HCC)

Identify all risks / areas with no (or) limited transparency

Data Elements:
• Financial Implications
• Health Implications
• Operational Implications

Consequences Continuum (C-HCC)

Identify all consequences and damages

Data Elements:
• Economic Business Impact
• Serviceability & Service Integrity
• Service, Medical and Financial Errors
• Legal Consequences

* Chapters 7 and 10 of this book
cover Behavioral Continuum Concepts

Exhibit 12.6   Behavioral continuum model.

Endnote

1 Busch, R. *Patient's Healthcare Portfolio: A Practitioner's Guide to Providing Tools for Patients.* CRC Press Taylor Francis, Boca Raton, FL, 2017.

Appendix: Professional Associations and Credentials

The infomediary specialist professional has several resources for consideration to stay current on emerging issues and continuing education support. These resources include:

- **American Association of Big Data Professionals, Inc. (AABDP):** AABDP advances social and economic causes by developing and responsibly applying capabilities of big data practitioners through education, advocacy, innovation, and cooperation (http://aabdp.org/).
- **American Health Information Management Association (AHIMA):** AHIMA is the premier association of health information management (IS) professionals worldwide and plays a leadership role in the effective management of health data and medical records needed to deliver quality healthcare to the public (https://www.ahima.org).
- **American Medical Informatics Association (AMIA):** AMIA serves as the key to discovering insights that help patients, increase effectiveness, improve safety, and reduce care costs. These insights help to accelerate healthcare's transformation (https://www.amia.org).

- **American Nursing Informatics Association (ANIA):** ANIA is an organization for informatics nurses promoting networking, education, and communication to advance the practice of informatics (https://www.ania.org).
- **Association for Strategic Planning (ASP):** ASP is a non-profit professional society whose mission is to help people and organizations succeed through improved strategic thinking, planning, and action (http://www.strategyassociation.org/).
- **Association for Veterinary Informatics (AVI):** AVI is a non-profit international and interdisciplinary organization comprised of individuals involved in biomedical informatics research, design, implementation, education, and advocacy within the domain of veterinary medicine (https://avinformatics.wildapricot.org/).
- **Council of European Professional Informatics Societies (CEPIS):** CEPIS is a non-profit organization seeking to improve and promote a high standard among informatics professionals in recognition of the impact that informatics has on employment, business, and society (https://www.cepis.org/).
- **Data Management Association International (DAMA-I):** DAMA-I is an international professional association to support an empowered global community of information for data modelers, analysts, and information resource managers (https://dama.org).
- **Digital Analytics Association (DAA):** DAA aims to advance the usage of data to understand and improve the digital world through professional development and community (https://digitalanalyticsassociation.org).
- **Enterprise Data Management Council (EDM Council):** DCAM was created on a collaborative basis by the members of the EDM council as a standard set of evaluation criteria for measuring data management capability (https://www.edmcouncil.org/dcam).

- **Health Informatics Forum:** This page contains links to professional health informatics associations and societies (http://www.healthinformaticsforum.com/ health-informatics-associations-and-societies).
- **Healthcare Information and Management Systems Society (HIMSS):** HIMSS is a global, cause-based, not-for-profit organization focused on better health through information technology (IT). HIMSS leads efforts to optimize health engagements and care outcomes using information technology (https://www.himss.org).
- **International Institute for Analytics (IIA):** International Institute for Analytics is an independent research firm that works with organizations to build strong and competitive analytics programs. IIA has worked with more than 200 organizations, sharing the keys to analytics maturity so that our clients gain an edge in an economy increasingly driven by data (https://www. theiia.org).
- **International Medical Informatics Association (IMIA):** International not-for-profit organization promoting medical informatics in healthcare and biomedical research (http://imia-medinfo.org/wp/).
- **National Association of Health Data Organizations (NAHDO):** National Association of Health Data Organizations (NAHDO) is a national non-profit membership and educational association dedicated to improving healthcare data collection and use. NAHDO's members include state and private health data organizations that maintain statewide healthcare databases and stakeholders of these databases (https://www.nahdo.org).

Index